ELEGIAC
ROMANCE

ELEGIAC ROMANCE

*Cultural Change and Loss of
the Hero in Modern Fiction*

Kenneth A. Bruffee

Cornell University Press

ITHACA AND LONDON

International Standard Book Number 0-8014-1579-9
Library of Congress Catalog Card Number 83-5354
Printed in the United States of America
Librarians: Library of Congress cataloging information
appears on the last page of the book.

The paper in this book is acid-free and meets the guidelines
for permanence and durability of the Committee on Production
Guidelines for Book Longevity of the Council on Library Resources.

Contents

CONTENTS

Acknowledgments

I first encountered the issue of "the modern hero," many more years ago than it is decreet to mention, in the seminars of Richard Ellmann, Zera Fink, and Jean Hagstrum. The excitement and erudition these teachers brought to the subject heavily influenced my thought. Shortly thereafter, the idea presented in this book precipitated rather suddenly and surprisingly out of what had by then become rather an odd concoction of Milton, Byron, Conrad, and an obscure eighteenth-century aesthetico-psychological notion called "the sublime."

Since that time, in developing the idea, I have enjoyed the help of a great many friends. I cannot possibly mention them all, but several deserve special thanks. Russell Hart, Robert Langbaum, and Phillip Stevick encouraged me in the early stages to pursue what was at that time little more than uninformed speculation and curiosity about the disappearance of the traditional hero in modern literature. The editors of *Studies in English Literature* found a place in their pages for the first examination of what I then called the "synthetic hero." When the idea had taken firmer shape and acquired a more suitable name, Richard Ohmann and William Machette published my first attempts to formulate it, in *College English* and the *Modern Language Quarterly*.

At the same time, other friends and colleagues helped generously in many ways. Some proposed works of fiction that seemed to fit the formulation I was drafting. I am grateful for the suggestions of Julian Kaye, Susan Fromberg Schaeffer, and Lanford Wilson. Others helped crystallize the formulation itself. Lawrence Buell's independent discovery of the larger formal category "observer-hero narrative," for example, confirmed my views. Marian Arkin read the manuscript with great care and helpfulness. Diana Feste-McCormick cheerfully shored my sagging French. And it was through William B. Coley's generous guidance that the project was brought at long last to fruition.

Still more friends, Edwin Eigner, Thomas Friedmann, Jack Kitch, Bernard Nemerson, Patricia Merivale, Eric Steinberg, and many others, deserve thanks variously for their patient interest in the project over the years, for making themselves available for discussion, and for reading numberless drafts. Professor Merivale's concern has remained particularly active and her encouragement enthusiastic for almost a decade. It was she who gave me the opportunity to debate my idea publicly for the first time at a conference session of the 1975 MLA meeting in San Francisco. Participants in that session or in the correspondence that preceded and followed were John Hagopian, Peter L. Hays, Thomas A. Hanzo, and Joseph Hynes. Naturally not everyone involved agreed with my point of view, and the resulting lively exchange contributed in memorable ways to my thinking.

Thanks are especially due also to Hudson White for his meticulous help in the final phases of research; to the several readers for Cornell University Press who contributed so much to the final revision of the manuscript; to Elsie Myers Stainton for her sympathetic, intelligent, and knowledgeable editing; and to Bernhard Kendler, Carol Betsch, and others on the editorial staff of Cornell University Press for their guidance in bringing the manuscript to publication.

Finally, I must express deepest gratitude once again to two very close friends: to Sophia Lauterbach for unflagging devotion, kindness, and expertise, without which the book would quite literally never have been written; and to Anthea Hemery Bruffee for expert editorial help and for holding my hand patiently and lovingly through so much of the seizure.

Portions of this book have been published previously. I am grateful for permission to reprint material (in most cases somewhat altered in form) from the following: "The Lesser Nightmare: Marlow's Lie in *Heart of Darkness*," *Modern Language Quarterly*, 25 (September, 1964), 322-29; "The Synthetic Hero and the Narrative Structure of *Childe Harold* III," *Studies in English Literature*, 4 (Autumn, 1966), 669-78; "Elegiac Romance," *College English*, 32 (January, 1971), 465-76 (published by NCTE); and "Nabokov's *Sebastian Knight*: An Example of Elegiac Romance," *Modern Language Quarterly*, 34 (June, 1973), 180-90.

K. A. B.

Brooklyn, New York

Abbreviations

Throughout this book I make parenthetical reference to editions of ten major works of elegiac romance according to the following abbreviations. Except in the case of *Doctor Faustus*, numbers found in parentheses—(*AKM* 23)—refer to pages in these texts. In the case of *Doctor Faustus*, to make cross reference between the translation and the German original easier, numbers in parentheses refer to chapters, e.g. (*DF*, Ch. 45).

AKM   Robert Penn Warren, *All the King's Men*. New York: Bantam, 1959.

DF   Thomas Mann, *Doctor Faustus*. Trans. H. T. Lowe-Porter. New York: Modern Library, 1948. *Doktor Faustus*. Frankfurt am Main: S. Fischer Verlag, 1967.

GG   F. Scott Fitzgerald, *The Great Gatsby*. New York: Scribner, 1925.

GS   Ford Madox Ford, *The Good Soldier*. New York: Vintage, 1955.

HD   Joseph Conrad, *Heart of Darkness*. Revised Critical Edition, ed. Robert Kimbrough. New York: W. W. Norton, 1971.

LJ   Joseph Conrad, *Lord Jim*. Cambridge, Mass.: Riverside, 1958.

LT   F. Scott Fitzgerald, *The Last Tycoon*. Ed. Edmund Wilson. Harmondsworth, Middlesex: Penguin, 1965.

SI   J. D. Salinger, "Seymour: An Introduction," in *Raise High the Roof Beam, Carpenters and Seymour: An Introduction*. New York: Bantam, 1966.

SP   John Knowles, *A Separate Peace*. New York: Bantam, 1966.

SK   Vladimir Nabokov, *The Real Life of Sebastian Knight*. Norfolk, Conn.: New Directions, 1941.

ELEGIAC
ROMANCE

/

A Note on Defining Genres

In this book I pursue an inquiry that may be read in several ways. It may be read as a limited and, I would hope, well-defined study in literary genre; I identify the form in which the heroic quest romance tradition endures in twentieth-century fiction. In this form, quest romance has become the story of its own failure to represent adequately in traditional terms modern human needs and aspirations. This study in literary genre, however, has a literary-historical dimension also. In this respect, I take the position that heroism and hero-worship have ceased to be viable themes in Western literature. Together they are a (largely nine-teenth-century) delusion, and both have been profoundly discredited in the twentieth century. There is no "modern hero," although there is in the novels and short stories discussed in this book an exemplary modern figure, one who exposes and copes with the delusion of hero-worship and outgrows it. Finally, this corner of literary history approached from the point of view of genre study has some larger cultural implications. In all the major works of twentieth-century fiction I examine, the central figure expresses an unavoidable fact of modern life—the experience of catastrophic loss and rapid cultural change, and the need to come to terms with loss and change in order to survive.

The discussion here demonstrates how these three thematic strands—the quest romance tradition, the discrediting of hero-worship and heroism, and the impact of loss and change—appear together initially in the narrative form that emerges in the early fiction of Joseph Conrad. This narrative form is found subsequently in fiction by several authors whom Conrad influenced, such as Ford Madox Ford, F. Scott Fitzgerald, Robert Penn Warren, Thomas Mann, and Vladimir Nabokov. As literary criticism, therefore, my argument traces the inception and development of a literary genre that has not heretofore been clearly defined or fully recognized. As an aid to understanding, it shows that a number of important works of modern literature are similar in basic and revealing ways.

Inevitably in the course of this discussion I make certain assumptions. I assume that works of literature (or of any other art) may indeed be classified according to what seem to be common traits, and that to see literary works as members of a class or genre may yield insights into the meaning and value of the works as individual products of the human imagination. Of course, anyone who sets out to classify literature in this way takes a serious aesthetic risk. That risk is the potential loss, at least for the moment, of one aspect of works of literary art that delights us most, their distinctiveness, their particularity, their unpredictable, unrepeatable orginality. The first vice of genre classification is presumption. It can be used as a blunt instrument to hack and chop, obliterating what makes works of art distinctive, in order to fit them willy nilly into abstract patterns, frozen categories, a priori types.

In defense of taking this risk I would argue that the attempt to classify can add to our delight in the particularities of art in the long run by leading us to a better understanding of how those particularities are organized to produce meaning. Robert Scholes has said that "the most serious misreadings of literary texts and most instances of bad critical judgment are referable to generic misunderstanding."[1] If this is so, it may be, E. D. Hirsch, Jr., would say, because our first surmise or assumption about what a thing is tends to color everything else we understand about it, and our understanding is likely to change substantially only when that initial assumption changes.[2]

---

1. *Structuralism in Literature* (New Haven: Yale University Press, 1974), p. 130.
2. *Validity in Interpretation* (New Haven: Yale University Press, 1967), p. 74.

But genre classification not only can improve our understanding directly. It also can help us indirectly by demonstrating concretely that every artist works in a community of artists, whether the other members of that community live down the street or a hemisphere away, or have lain in their graves perhaps for centuries. Harold Bloom has recently reminded us that writers write both for and in the teeth of other writers, living and dead. Genre classification illuminates that insight by helping us to delineate the mores, the heritage, and the limits of communities of writers. Thus, although genre classification can of course oversimplify and pigeonhole works of art, done carefully and judiciously it becomes an important branch of literary and cultural history. As a critical and historical tool, genre study can help to explain aspects of works that had heretofore seemed problematical. It can, as Thomas Friedmann has observed, "disentangle old knots as well as . . . [spin] new threads."[3]

In attempting in this book to do both, I examine relatively few but important works among what is in fact a large and growing canon of fiction identifiable as elegiac romance.[4] I point to the evidence, where I know it to exist, that suggests direct historical relationships among these works. And I argue both analytically and historically that, although the works differ widely in superficial ways, what they have in common is what is most fundamental to their significance as works of literary art.

Except for the novels of Conrad, I consider no work here in the context of its writer's corpus. My main purpose is not to show through close textual analysis how these particular works of fiction were written or (except briefly in the Epilogue) to show what significance they may have in the literary careers of the people who wrote them. My purpose is to point out important similarities among the works I discuss, and to demonstrate ways in which they shed light on one another's meaning when read as a group.

In the current critical climate, this effort may strike some

3. Private correspondence.
4. In using this term I have been anticipated by Northrop Frye, who applies it in passing as a modal designation. *Anatomy of Criticism* (Princeton, N.J.: Princeton University Press, 1957), p. 37. I am indebted to Martin Elsky for calling my attention to this passage.

readers as old-fashioned. It may seem so in the sense that although I respect many of the issues and developments in literary criticism in the past decade, I have sidestepped them. My argument is based instead on reading, over the years, the work of critics such as Wayne C. Booth, Alastair Fowler, Northrop Frye, E. D. Hirsch, Jr., and Robert Scholes.[5] And it is most comprehensively served by the two central chapters in Claudio Guillén's *Literature as System*, "Toward a Definition of the Picaresque" and "On the Uses of Literary Genre."[6]

In these essays Guillén defines genre from two complementary points of view. From the writer's point of view, a literary genre is a "traditional model or conventional pattern" that functions as a standing "invitation to the actual writing of a work, on the basis of certain principles of composition" (72). This model or pattern is a "problem-solving" device (120) or "working hypothesis" (130) that writers find "convenient" (72) to their purposes. Writers do not of course "take over" genre models ready made. Each writer's "concrete manifestation of the model must be achieved all over again from the start with each single work" (129). The function of previously existing models for any given generation of writers is to give them "a very special sort of assistance": "to discern or recommend not a certain matter or a certain form but a principle for matching one to the other" (111).

Thus a genre concept may help writers by stimulating or mak-

5. Booth, *The Rhetoric of Fiction* (Chicago: University of Chicago Press, 1961); Fowler, "The Life and Death of Literary Forms," *New Literary History*, 2 (Winter, 1971), 199-216, reprinted in *New Directions in Literary History*, ed. Ralph Cohen (London: Routledge, 1974), pp. 77-94; Frye, *Anatomy of Criticism*; Hirsch, *Validity in Interpretation*; Scholes, *Structuralism in Literature*. Other studies I have found helpful are Charles E. Whitmore, "The Validity of Literary Definitions," *PMLA*, 39 (1924), 722-36; Irvin Ehrenpreis, *The "Types" Approach to Literature* (New York: King's Crown Press, 1945); Harry Levin, "Literature as an Institution," in *The Gates of Horn* (New York: Oxford University Press, 1963), pp. 16-23; Robert Scholes and Robert Kellogg, *The Nature of Narrative* (New York: Oxford University Press, 1966); Paul Hernadi, *Beyond Genre* (Ithaca: Cornell University Press, 1972); Fredric Jameson, "Magical Narratives: Romance as Genre," *New Literary History*, 7 (1975), 135-63; and Jonathan Culler, "Towards a Theory of Non-Genre Literature," in Raymond Federman, ed., *Surfiction* (Chicago: Swallow Press, 1975), pp. 255-62.

6. Claudio Guillén, *Literature as System* (Princeton, N.J.: Princeton University Press, 1971). Parenthetical page numbers in "A Note on Defining Genres" refer to this volume.

ing possible the writing of a new work. Similarly, "an a posteriori description . . . of a group of works as they appear and are available to the contemporary reader" may also help readers, by motivating them to approach new or unfamiliar works in a specially informed way or to question known works in newly enlightening ways (97-98). A genre concept can help readers at two levels. First, it provides readers with the means to make what in Hirsch's terms might be called a genre guess.[7] This is a way of getting started, a working hypothesis that readers can then confirm, modify, or reject as their familiarity with the work increases. Genre identification is in this respect parallel to the process of generic identification in the sciences.[8]

Second, the idea of a genre helps by providing a sort of leverage readers can use to get at the meaning of a set of literary works taken as a whole and thus, by association, of individual works within the set. The principle involved here is that it is reasonable to suppose that a trait found in one work will exist also, at least hypothetically, in a structurally similar work, even though in the latter the trait may be difficult to recognize because it has been minimalized, distorted, or disguised. Again the scientific analogy is apt. Finding structural similarities among several literary works may lead us, therefore, to bring insights into one of them fruitfully to bear on others of the same type; then, by a process of compounding, Guillén suggests, we may be led further to a still more general meaning, a "larger significance" (100) implicit in the genre concept itself.

One of several tasks that a critic may undertake with respect to genres is to provide both writers and readers with new tools of this sort to work with. That is, the critic may undertake to identify and to define explicitly resources that have remained,

7. Hirsch, *Validity in Interpretation*, pp. 75-78.
8. The scientific analogy in discussing literary generic classification has limitations. Scholes argues, for example, paraphrasing and quoting Todorov, that "a literary genre is fundamentally different from the generic classifications of zoology and even of linguistics. In literature . . . 'each work modifies the whole set of possibilities. Each new work changes the species.' . . . Every literary text is a product of a pre-existing set of possibilities, and it is also a transformation of those possibilities" (*Structuralism in Literature*, p. 128). The analogy seems nevertheless to have useful explanatory value in the context of Guillén's theoretical outline.

so far, part of what Renato Poggioli has called the "unwritten" or tacit poetics of an age,[9] and then to show readers in particular how that genre concept now made newly explicit can help to produce still further questioning of relevant works. To be adequate to both historical fact and the needs of informed and inquiring readers, however, a genre concept so defined and expressed must be "sufficiently flexible" to allow for changes that conventions almost inevitably undergo as they pass from purpose to purpose and technique to technique among individual writers who use them; as they pass from epoch to epoch, nation to nation, ethnic group to ethnic group, and value system to value system within the variety of cultures that welcome them; and as they are reshaped by use in context with other genres or hybridized with them (98-99).

As a posteriori notions, genre concepts must be flexible also because in reality, as Guillen puts it, a "so-called new genre" comes into being only through a slow, "peculiar process of acceptance" (125). Guillen uses the phrase "so-called new genre" here because by the time the form is familiar enough to be named, defined, discussed, and explicitly accepted by a community of readers and writers, it is far from new. Its effect may have been felt in the literature of that community for decades. The "new" genre discussed in this book, for example, first became fully explicit during the mid-1960s and early 1970s with the publication of articles attempting to sketch a definition of the form and with a brief discussion of the form at a convention of literary scholars and critics.[10] But by that time, the genre had

9. Poggioli's phrase is quoted in Guillén, p. 125.
10. Kenneth A. Bruffee, "The Synthetic Hero and the Narrative Structure of *Childe Harold* III," *Studies in English Literature*, 4 (Autumn, 1966), 669-78; "Elegiac Romance," *College English*, 32 (January, 1971), 465-76; and "Nabokov's Sebastian Knight: An Example of Elegiac Romance," *Modern Language Quarterly*, 34 (June, 1973), 180-90. The public discussion mentioned here took place at the 1975 annual convention of the Modern Language Association in a session entitled "Comparative Literature I: Prose Fiction" led by Patricia Merivale. Earlier suggestions, largely ignored so far as I know, had been offered by Jerome Thale in "The Narrator as Hero," *Twentieth Century Literature*, 3 (1957), 69-73, and "Marlow's Quest," *University of Toronto Quarterly*, 24 (1955), 351-58; by Albert Guerard in *Conrad the Novelist* (Cambridge, Mass.: Harvard University Press, 1958), pp. 126-27; and by Murray Krieger in *The Classic Vision* (Baltimore, Md.: Johns Hopkins Press, 1971), p. 306. Separately, several critics have noticed im-

been available as a "repertory of norms" (125) to two generations of writers—since roughly the first decade of the twentieth century. Furthermore, long before it was defined explicitly, elegiac romance had undergone a complete process of development of the sort Alastair Fowler describes, from synthesis and refinement through variation and parody.[11]

Thus the history of elegiac romance tends to confirm at least three of Guillen's observations about the nature and development of genres. The first is the one I have just been discussing, that a genre may exist tacitly long before critics define and discuss it. The second is that genres are dynamic, protean models, not static, graven ones. The writer, Guillen says, "is obliged to face . . . the necessity of an active dialogue with the generic models of his time and culture. This dialogue is active in the sense that the writer does not merely choose among standards that are accessible to him—he makes possible their survival; and he determines *which* are preferable or pertinent to the potentially new norms" (128). This "active dialogue" is clearly evident in the history of elegiac romance. As the ensuing chapters attempt to show, Conrad first patched together his new form by adopting and synthesizing "certain already existing prototypes" (73)—older forms that he knew as part of the baggage that well-read readers carry with them. In Conrad's case, some of these prototypes were, for instance, seafarer fiction, voyage literature (and other examples of exotic, quest literature), fictional autobiography, and the heroic tale. Conrad in fact put several of these older types to rest by submerging them in the new form he invented. But exactly by putting them to rest in this way, he also ensured their survival in the new guise. The exotic tale, for example, is today (perhaps, and for the moment) moribund. Yet it lives on in its supreme manifestation, *Heart of Darkness*. Following Conrad's lead, then, other writers such as Ford and Fitzgerald found the new form useful to their own ends and refined it still further.

---

portant traits of elegiac romance in some of the works discussed in this book. See for example Hynes on Ford (Chapter Five, note 5), Baumbach and Girault on Warren (Chapter Five, note 8), Warren on Warren (Chapter One, note 11), Bruss on Conrad (Chapter Four, note 3), Hatfield on Mann (Chapter Five, note 13), Peirce on Ford (Chapter Five, note 5), and Kuhnle on Fitzgerald (Chapter One, note 25).

11. "Life and Death of Literary Forms," p. 212. See Chapter Seven, note 1.

In trying to describe this "active dialogue" between writers and one of the genre models tacitly available to them, in defining explicitly the genre that appears to have resulted from this dialogue, and in reading several major literary works from that point of view, I have taken certain calculated risks, risks every genre critic more or less consciously takes. Apart from the larger aesthetic risk, the most serious of these is circularity. "The idea of a genre must come into existence or be detected," Guillén points out, "before it can be operative as a norm or as a practical model" (123). This means that "logically speaking," genre studies attempt "to define a being whose limits and character are largely dependent on the results of the definition" (129). In literary studies, furthermore, this logical circularity cannot easily be broken by recourse to fact, as it can sometimes be in the sciences. As Robert C. Elliott points out, a generic question in science is "a question to be settled by examining the [object] for the necessary and sufficient properties which would automatically entitle it" to be placed in one category rather than another.[12] But whether, say, Wordsworth's *Prelude* is epic or lyric poetry is not a question to be settled in this way. Rather, it is to be settled by establishing that the "resemblances" among a number of works is "sufficient" for us to include them in the same category.

Guillén provides two rules of thumb to help critics overcome the circularity implicit in genre classification. One is to look at a genre concept from the point of view of a writer. If the concept seems to be a "model that could have affected the writer (exerted an influence upon the work in progress)" (147), then what we are looking at is likely to be genotypic. In accordance with this rule of thumb, I have stressed in my study of Conrad's development of the basic elements of elegiac romance how these elements suited his formal and thematic needs as a writer "matching matter and form." Then, in discussing works that seem to follow Conrad's new form, I have tried to show how the new form served in turn as an "invitation to the actual writing" of several works, "on the basis of certain principles of composition" (72).

12. "The Definition of Satire," *Yearbook of Comparative and General Literature*, 11 (1962), 23, cited in Guillén, pp. 130-31. For another view of circularity in genre definition, see Hirsch, *Validity in Interpretation*, p. 70.

A Note on Defining Genres

The second rule of thumb Guillén provides is adapted from Elliott's general point that a question of literary genre is not a question of fact. A genre question "is a *decision* question," that is, a question of warranted judgment. We establish that the "resemblances" among a number of works is "sufficient" for us to include them in the same category by taking "a position based on an aesthetic experience" (131). The validity of our judgment is determined finally by whether or not the genre category we decide upon in this way feels right, so to speak, to the members of the community of sensible, well-educated, broadly experienced readers. In this book I suggest that resemblances among the works discussed here are sufficient to include them in a single genre category. The validity of that suggestion, however, is for my readers, not for me, to decide.

The development of elegiac romance as traced here also lends further credence to a third argument Guillén makes about genres. This argument is a corollary of his description of the "peculiar process of acceptance" that genres undergo. Guillen suggests that because that process is slow and erratic, in any given period there may exist two modes of aesthetic practice. One of them is a "codified" or explicit poetics that critics use as tools of analysis. The other is a (usually) much larger set of "literary possibilities," the "unwritten" or tacit norms that writers and readers apply unsystematically and often with little if any self-awareness. Critics of any given age for the most part fail to perceive this set of tacit norms. Some measure of disjunction always exists between the norms critics apply in choosing what to read and how to read it and the norms affecting what writers who are their contemporaries choose to write. Naturally this disjunction is sharper in some epochs than in others. But to the extent that it exists in any epoch, the breadth of the gap at any time between explicit and tacit norms profoundly affects the nature and limits of critical awareness.[13] With possibly the rare

13. Genre studies of recent literature, such as Culler's "Towards a Theory of Non-Genre Literature," attempt to close this gap, but the shots they bravely call are notoriously difficult. The "non-genre" convention-free fiction Culler discusses, for example, may seem a good deal more convention-bound fifty years from now than it seems today, as its counterpart, surrealism, another era's rebellion against another era's prevailing conventions, seems now.

23

exception of practicing artists who are also critically aware and articulate, such as Pope, Coleridge, or T. S. Eliot, the critical discussion of every age will almost inevitably overlook some of the important determining generic forces acting upon contemporary writers and perhaps as well those acting upon the writers of immediately preceding epochs.

This disjunction may be one root of the troubled frustration that some critics in almost every age express. But there does exist a satisfactory and perhaps potentially relieving explanation of the gap between the characteristics of a literary epoch and what any generation of critics can perceive. Thomas Kuhn has shown that although the assumptions, values, and disciplinary matrices of a knowledge community (of which a critical generation, or to use Stanley Fish's term, an "interpretive community," is one type) make certain kinds of study and certain insights possible, they also make other kinds of study and other insights impossible.[14] Richard Rorty has generalized Kuhn's position so far as to argue that even what a community considers to be knowledge itself is determined by the accepted critical language, the "normal discourse," of the day.[15] For most of us as practicing critics, insight is restricted by the values, goals, and interests of the critical community of which we are members.

Thus it is a striking fact, but one that should surprise no one, that the set of literary norms that this book now points to and calls characteristics of elegiac romance developed almost unobserved by literary critics during an age as critically self-conscious as the twentieth century. Dominated by highly academic and hermetic traditions, criticism for the past half century has brought to bear on certain kinds of literature vast erudition and ingenious verbal analysis. But since such a narrow focus, however fruitful, also limits critical vision, during this period the repertoire of norms represented by the term elegiac romance escaped recognition almost entirely. Elegiac romance remained unrecog-

14. Kuhn, *The Structure of Scientific Revolutions* (Chicago, Ill.: University of Chicago Press, 1970); Fish, *Is There a Text in This Class?: The Authority of Interpretive Communities* (Cambridge, Mass.: Harvard University Press, 1980), pp. 14-15, 303-71.
15. *Philosophy and the Mirror of Nature* (Princeton, N.J.: Princeton University Press, 1979).

nized for at least two reasons. First, its characteristics tend to elude identification by the methods—close verbal analysis, for example—most native to the dominant community of twentieth-century criticism. And, second, as a form, elegiac romance depends on the ironic integration of certain literary conventions—the integration of, for example, the heroic tale and the first-person "autobiographical" quest narrative—conventions that tend to be neglected by the explicit poetics of that dominant twentieth-century critical community.

Inevitably, the point of view taken in this book suffers from similarly limited critical vision. I believe I can do no better in setting forth the conditions of this study, therefore, than to quote at length the major clause of Claudio Guillén's own contract with the reader. In attempting to define elegiac romance as a genre,

> I am not proposing an absolute norm, to which one might be tempted later to subordinate the actual works under study. On the contrary, my definition is entirely relative to its possible usefulness in two ways: as a procedure for ordering the continuum of individual facts; and as a critical perspective, perhaps fruitful at the moment of reading. . . . The target of this discussion is a series of literary works, not a definition. The definition itself, like any critical set, is merely a limited perspective. [74]

I hope readers will feel that the task undertaken in this book has been done with these goals and limitations consistently in mind.

CHAPTER 1

Elegiac Romance: A Modern Tradition

Commenting on Saul Bellow's *Humboldt's Gift*, Leslie Fiedler has pointed out that the central character in that novel is not its title character, Von Humboldt Fleisher. "Bellow's book is called not *Humboldt* but *Humboldt's Gift*; and the recipient of that gift, . . . the narrator Charlie Citrine, is its real hero. For a little while, Citrine (who at times seems scarcely distinguishable from his author) finds in Humboldt's death and his own survival, an occasion for guilt. . . . But in the end, he succeeds in convincing himself that Humboldt has died for him, . . . leaving Citrine as a heritage not empty regrets but a saleable story; Humboldt's story once, [Citrine's] story now, the book we are reading."[1]

Fiedler has deftly condensed here what is an important part of my argument in this book. The narrator of *Humboldt's Gift*, and of novels like it, is distinctive by virtue of the unique role he plays in the fiction and by virtue of his characteristics and motivation. What Fiedler's remarks omit is recognition that neither the narrator nor the narrative form of Bellows's novel is new in modern fiction. Both follow closely a well-developed modern tradition. It is this tradition that I have set out to define here as a coherent genre—elegiac romance. The elegiac romance tradition is important because it provides a complex, flexible form for expressing many themes central to modernism and the modern sensibility.

1. "Literature and Lucre: A Meditation," *Genre*, 13 (Spring, 1980), 10.

26

Elegiac romance as a formal entity is congruent in many respects with the category of "observer-hero narrative" defined by
Lawrence Buell.[2] Buell has made a rigorous case for this broad
class of fiction. In doing so he takes an important step beyond
Walter L. Reed's view that twentieth-century observer-hero narratives are identifiable as parodies of nineteenth-century heroism, but otherwise lack coherence as a genre.[3] Reed is right that
the residual influence of an archaic heroism is at issue in these
works, but I would insist with Buell that the broad class of fiction
Buell describes does clearly and demonstrably exist. In this book
I discuss a few novels and shorter works of fiction that lie at the
epicenter of the class. These key works, those I call elegiac romances, are distinguishable from other works of observer-hero
narrative by the clearly definable conditions of the narrator's
tale—its occasion and purpose—and by the development of thematic material that these constraints imply.

Viewed generally, Buell argues, twentieth-century observer-
hero narrative seems to concern, "the interplay of . . . complementary psychic universes," the narrator's and his hero's. The
narrator's state of mind seems wholly rational, and his enterprise
is accurately described as a "meditation on the hero" in Reed's
sense. In these novels, Buell says,

> the hero is characterized in such a way as to renew the observer's
> (and the reader's) faith in the possibility of a degree of grandeur
> we had more or less assumed to have faded from the contemporary
> world; to indulge that dream for awhile; and yet finally to keep
> from full identification with it by viewing it as illusory and/or de-
> structive. Thus the encounter with the hero is finally turned into
> a learning experience for the observer. It is significant in this
> regard that a number of observer-hero narratives play upon the
> old-fashionedness of the hero in contrast to the up-to-date ob-
> server. . . . The observed heroes reflect both the dream of a nobler
> life-style and the feeling that it would be quixotic to act out such
> a dream.[4]

2. "Observer-Hero Narrative," *Texas Studies in Literature and Language*, 21
(Spring, 1979), 93-111.
3. *Meditations on the Hero: A Study of the Romantic Hero in Nineteenth-Century
Fiction* (New Haven: Yale University Press, 1974).
4. "Observer-Hero Narrative," p. 101.

Although this description is accurate for the category of observer-hero narrative as a whole, the central works in that category focus much more intensively than Buell implies on the narrator's own complex state of mind, the narrator's own peculiar "universe." In these central works, the narrator's enterprise and the "learning experience" that results from it constitute not so much a meditation as a concerted, conscious effort to work through an obsession. The narrator has carried his tendency to "mythologize" his hero to an extreme, so that the narrator's hero, as the narrator presents him to us in his tale, must be read largely as a product of the narrator's fantasy. The reader has no way of knowing for sure where the narrator's fantasy leaves off and the factual reality of the hero's existence begins. What the narrator "dissociates" himself from through telling the tale is not his hero's "life-style." It is something a good deal more serious: an aspect or version of the narrator's own inner self. By telling the tale, the narrator manages, as Fiedler suggests, to gain some control over the underlying problem that fueled his obsession, the problem he has revealed by projecting it onto the hero of the tale.

The underlying problem the narrator faces as the novel begins and the change he under goes as he attempts to solve it by telling the tale are what distinguish elegiac romance from other works of observer-hero narrative. The problem the narrator faces is that although his hero is now dead or irretrievably lost, his hero's influence remains unaccountably alive in the narrator's mind. The narrator attempts to solve this problem by coming to terms, through telling the tale, with the debilitating influence that his hero continues to exert over him.

This criterion makes it possible to differentiate elegiac romances from other works of observer-hero narrative. For example, when we compare Mann's *Doctor Faustus* with Conrad's *Under Western Eyes*, it is clear that they are structurally similar. In both, a narrator tells a tale about another, more active, seemingly more interestng character. In both, this second character is a heroic figure drawn on nineteenth-century lines. But *Under Western Eyes* is not an elegiac romance. It is a story of guilt and intrigue told by a narrator otherwise implicated only incidentally action of the novel. In *Doctor Faustus*, as in any elegiac romance, what happens to the narrator as he tells the tale governs the central action of the novel. One could argue indeed that what happens to the narrator *is* the central action of the novel. The importance of everything that happens to the narrator's hero in *Doctor Faustus* is proportionate to its relevance to the process of change in the narrator's mind effected by and evidenced in the tale he tells. In *Under Western Eyes*, the narrator is not affected by the telling of the tale in this way. The narrator is an observer. He finds Razumov a curiosity. He is not a victim of the obsessive relationship of hero-worshiper to hero that is essential to elegiac romance. Telling the tale does not affect his understanding of himself. He feels little sense of loss when Razumov disappears.[5]

Another type of observer-hero narrative that is not elegiac romance is represented by Alain-Fournier's *The Wanderer (Le Grand Meaulnes)*. Here the narrator is unquestionably an obsessed hero-worshiper, but telling the tale has no effect on the narrator's obsession. He is still as emotionally dependent on his boyhood hero when he concludes his tale as he was when he began it. He tells the tale not to overcome dependency but to indulge it. He is overwhelmed by the possibility of losing his hero, but the tale ends with his hero still alive and living tantalizingly near by. The result is that the novel nostalgically celebrates and attempts to rehabilitate nineteenth-century heroic virtues. It does not question or reject them.[6]

At the same time that we make these distinctions between certain kinds of observer-hero narrative and elegiac romance, however, we must continue to see that observer-hero narrative taken as a whole, including elegiac romance, does constitute a coherent category of twentieth-century fiction. Buell's essay suc-

5. Examples of twentieth-century observer-hero narrative that, like *Under Western Eyes*, lack some or all of the essential characteristics of elegiac romance might include Earle Birney's "David," Willa Cather's "Tom Outland's Story," R. V. Cassill's *Clem Anderson* and *Doctor Cobb's Game*, Robertson Davies's *Fifth Business*, Graham Greene's *The Quiet American* and *The Third Man*, and Henry James's "Brooksmith" and "The Author of 'Beltraffio.'"

6. Examples of twentieth-century observer-hero narratives that, like *The Wanderer*, exemplify nostalgia for nineteenth-century heroic virtues might include Vladimir Arsenyev's *Dersu Uzala*, Konrad Bercovici's "Revenge," Ricardo Guiraldes's *Don Segundo Sombra*, and Jack London's *The Sea Wolf*.

cessfully and instructively argues this coherence. And the existence of elegiac romance at the center of the category lends still further credence to Buell's argument. Buell concedes it as a weakness in his argument that on the basis of the evidence available to him he "cannot prove that the authors [of observer-hero narratives] were consciously aware of working with preestablished norms."[7] This weakness disappears, however, when we focus on the central works in the category, where it is demonstrable that a number of authors were aware of the formal and thematic norms of the sort of fiction I am calling elegiac romance.

There is little doubt that the preestablished norms most twentieth-century authors of elegiac romance work within are traceable to Joseph Conrad. The evidence is clear that Conrad is responsible for making these central works viable and meaningful as a twentieth-century medium, and that following Conrad there is a clear line of writers—among them Ford, Fitzgerald, Warren, Mann, and Nabokov—who consciously imitated Conrad's form and central theme "in the Renaissance sense," as Alastair Fowler puts it.[8] Ford worked closely with Conrad for six years, so that the effect of Conrad's interest in form on Ford's elegiac romance, *The Good Soldier*, is hardly surprising.[9] Fitzgerald cites Conrad explicitly in notes to his unfinished *The Last Tycoon*, a novel Fitzgerald intended to make "like *The Great Gatsby*" and to structure narratively "as Conrad did."[10] Both Warren and

7. Buell, "Observer-Hero Narrative," p. 102.
8. "Life and Death of Literary Forms," p. 212. I am aware I have left unaddressed here tensions that may be implicit in imitation, the issue raised in Harold Bloom, *The Anxiety of Influence* (New Haven: Oxford University Press, 1975).
9. Ford Madox Ford, *Return to Yesterday* (New York: Liveright, 1932), pp. 186-201; and H. Robert Huntley, *The Alien Protagonist of Ford Madox Ford* (Chapel Hill, N.C.: University of North Carolina Press, 1970), pp. 168ff. See also my discussion of Ford's *Joseph Conrad: A Personal Reminiscence* in the Epilogue.
10. See also Robert Emmet Long, "*The Great Gatsby* and the Tradition of Joseph Conrad," *Texas Studies in Literature and Language*, 8 (1966), 257-76, 407-22, and "*The Great Gatsby* and Conrad," in *The Achieving of "The Great Gatsby"* (Lewisburg, Pa.: Bucknell University Press, 1979), pp. 79-188; R. W. Stallman, "Conrad and *The Great Gatsby*," *Twentieth Century Literature*, 1 (April, 1955), 5-12; James E. Miller, *The Fictional Technique of F. Scott Fitzgerald* (The Hague: Mouton, 1957); and Thomas A. Hanzo, "The Theme and the Narrator of *The Great Gatsby*," *Modern Fiction Studies*, 2 (Winter, 1956-57), 183-90.

Mann wrote critical essays on Conrad.[11] Mann tells us in *The Story of a Novel*, his account of writing *Doctor Faustus*, that at the time he was working on that novel he read through once again Conrad's collected fiction.[12] And Nabokov alludes to the "Conradish" nature of *The Real Life of Sebastian Knight* (*SK*, 42).

This evidence of Conrad's influence on later writers of elegiac romance is convincing enough to lead us to examine the way elegiac romance developed as a form in Conrad's fiction. I have attempted this analysis in Chapters Two, Three, and Four of this book. In Chapters Five, Six, and Seven, I have undertaken to examine later fiction that shows signs of being influenced, directly or indirectly, by the form Conrad developed.

As for influences on Conrad, we shall see in the next section of this chapter that elegiac romance is part of the quest romance tradition, to which many works of nineteenth-century literature are also more or less consciously related. Structurally, some of these are similar in some ways to elegiac romance. *Moby-Dick* is one important example, as is Melville's short story "Bartleby the Scrivener," Pushkin's "The Shot," and Poe's "The Fall of the House of Usher." For the most part, however, as Edwin Eigner has found in his wide-ranging survey of nineteenth-century minor fiction, works with a structure similar to that of elegiac romance seem otherwise all but nonexistent before Conrad.[13] So there seems at present no evidence that Conrad depended directly on the work of any earlier writers, with the possible exception of Byron, in developing his new form. In fact, the tortuous, slow development of the form in Conrad's early fiction suggests quite the opposite. This is not to say that the form Conrad devised is to be regarded as *sui generis*. On the contrary, Conrad successfully fused in the medium of modern prose fiction two major strains of the Western literary tradition: elegy and quest romance.

11. See for example Warren's introduction to *Nostromo*, *Sewanee Review*, 59 (1951), 363-91; also, Seymour L. Gross, "Conrad and *All the King's Men*," *Twentieth Century Literature* 3 (1957), 27-32.
12. *The Story of a Novel*, trans. Richard and Clara Winston (New York: Knopf, 1961), pp. 191-212.
13. Private correspondence.

be alive, and to be young is very heaven. And it is the age when the "artificial" conventions of courtly love are likewise rejected in favor of sincere love for gentle Lucy in her simple cottage. As for the heroic quest, it disappears from public view. It becomes, as Harold Bloom points out, "internalized." For the Romantics, the goal of the quest is now a "humanizing" one, with the hope of leaving the central figure, now in most cases the poet himself, "twice born." Bloom offers the following thumbnail sketch of this development:

> The movement of quest romance, before its internalization by the High Romantics, was from nature to redeemed nature, the sanction of redemption being the gift of some external spiritual authority, sometimes magical. The Romantic movement is from nature to the imagination's freedom (sometimes a reluctant freedom), and the imagination's freedom is frequently purgatorial, redemptive in direction but destructive of the social self. [This is] the high cost of Romantic internalization. . . . The quest is to widen consciousness as well as intensify it, but the quest is shadowed by a spirit that tends to narrow consciousness to an acute preoccupation with self.

What makes internalizing the quest romance seem worth the price most Romantics pay for it is that Romantic preoccupation with self is a preoccupation with personal growth. "The internalization of quest-romance," Bloom says, makes the poet-hero "a seeker [not] after nature but after his own mature powers."[15]

Bloom's insightful analysis of the internalized Romantic quest has one limitation, however. It confuses two quite different types of quest. It does not pause to ask, in terms of history of the dramatic structure of the quest story since Cervantes: In whom is the quest internalized, the knight or the squire? In the work of many of the High Romantics the answer to this question is not clear, although it is always relevant. But one English Romantic poet, Byron, perhaps somewhat more deeply imbued with the quest tradition than others, does answer the question clearly by dramatizing the very moment of internalization. This

15. Harold Bloom, "The Internalization of Quest Romance," in *The Ringers in the Tower: Studies in Romantic Tradition* (Chicago, Ill.: University of Chicago Press, 1971), pp. 15-16.

dramatization occurs in the tightly structured Canto III of Byron's otherwise loose and desultory narratve poem *Childe Harold's Pilgrimage*. In the first two cantos of *Childe Harold*, Byron maintains the Cervantean two-character structure of the quest story. He renders the heroic role, values, and aims of the traditional questing knight in the character of Harold, peregrinating across the face of early nineteenth-century Europe. He renders the everyday role, interests, and needs of the knight's squire in the character of the poem's narrator. The narrator follows Harold closely and comments on his experience, achieving, like Sancho Panza, a "sympathetic penetration" of Harold's world. As late as Stanza 72 of Canto III the narrator tells us, "I live not in myself, but I become/ Portion of that around me."

In the climactic passage of the poem (Stanzas 85-97), the direction of this "penetration" undergoes a reversal. During an intense experience of "the sublime," in a thunderstorm at night on Lake Geneva, the narrator ceases to feel "Portion" of everything around him. He feels instead that everything around him is suddenly "concentered" in himself (Stanza 89). This reversal is crucial to the significance of the poem because it means that unlike Sancho Panza, Byron's squire-narrator is not passively assimilated into his knight's identity and world. The narrator actively assimilates Harold and Harold's world, and he subordinates them to his own aims, interests, and needs. After this scene, the text of the poem never mentions Harold again. The narrator carries on alone in the world as he perceives it.[16]

16. *The Works of Lord Byron: Poetry*, ed. Ernest Hartley Coleridge, vol. 2 (London: John Murray, 1922), pp. 262, 269-76. My analysis of the climactic passage in *Childe Harold* III revises somewhat my first attempt to examine Byron's "confusion" of narrator and hero (and to formulate the thesis of this book) in "The Synthetic Hero and the Narrative Structure of *Childe Harold* III," *Studies in English Literature*, 4 (Autumn, 1966), 669-78. In reading *Childe Harold* III, I am indebted to Robert Gleckner's *Byron and the Ruins of Paradise* (Baltimore, Md.: Johns Hopkins Press, 1967) and to Jerome McGann's textual study of the manuscript, "The Composition, Revision, and Meaning of *Childe Harold's Pilgrimage* III," *Bulletin of the New York Public Library*, 71 (1967), 415-30.

I differ with McGann's interpretation, however. In *Fiery Dust: Byron's Poetic Development* (Chicago: University of Chicago Press, 1968), he argues that because "both external and internal evidence . . . are clear" that the first draft of the poem was "written sequentially," and because Byron lacked "models to guide him in techniques for handling ego-projections in a first-person confessional form," the narrator in *Childe Harold* III must be identical with Byron and the poem

Thus in dramatizing this moment of internalization in the Romantic quest for self-regeneration, Byron reveals a crucial fact of the underlying nature of that internalization. The questing, truth-seeking, Romantic "I" of the internalized quest absorbs the traditional consciousness and emotional agenda of heroic selfhood into its own agenda of common everyday emotional needs, selfhood, and consciousness, and then gets on with its own quest on its own terms. To say this is of course only to repeat a commonplace: the Romantic quest is the inner counterpart of the great political upheavals of the times, the common person seeking freedom. But to remind ourselves that the quest of the Romantic "I" is the quest of a common everyday sensibility to fulfill common everyday needs is also to caution ourselves against taking too literally in their traditional sense some of the phrases it is difficult to avoid in a discussion of this topic: the "internalized quest" of the "Romantic hero" and the "poet-hero."[17] The Romantic hero does not pursue internally a traditional knightly quest reformulated in Romantic terms. The poet-hero is not heroic in traditional terms and the quest he internalizes is not the traditional quest. The traditional hero of aristocratic lineage, values, and aims, and the traditional adventurous quest for admission into a privileged state of being disappear from the scene in the Romantic period. The problems that the questing knight traditionally faces are set aside unsolved. The goal of the knight is supplanted by the goal of the heretofore subordinate and, still more to the point, the heretofore dependent squire. And the goal of the squire is a function or product of that dependent

must be an unequivocally "subjective" statement (pp. 69-70 and 69n). McGann also thinks that the narrator disappears from the poem and Harold remains. My position is of course the reverse on this point. The eighteen stanzas Byron inserted after completing the first draft affected the poem structurally, changing it from a confessional travelogue to a distanced fictional artifact of considerable formal sophistication. A thorough examination of Byron's influence on nineteenth- and twentieth-century fiction would show that Byron has had as much of an impact as a resource for formal innovation as for theme and character type.

17. Another confusing term in this context is "the Byronic hero." Harold is a "Byronic hero," as are other figures of Byron's creation such as the Corsair and Manfred. But the narrator of *Childe Harold's Pilgrimage*, in my view, is not a Byronic hero. He is a Byronic figure of another, and perhaps greater, importance. See Peter L. Thorslev, Jr., *The Byronic Hero* (Minneapolis, Minn.: University of Minnesota Press, 1962).

status. The squire's quest for independence requires him to seek vigorously to gain not a privileged state of being but a common human birthright, his freedom and "his own mature powers."

The importance to my argument of Byron's revelation about the centrality of the squire-narrator to the Romantic quest is that with it he makes possible the fundamental structural change necessary for modern writers to adapt the quest romance tradition to the needs of twentieth-century fiction. In Cervantes, the squire joins the knight as the dramatic focus of attention, pursuing the knight's agenda. In the Romantic quest the squire and the squire's agenda replace the knight as the dramatic focus of attention. The squire swallows the problematic elements in the traditional agenda of the heroic quest, although he does not necessarily digest them. They remain dormant but potentially troublesome. In the twentieth-century version of quest romance, elegiac romance, the knight returns to the scene, but alive only in the vivid memory of the squire-narrator. The squire narrator is solely responsible for bringing up again the agenda of traditional heroism. He raises it because, brought to the surface now from the deep recesses of his own emotional life, traditional heroism can at last be exposed, confronted, and cast aside.

Byron may have realized dimly this latent potential involved in replacing the knight with the squire as the central figure in the Romantic internalized quest. Evidence for this possibility is the fact that he dramatizes the same sort of replacement in an obscure work, his "Fragment of a Novel," written about the same time as *Childe Harold* III, during summer, 1816, when he was living in Switzerland with Percy Bysshe and Mary Shelley. These three, along with Byron's physician John Polidori and friend Claire Clairmont, staged a "contest" during a spell of bad weather to see who could write the story that would most frighten and disturb the others. It was this contest that led to Mary Shelley's *Frankenstein*.[18]

For his part, Byron began a novel on the theme of vampirism. As it is left to us, this fragment has, perhaps inadvertently, the structure of elegiac romance. In it, a young man tells the tale of

---

18. Leslie A. Marchand, *Byron: A Biography* (New York: Knopf, 1957), pp. 628-29.

a strong-willed older man who had persuaded the young man to travel with him into the Levant. There, the older man suddenly died. At just this point Byron left the story unfinished. But for this reason, even in its fragmentary state the story gives the reader an odd sense of resolution. Although the older man is unquestionably fascinating, the younger man's feelings seem clearly the story's focus. The most significant of these feelings is his choked, static ambivalence at the end of the tale when the older man dies: "I was tearless," he tells us, "between astonishment and grief." It is this extreme ambivalence about his hero, the fragment seems to suggest, that drives the young man after his hero's death to tell the tale.[19] The death of the narrator's hero and the story's focus on the narrator's response to that death seems especially significant when we contrast Byron's "Fragment" with the story Polidori wrote for the contest on the same subject. Polidori's work follows the conventions of vampire literature closely. It focuses on the conventional central figure, the vampire. Nothing in the story suggests that the narrator suffers anything more remarkable or profound than stock horror-tale chills.[20]

The potential for structural evolution of the quest tale implicit in Byron's *Childe Harold* III and "Fragment of a Novel" becomes actual in the fourth major phase of the quest romance tradition, the phase of elegiac romance.[21] Here, consistent both with Cer-

---

19. *The Works of Lord Byron: Letters and Journals*, ed. Rowland E. Prothero, vol. 3, (London: John Murray, 1901), pp. 446-53.

20. *The Vampyre, A Tale* (London: Sherwood, Neely, and Jones, 1819). See also *The Diary of Dr. John William Polidori, 1816, Relating to Byron, Shelley, Etc.* ed. William Michael Rosetti (London: E. Matthews, 1911), pp. 23-24.

21. The structure of Byron's "Fragment of a Novel" illustrates the potential of Byron's thinking about narrative structure. I do not of course mean to imply that the "Fragment" had any literary influence. A historical relationship between *Childe Harold* and elegiac romance is suggested, however, by the structural similarities outlined here. A historical relationship of a somewhat more general sort between Byron and elegiac romance is suggested also by allusions to Byron in at least three major elegiac romances. In *The Great Gatsby*, Gatsby's fabricated autobiographical tale is patently Byronic: "I lived like a young rajah in all the capitals of Europe," Gatsby tells Nick, "trying to forget something very sad that happened to me long ago" (*GG* 66). In *The Real Life of Sebastian Knight*, Nabokov's narrator says when he describes certain passages in Sebastian's life that they seem to take on the character of "Byron's dream," a reference to the unusual

vantes's precedent in structure and theme and with the Romantic internalization of quest romance as dramatized by Byron, the story is once again highly ironic. As in Cervantes, it may be unclear at first reading whose values the reader is meant to share. The knights of elegiac romance (whom Jerome Thale calls "princes")[22] are obsessed by the goal of their quest, just as Parzival and Don Quixote are. They are the narrators' heroes of elegiac romance: Kurtz and Jim, Ashburnham, Sebastian Knight, Gatsby, Leverkühn, and so on. Their theater is adventurous action both physical and mental. They explore wildernesses of sea and land, art, sport, business, and sex, striving to fulfill their own fantasies of singular glory and lonely self-satisfaction.

The squires of elegiac romance share their knights' obsessions vicariously, serving them in attendance as ordinary seamen, servants, nurses, advance men, executors, toadies, and dupes. They are the narrators of elegiac romance--such characters as Nabokov's "V.", Ashburnham, Marlow, Zeitblom, Gene Forrester, Jack Burden, and Nick Carraway. Like Sancho Panza, each of these squire-like figures has in some sense "fallen in love with his master's madness and his own role." Each has "live[d] himself into" his hero's life and experience. Each has internalized the hero's madness. But now, by virtue of the tale the narrator tells, that madness becomes both obsessive and productive in the narrator himself.

In the first phase of the quest romance tradition, then, the

---

narrative structure of Byron's short poem, "The Dream," contemporaneous with *Childe Harold* III (*SK* 139). Nabokov's narrator also refers to a "club-footed shadow" in a portrait of Sebastian and to Sebastian's "Byronic langour" (*SK* 120). And in *Lord Jim*, Marlow alludes to Byron's physical defect, a kind of hallmark of the Byronic hero, when he suggests that in pacing the room Jim "gave a curious impression of an invisible halt in his gait" (*LJ* 169). Byron is the only author besides Shakespeare that Conrad's early persona, the Marlow of "Youth," has in his possession.

22. Jerome Thale, "Narrator as Hero," pp. 69-73. One of the characters in Nabokov's *The Real Life of Sebastian Knight* tells the narrator that he ought to write Knight's biography as "a fairy-tale with Sebastian for prince. The enchanted prince" (*SK* 23). Saint-Exupéry calls his narrator's child-hero "the little prince." In *Doctor Faustus* the narrator tells us that his hero had "the education of a young prince" (*DF*, Ch. 9). And Warren's narrator's hero is a "king." But Conrad calls Jim a "knight" (*LJ* 224), and "Knight" obviously seemed more suggestive to Nabokov, as it does to me, of the historical origins of the elegiac romance narrator's hero and his function in the genre.

knight alone undergoes the pain of change brought on by the rigors of the quest. In the second phase, the relationship between Cervantean knight and his squire is reciprocal, so that they undergo development together in the course of the story. In the third phase, the internalized Romantic quest, the knight plays no active role and change occurs only in the squire. In the fourth phase, the phase of elegiac romance, the knight again becomes conspicuous, but still undergoes no change. Or rather, he undergoes only one all-important change: at the end of the narrator's tale he dies. He does not mellow. He experiences no enlightenment or, at best, very little. His character remains constant. The squire-narrator is the true center of attention, because it is his character that develops. As in the third, the Romantic, phase of the tradition, the squire-narrator's quest is still a quest for independence. He is still the seeker after his birthright: freedom and "his own mature powers." Now, however, the dramatic situation and the reassertion of traditional heroic values in the person of the narrator's hero acknowledge that the squire-narrator's quest may be more difficult and complex than the Romantics quite allowed. The squire-narrator himself still seems to believe that his hero and his hero's agenda, not himself and his own agenda, are the proper focus of his attention, and what is more the proper focus of ours, the audience. Yet despite this appearance, in fact the squire-narrator is himself his own central concern in elegiac romance. And in reading elegiac romance it is the enlightenment of the squire-narrator that we, his audience, must strive to understand.

We know this for certain because in elegiac romance, since the squire tells us the story, our view of his hero is inevitably his view, an exterior view heavily obscured by the narrator's own concerns, biases, and fantasies. Thus we must assume that a good deal of what we seem to understand of the narrator's hero's character is a projection instead of the narrator's own complex personality. Although in this phase of the quest romance tradition we cannot therefore really share the knight's values or understand his inner life, we can know the values and inner life of the squire. By telling the tale, in fact, he invites us to share his inner life. Just as he, the narrator, was once imaginatively engaged in the life of his hero, he tries to engage us the readers imaginatively in adulation of his hero and in coping with his own life and problems, of which adulation of his hero is the central fact. If he is successful in this effort, we will assume along with the narrator the "active, exploratory, organizing role" that Albert Guerard says novels of this type require of their readers.[23] In short, the narrator tries to seduce the reader into sharing first his illusion and then his disillusionment, so that the reader will not just "respond" but instead gain a sort of self-knowledge that will be, as Thale puts it, "coincident" with the self-knowledge the narrator gains as he tells the tale. In elegiac romance, the quest of the squire-narrator becomes our quest.

Pastoral Elegy

Both this basic theme of elegiac romance and the structure that renders it are also recognizable in another traditional genre, the classical poetic form pastoral elegy. The similarity of the two forms lies in the putative origin of the fiction they render, the death of a valued friend; in their structure, the plaint for the lost friend that turns into a medium for introspection; and in their willingness to confront the issue of death and grief head on, rather than to avoid it in bouts of sentimentality, nostalgia, euphemism, and transcendental flight.

In addressing the issue of death and grief, elegiac romance differs strikingly from realist novels of the nineteenth century. These novels, as Robert Alter points out,

> though they may be filled with scenes of disease and dying, are in another sense also an implicit evasion of death because . . . behind the vast effort to represent in fiction a whole society . . . was a dream of omnipotence, the novelist creating a fantasy world so solid-seeming that he could rule over it like a god. When the writer, on the other hand, places himself or some consciously perceived surrogate within the fiction's field of probing consideration, his own mortality is more likely to be an implicit or even explicit subject of the novel. [Such a novel would] put us in touch with the im-

23. *Conrad the Novelist*, pp. 126-27.

ponderable implications of life implicit in the building of vivid and various fictions.[24]

To affirm life in response to the intense feelings of personal vulnerability that are an aspect of grief is of course an act of courage. Defiant courage of this sort is a central theme of the pastoral elegiac tradition. In a pastoral elegy, the speaker does not evade the fact of death. He faces it down through a creative act, the elegiac poem itself. The poem gives loss its full due by memorializing the speaker's friend as seeming in death almost larger and more affecting than in life. John H. Kuhnle has pointed out in discussing *The Great Gatsby* that in pastoral elegy the elegist traditionally treats "the elegized character as embodying special, even heroic significance. And, though the formal occasion of elegy traditionally has been the celebration of the noble life and death of an important person, the more subtle theme has concerned the effect of that death upon his survivors."[25]

Elegiac romance similarly gives loss its due and is similarly life-affirming and self-reflective. At the core of elegiac romance, as of other truly elegiac forms such as pastoral elegy, is the mode of self-discovery, self-revelation, and self-disclosure that Abbie Findlay Potts calls *anagnorisis*. Anagnorisis, Potts argues, "is the very goal of elegiac poetry, determining the whole procedure. . . . Elegy is the poetry of skeptical and revelatory vision for its

24. *Partial Magic: The Novel as a Self-Conscious Genre* (Berkeley: University of California Press, 1975), pp. 243-44.
25. "*The Great Gatsby* as Pastoral Elegy," in Matthew J. Bruccoli and Richard Layman, eds., *Fitzgerald/Hemingway Annual: 1978* (Detroit, Mich.: Gale, 1979), pp. 141-54. See also Richard P. Adams's list of seventeen conventions of pastoral elegy in "Whitman's 'Lilacs' and the Tradition of Pastoral Elegy," *PMLA*, 72 (1957), 479; J. H. Hanford, "The Pastoral Elegy and Milton's 'Lycidas'," *PMLA*, 25 (1910), 403-47; and George Norlin, "The Conventions of the Pastoral Elegy," *American Journal of Philology*, 32 (1911), 294-312; David Stouck, "White Sheep on Fifth Avenue: *The Great Gatsby* as Pastoral," *Genre*, 4 (1971), 335-47; Renato Poggioli, "The Oaten Flute," *Harvard Library Bulletin*, 11 (1957), 147-84; Erwin Panofsky, "Et In Arcadia Ego: On the Conception of Transience in Poussin and Watteau," *Philosophy and History: Essays Presented to Ernst Cassirer* (Oxford: Clarendon Press, 1936), pp. 223-54, reprinted in *Pastoral and Romance*, ed. Eleanor Terry Lincoln (Englewood Cliffs, N.J.: Prentice Hall, 1969); and Thomas G. Rosenmeyer, *The Green Cabinet: Theocritus and the European Pastoral Lyric* (Berkeley, Cal.: University of California Press, 1969). Passages from "Lycidas" in this section are from Merritt Y. Hughes, ed., *John Milton: Complete Poems and Major Prose* (New York: Odyssey Press, 1957), pp. 116-25.

own sake, satisfying the hunger of man to see, to know, to understand. Whether the reader be purged or indoctrinated, he must be enlightened. In its latest as in its earliest guise elegy labors toward human truth as its end in view."[26] Harold Bloom has extended this line of thought by suggesting that "the great pastoral elegies . . . do not express grief at all" but rather "center upon their composers' own creative anxieties." "The largest irony" of the pastoral elegist's effort, Bloom says, may be that by "confronting the imminence of death" he works "to subvert the immortality" of his precursor, to whose memory he ostensibly devotes his verse.[27]

Each of these elements is evident in one of the most familiar pastoral elegies in English, Milton's "Lycidas." Here, the occasion of the speaker's "song" is the death of a friend, "For *Lycidas* is dead, dead ere his prime,/ Young *Lycidas*, and hath not left his peer." The speaker's ostensible purpose in the poem is to celebrate the life and accomplishments of his friend and the pleasures of their friendship. The speaker indentifies with Lycidas, because they grew up together, "nurst upon the self-same hill,/ Fed the same flock, by fountain, shade, and rill"; and because they shared the same interests and talent, Lycidas too, like the speaker, knew how to "sing, and build the lofty rhyme."

Thus the speaker in pastoral elegy sets out to eulogize his dead friend, and does return to this purpose intermittently. It soon becomes clear, though, that his mind is more troubled by another subject, one he is led to by reflecting on the loss of his friend. This subject is the short, rapid flight of the speaker's own life and the nearness and inevitability of his own death. His plaint is saturated with feelings of inadequacy, impotence, spiritual emptiness, and, perhaps, rage in the face of inevitable death:

> Alas! what boots it with uncessant care
> To tend the homely slighted Shepherd's trade,
> And strictly meditate the thankless Muse?
> . . . . .

26. *The Elegiac Mode* (Ithaca, N.Y.: Cornell University Press, 1967), pp. 36-66.
27. *The Anxiety of Influence* (New York: Oxford University Press, 1973), p. 151.

43

> *Fame* is the spur that the clear spirit doth raise
> (That last infirmity of Noble mind)
> To scorn delights, and live laborious days;
> But the fair Guerdon when we hope to find,
> And think to burst out into sudden blaze,
> Comes the blind *Fury* with th'abhorred shears,
> And slits the thin-spun life.

This subject—the foreseen loss of the speaker's own life, energy, and oppportunity, the imminence of old age and death—in one form or another dominates many pastoral elegies, as it does most elegiac romances. In pastoral elegy especially, the speaker's friend, whose life and character never do come through very clearly, is either displaced altogether by these concerns, or else transformed in the speaker's meditation into a symbol of them.

Pastoral elegy does not end, however, with the expression of anxiety over loss. By "singing," by symbolizing his anxiety in the figure of his lost friend and expressing his grief, the elegist overcomes his depressed state of mind. Through this imaginary, symbolic act, he puts behind him not only the lost past but also his fear of future loss. He restores his own vitality, once sapped by anxiety and grief, and prepares his mind for action. Refreshed, he sets out to remake his life. On this optimistic note "Lycidas" ends:

> Thus sang the uncouth Swain to th'Oaks and rills,
> While the still morn went out with Sandals gray;
> He touch't the tender stops of various Quills,
> With eager thought warbling his *Doric* lay:
> And now the Sun had stretch't out all the hills,
> And now was dropt into the Western bay;
> At last he rose, and twitch't his Mantle blue:
> Tomorrow to fresh Woods, and Pastures new.[28]

28. In *The Green Cabinet*, Thomas Rosenmeyer points out that there are two currents in the pastoral elegiac tradition. In one, "nature is said to be exercising a refreshing or consoling power." In the other, "nature is shown to be dying with the man or woman lamented" (p. 113). If the structural parallel I have been arguing for here between pastoral elegy and elegiac romance is valid, then the revitalization of the speaker in "Lycidas" and of the narrator in most of the elegiac romances considered in this book would place all these works in the former of these two categories. In elegiac romances in the latter current of the

In structure and theme, elegiac romance is remarkably similar to this classic poetic form. The narrator in elegiac romance confronts his "astonishment and grief" by recreating his lost friend in a character of heroic proportions, a "vivid and various fiction," thereby making immutable both the person and his feeling for him, so that the narrator can in effect walk away renewed. At the same time, however, as I suggest later, the narrator in elegiac romance accomplishes something larger as well. The social psychologist Peter Marris has described grief as a response not just to loss of a particular person but to "the disintegration of the whole structure of meaning dependent on the relationship" with that person.[29] The task the elegiac romance narrator undertakes in telling his tale is therefore additionally burdensome, since the hero of the tale is more than a lost friend apotheosized. His loss represents the loss of aspects of the narrator's own inner life and also loss of aspects of "the whole structure of meaning" of the cultural epoch in which the narrator lives.

Like pastoral elegy, elegiac romance avoids the sentimentality, nostalgia, and transcendental speculation to which such a loss of meaning might tend, with an aesthetic form that helps overcome, as Marris puts it, the impulse merely "to restore the past." This aesthetic form allows us to assimilate loss and change "by placing them in the context of a familiar, reliable construction of reality."[30] It is not just that an act of narration helps the narrator survive a catastrophic loss. What helps him survive is the peculiar kind of narration undertaken in this elegiac tradition. The hero of the elegist's tale is cast in the role of a highly conventional, highly traditional, hence a highly reliable figure. The narrator or speaker knows, the author knows, we the readers know, on the one hand what is likely to happen to a classical pastoral figure—a Lycidas, an Adonais—and, on the other hand, what is

---

tradition, it would seem, narrators might seem to waste away and perhaps even die in sympathy with the heroic figures whose death they lament. The possible existence of this current in the evolution of elegiac romance seems evident in Fitzgerald's *The Last Tycoon* and in Joan Didion's *The Book of Common Prayer*. See Chapter Seven, note 9.

29. "Attachment and Society," in *The Place of Attachment in Human Behaviour*, ed. Colin Murray Parkes and Joan Stevenson-Hinde (London: Tavistock, 1982); as quoted in Anthony Storr, "The Bonding Process," *TLS*, July 30, 1982, p. 822.

30. Peter Marris, *Loss and Change* (New York: Pantheon, 1974), pp. 5-6.

likely to happen to a Faust, a Byronic hero, a Lohengrin, a Cid, a Chevalier Bayard. What the narrator, the author, and the reader together do not know is what is likely to happen to ourselves, except of course that eventually we too are sure to die.

The fictional hero in a pastoral elegy or an elegiac romance, together with the poem or the fiction as a whole, serves, therefore, as a temporary point of reference in the face of unavoidable, catastrophic loss, change, or uncertainty. It is just here, then, that we get our first hint of the way elegiac romance as a cultural artifact may contribute its own insight to our understanding of how human beings cope in the face of loss. Marris argues that, normally, we respond to loss in one of two ways. We may formulate "the principles of the fundamental structure of meaning each of us has grown up" with "in terms abstract enough to apply to any event we encounter." This, Marris suggests, is the option offered by the social sciences. Or we may choose instead to try to "ignore or prevent experiences which would not be comprehended in terms of" the fundamental structure of meaning each of us has grown up with. This is the option offered by political and religious extremism.[31]

The elegiac tradition, as developed in elegiac romance, however, offers a third option. That option is to undertake through an aesthetic act an imaginative "research" into the past, a *recherche du temps perdu*, to discover the roots of the fundamental structure of meaning that each of us has grown up with. The central virtue of this aesthetic act is, so to speak, safely to preserve that traditional or conventional structure of meaning in amber, in the aesthetically satisfying form of the elegist's tale about his hero and his hero's career. Preserving in this form the fundamental structure of meaning we have grown up with, then, frees us—the narrator, the reader, even perhaps the author himself—from the hold it has upon us. It frees us to change, that is, because in a single gesture it both acknowledges that what is lost is lost, finally and irrevocably—the hero is dead—and provides a means by which, to quote Marris once again,"the lost attachment can still give meaning to the present."[32]

31. *Loss and Change*, p. 17.
32. Page 149.

We must of course take care in making this comparison between elegiac romance and pastoral elegy. Elegiac romance is a genre of the infinitely free form of prose fiction, unbounded by the rigorous conventions of pastoral poetry. Its mode is quest romance not pastoral friendship, so that Arcadian languor and sentiment rarely appear, and instead the heroic mode dominiates. In pastoral elegy, furthermore, lyric self-concern overtakes and subordinates selfless eulogy, whereas in elegiac romance it is autobiographical self-concern that overtakes and subordinates the selfless biographical urge. There may well be other differences. But the similarities between pastoral elegy and elegiac romance are nevertheless striking enough to suggest that historically an elegiac literary form with the characteristics basic to these two genres is endemic to Western culture, and perhaps even to suggest that elegiac romance serves today something of the same function served at various moments in the past by pastoral elegy.

An Outline of Elegiac Romance

On the surface, modern works of fiction expressing these themes and written in the narrative form I have been discussing tend to be deceptively diverse. This diversity may make it hard at first to see their underlying similarity. The canon of elegiac romance includes some short fiction such as Faulkner's "Uncle Willy," Stefan Zweig's "Buchmendel," Bernard Malamud's "The German Refugee," Indro Montanelli's "His Excellency," Willa Cather's "My Mortal Enemy," Julio Cortazar's "The Pursuer," Truman Capote's *Breakfast at Tiffany's*, and Saint Exupéry's *The Little Prince*.

The canon of elegiac romance also includes a number of major works of modern fiction. Some of these longer elegiac romances are novels of exotic adventure, such as Conrad's *Heart of Darkness* and *Lord Jim*. Others run to the conventions of true-love-confession and sentimental realism, for example Fitzgerald's unfinished novel, *The Last Tycoon*. There are anatomies of human monstrosity, such as Nabokov's *Pale Fire*, and examinations of the creative personality, such as his *Real Life of Sebastian Knight*.

Some elegiac romances, such as *The Great Gatsby* and Warren's *All the King's Men*, undertake to analyze explicitly a corrupt cultural ideal. Others, such as Salinger's "Seymour: An Introduction" and John Knowles's *A Separate Peace*, study the agonies of adolescence. In sharp contrast still another, Ford Madox Ford's *The Good Soldier*, renders satirically the trials of marital infidelity. One of the most complex of all elegiac romances, Mann's *Doctor Faustus*, manages to accomplish many of these thematic tasks all at once.

In this rapid survey of elegiac romance fiction we may observe several common traits. One is that each is characteristically elegiac on two levels and also on two levels characteristically a work of quest romance. Hence the term I have applied to the form—elegiac romance. The form is on two levels a quest romance because the narrator's hero as the narrator remembers him, modeled on the knightly hero of traditional romance, is involved in a quest on the grand scale. And the narrator, modeled on the poet-squire of Romantic internalized romance and on the ironic role played by Cervantes's Sancho Panza, is launched on a more modest, but ultimately more interesting, inner or metaphysical quest of his own.

The form is on two levels elegiac too, because the quest of both characters, narrator and narrator's hero, is generated by a sense of loss. The narrator's hero, as the narrator remembers him, in almost every case regards the past as something external to himself that stands as a barrier to his own success. He therefore futilely rejects the past, overvalues it, or finds it an intolerable burden—or all of these at once. This effort is futile because in most cases the values of the narrator's hero are irredeemably fixed in the past. Nevertheless, he regards his own quest, typically, as an attempt to recapture, rectify, challenge, or throw off the past by struggling heroically with its present results, representatives, or other unfortunate residue. The narrator, more modestly, regrets mainly his own past and seeks only to come to terms with that past by remembering it and telling a tale adequate to the complexity of feeling that that memory evokes.

A second trait we may observe in a rapid survey of elegiac romances is that even the titles of many of them, especially major ones, tend to be deceptive or ironic. Like the title of *The Great Gatsby*, the title of an elegiac romance often calls attention to the ostensible hero of the narrator's tale, but at the same time qualifies that attention so as to cast doubt even before the tale begins on the ostensible hero's legitimacy both as *a* hero and as *the* hero, that is, both on his genuineness and integrity and on his role as the true central figure in the work: "Lord" Jim "the great" Gatsby, all the "king's" men, "Doctor Faustus," the "last tycoon." The title of an elegiac romance often reveals right away, perhaps sooner than we really expect it, the narrator's point of view. In doing so, the title of an elegiac romance itself may be the first gesture in the complex rhetoric of the narrator's tale.

A third characteristic of elegiac romance fiction revealed by a rapid survey of the canon is a typical sequence of events presented systematically out of their proper chronological order. In chronological order, the sequence of events in an elegiac romance run roughly as follows. In the fictional past, a self-effacing young or middle-aged person, in most elegiac romances to date a male (Marlow, John Dowell, Nick, Buddy Glass, Jack Burden, Serenus Zeitblom), at one time encountered another person, usually older than himself and also in most cases male (Kurtz, Jim, Edward Ashburnham, Gatsby, Seymour, Willie Stark, Adrian Leverkühn), and transformed him into a heroic figure by projecting onto him his own private wish-fulfilling fantasies. The friend, apparently gratified by this adulation or (more usually) apparently indifferent to it. accepted the heroic role but did little to return the other's affection. Eventually the "heroic" friend died. Crushed by his loss, the hero worshiper sets out in the dramatized fictional present to memorialize his hero by writing his biography. That biography is the narrator's tale that we read. In the course of ostensibly telling the story of his hero's life, however, the hero worshiper, now the apparently self-effacing narrator, manages to reveal a good deal of himself. His biography of his hero turns out in fact to be an *auto*biography, or sometimes an autobiographical fragment, that both explores a crucial phase in the narrator's own emotional development and ends that phase by resolving the problem that gave rise to it. As he tells the tale, the narrator revaluates his hero and himself.

By this means, he frees himself from the burden of the obsessive attachment and from its concomitant state of arrested emotional development.

The formal order of elegiac romance differs considerably, however, from this chronological order of events. Formally, elegiac romance fiction divides the chronological sequence into two portions at a point some few months or years after the death of the narrator's hero, the moment at which the narrator begins to tell the tale. Thus the narrative structure of elegiac romance is contrapuntal. The fiction as a whole consists of two sets of parallel events: (1) events occurring in the dramatized fictional present, including character development and change in the narrator and his insight into his hero's nature and into his own; and (2) events that occurred in the fictional past and that are therefore part of the narrator's tale, usually events in the hero's life although sometimes also the narrator's earlier insights that he now remembers and to which he now can give new meaning.

If the narrator does not explicitly suggest a significant correspondence between these two sets of events, such a correspondence is usually implied through the formal order of the fiction. An elegiac romance begins in the dramatized fictional present: the narrator introduces himself as telling the tale that follows and announces, usually, that the hero of the tale is dead. The events in the tale have occurred in the narrated fictional past when the narrator met the person who now becomes the hero of the tale, and the tale ends in most cases with that person's death. While the narrator is telling this tale comprised of events in the fictional past, however, other still more important events are occurring in the dramatized fictional present. The narrator tells us about these events as well, not always (indeed, not usually) calling our attention to the difference between them. Through telling the tale, the narrator experiences one or more dramatized insights into himself and his hero, and he manifestly undergoes some degree of character development. The act of narration, the urge to explore his hero's experience and his own that engendered that act, and the insights that narration in turn engenders play off in a kind of narrative counterpoint against the past events in the tale itself. Toward the end of the fiction, as the tale he is telling approaches the moment of his hero's death, the narrator usually resolves the problem that motivated him to tell the tale in the first place, insofar as he is capable of resolving it.[33]

In many elegiac romances this contrapuntal structure is enhanced with appropriate modern narrative techniques such as reflective and reportorial digressions, memory slips, editorial commentary, and other seemingly capricious means of temporal disruption. These stylistic techniques further complicate the chronology, tailoring it to the narrator's particular, and sometimes rather peculiar, cast of mind.[34]

The *necessary conditions* for elegiac romance fiction are the narrator's protracted hero worship of his friend, and his friend's death before the narrator begins to tell the tale. The *occasion* of the narrator's tale is his irretrievable loss of his hero. The *ostensible purpose* of his tale is to memorialize his lost hero. The *real purpose* of his tale is to recover the coherence of his own interior world, lost when he lost the screen, so to speak, upon which he had projected his fantasies.

The Hero in Modern Fiction

In achieving this purpose, the narrator in elegiac romance becomes a new and distinctively twentieth-century figure. His

---

33. The counterpoint in elegiac romance of past events in the narrator's tale against present events occurring as the tale is told creates some minor stylistic difficulties for critics. Conventionally we talk about events in a literary work in present tense (Hamlet sees the ghost; Tom Jones marries Sophia). To discuss elegiac romance we have to use present and past tense to distinguish between what the narrator, the narrator's hero, and others *did* during the narrated past of the tale (Zeitblom followed Leverkühn to Halle; Gatsby watched the green light; Judge Irwin played with the toy canon); and what the narrator and others *do* as the narrator tells the tale (Marlow insults his listeners and they protest; Buddy Glass complains about his health). We may occasionally even have to use a past perfect tense to distinguish between what the narrator says the narrator's hero *did* and what the narrator says the narrator's hero *said he had done* (Marlow says that Jim told him Stein had offered him a second chance in Patusan). These distinctions will be maintained throughout this book.

34. This trait of the narrator's style is perhaps most evident in *The Good Soldier* and *The Real Life of Sebastian Knight*. But see also Erich Heller's comment on the opening sentence of Mann's *Doctor Faustus* in *Thomas Mann: The Ironic German* (Cleveland, Ohio: Meridian, 1961), p. 254; and Zeitblom's remarks on "the absence of a controlled and regular structure in my work" (*DF*, Ch. 21).

exemplary qualities are those of self-recovery and self-realization. The narrator recovers the coherence of his inner world by drawing the past out of himself in telling the tale. This method works for him, first, because to narrate is to transform remembered experience into symbol; and second, because this process of symbolizing does more than merely represent. To symbolize is to effect significant mental development. By symbolizing, Ernst Cassirer says in *Philosophy of Symbolic Forms*, we separate or extract the material symbolized from "the constant flux of the contents of consciousness." This extraction "fixes" the material so that we can then "confront it in imagination as something past and yet not vanished."[35] Thus in an elegiac romance the narrator, such as for example Nick Carraway, exercises what Cassirer calls "an original formative activity" in telling his tale. In doing so, he apprehends the experience that constitutes his tale, and at the same time apprehends a "formative law" that governs his own mental processes. In telling the tale, the narrator follows, and thereby discovers, what Nabokov's narrator in *The Real Life of Sebastian Knight* calls the "rhythmical interlacements" of his own thought and personality (*SK* 137).

Elegiac romance implies, therefore, an important contrast between the true symbolic act the narrator accomplishes in the fictional present in telling the tale, and the flawed symbolic act he indulged himself in during the fictional past when he encountered an impressive-seeming fellow and transformed him into a personal hero. This implicit contrast underlies the meaning of elegiac romance. The simplest and most general way to express this meaning is to say elegiac romance shows that a true symbolic act has power hero-worship lacks, the power to "fix" the contents of consciousness. The narrator's hero is a glimpse of the narrator's immature "picture" of the world "inside his head," as Robert Penn Warren's narrator Jack Burden expresses it (*AKM* 247). Telling the tale changes the mental picture, the perceptual paradigm, by which the narrator interprets the world.

To put it another way, the narrator's hero in elegiac romance is a static projection of the narrator's own "secret needs" (again

35. Vol. 1, *Language*, trans. Ralph Manheim (New Haven: Yale University Press, 1953), pp. 89-93.

Robert Penn Warren's term).[36] The narrator's tale tells us how in the past he projected those secret needs onto a heroic figure in order to try to satisfy them magically. Thus, each narrator's hero in elegiac romance is the perfect mirror in which the narrator and his audience can see reflected what Nabokov's narrator calls "the close fitting dream of his [that is, the narrator's] own personality" (*SK* 179). Hero making did not free the narrator from narrow, immature preconceptions of life and the world. It reinforced them. Worse still, the narrator projected his exaggerated, wish-fulfilling image on someone who is in fact a mortal being like himself. This is why the death of the narrator's hero was such a stunning blow, and why in the long run it turns out to be such a salubrious event as well.

His hero's death is salubrious because it forces upon the narrator the perspective he might otherwise not be strong enough to establish for himself. As Susanne Langer tells us, we symbolize in order to "develop a characteristic attitude toward" an object *in absentia*.[37] The death of the narrator's hero, by absenting him irremediably, establishes the very condition that the narrator of elegiac romance requires in order to engage in an act of true, that is effective not regressive, symbolic expression. The important result of the narrator's hero's death is that it makes the hero's mythic aura apparent to the narrator and hence to his audience. Gatsby alive—the pink-suited gangster Nick knew in West Egg whose Byronic glamour derived in large measure from Nick's own adolescent illusions—that Gatsby is not exactly the Gatsby of Nick's tale. The Gatsby of Nick's tale is Gatsby being reflected upon and being seen through. He is a product of Nick's maturing mind.

36. Warren uses the phrase "secret needs" in discussing the relationship between the demagogue and his people. The politician's success in *All the King's Men*, he says, was "based on the fact that somehow he could vicariously fulfill some secret needs of the people about him." Chief among the people around Willie Stark is of course Jack Burden. And in describing how the novel developed out of the earlier play, *Proud Flesh*, Warren says that "the story, in a sense, became the story of Jack Burden, the teller of the tale" ("Introduction to the Modern Library Edition of *All the King's Men*," reprinted in Robert H. Chambers, ed., *Twentieth Century Interpretations of "All the King's Men"* [Englewood Cliffs, N.J.: Prentice Hall, 1977], pp. 93, 96).

37. *Philosophy in a New Key* (Cambridge, Mass.: Harvard University Press, 1942), p. 31.

One significance of this underlying theme to elegiac romance as a twentieth-century fictional genre lies in what it says about modern attitudes toward heroes and heroism.[38] In Disraeli's *Coningsby*, one character gives another the following advice: "Nurture your mind with great thoughts. To believe in the heroic makes heroes."[39] To be fair to Disraeli and to the nineteenth century, we should of course read this passage "straight." Yet for twentieth-century readers it is hard not to read it ironically. Heroes are made by those who believe in heroes. Heroes are products of hero worship. Thus nineteenth-century heroism unilluminated and corrupted in a twentieth-century context is the motivating force behind the growth of elegiac romance as a genre. Elegiac romance attacks one aspect of the culture-lag from age to age that seems to be especially severe in the twentieth century. This is what Thomas Mann suggests when his character Leverkühn says in *Doctor Faustus*, "The nineteenth century must have been an uncommonly pleasant epoch, since it had never been harder for humanity to tear itself away from the opinions and habits (*Anschauungen und Gewohnheiten*) of the previous period than it was for the generation now living" (*DF*, Ch.4).

Elegiac romance as a fictional genre is part of the twentieth-century effort to tear ourselves away from the nineteenth century and replace outworn, conventional heroism (seen in the narrators' heroes of elegiac romance) with a new, more modest, effective set of exemplary values (seen in the narrators of elegiac romance). It is decidedly not another modern ironical attempt to rehabilitate and perpetuate the traditional notion of the Western hero, nor is it, as Walter Reed argues, an attempt "to protect the hero, to keep alive the hope for a hero in our time" by

38. For a useful survey of twentieth-century views of the nineteenth-century hero, see the first chapter of Reed, *Meditations on the Hero*.

39. Benjamin Disraeli, *Coningsby: Or the New Generation* (New York: Capricorn, 1961), p. 145 (book 3, chapter 1). Some readers may wonder at this point in my argument why I have not mentioned Carlyle. One reason is that I think the sentence quoted from Disraeli encapsulates adequately for my purposes the viewpoint Carlyle represents. The second reason is that because Carlyle assumes the potential value of heroic virtues, for literary critics having difficulty understanding "the twentieth-century hero," reading Carlyle almost seems to be part of the problem. It seldom seems to be part of the solution. See for example Chapter Three, note 1, and Chapter Seven, note 7.

mounting "a problematical defense of heroism, a lament over its corruption and demise."[40] On the contrary, elegiac romance is an effort to dispense with heroes and heroism entirely. The elegiac romance narrator's hero is an atavism representing adherence to outworn values and archaic modes of thought. In many cases he is an almost purely nineteenth-century Romantic figure, the sort Harry Levin describes as being imbued with "proud, uncompromising, absolute individualism,"[41] a character like Conrad's Jim, about whom Marlow says "of all mankind [he] had no dealings but with himself" (*LJ* 251). The narrator's hero in elegiac romance combines traits of both the traditional hero and the Byronic hero. In most cases he is drawn "bigger than life," above the level of common everyday life in every virtue and every flaw, and he is drawn apparently profound in sensibility and apparently Satanic in arrogant resistance to the needs, virtues, and possibilities of everyday life.[42]

The narrator in elegiac romance, in contrast to the narrator's hero, is the sort of modern figure Joseph Campbell describes who "in the absence of an effective general mythology . . . has his private, unrecognized, rudimentary, yet secretly potent pantheon of dreams."[43] He embodies these dreams in the hero of his tale. The narrator admits, in short, that he was at one time enthralled by what he took to be his hero's virtues and attractive qualities of character. But the values and the state of mind that the narrator arrives at in the course of telling the tale are not those he began with, and they are not ones his hero would share.

As a representative figure, therefore, it is narrators of this kind of fiction—Marlow, Nick, Jack Burden, Zeitblom—not their heroes, who tend to be the sort of exemplary modern personages Ortega y Gasset describes, those who aim "at altering the course of things" by refusing "to repeat the gestures that custom, tradition, or biological instincts force them to make," and for whom an exemplary life results from the "will to be oneself."[44]

40. *Meditations on the Hero*, pp. 190-92.

41. "From Priam to Birotteau," in *Gates of Horn*, p. 61.

42. Thorslev succinctly summarizes and contrasts traditional and Romantic or Byronic heroic values in *The Byronic Hero*, pp. 186-90.

43. *The Hero with a Thousand Faces* (Princeton, N.J.: Pantheon, 1949), p. 4.

44. *Meditation on Quixote*, trans. Evelyn Rugg and Diego Marin (New York: Norton, 1961), p. 149.

That is to say, the elegiac romance narrator is not to be confused with the modern "anti-hero." He is no Willie Loman, no
underground man. If the narrator's mood as he begins his tale
in some cases seems depressed and subservient, this is because
although his hero is gone before the tale begins, he is not yet
sufficiently forgotten. It is not accurate either to describe as anti-
heroic the state of mind and the values the narrator arrives at
in the course of telling the tale, although the fiction as a whole
might be fairly described in that way. The narrator's final state
of mind and values do not take issue with heroism or contend
with it directly. A more appropriate term for the state of mind
and values that elegiac romance narrators arrive at in telling the
tale might be "a-heroic." It is what we tend to think of as the
state of mind and values of realistic, mature, everyday life. What
is exemplary about the narrators of elegiac romance is that eventually they are able to step around heroism, as if finally, mer-
cifully, heroism just wasn't of much importance any longer.

The narrator's new values and state of mind arrived at in the
course of telling his tale may not seem exemplary at first to most
readers. We the readers, the narrator's audience, are accultur-
ated much as he has been. We too tend to be imbued with the
conventional themes and values of traditional nineteenth-century heroism. We are likely at first, therefore, to identify with
the narrator's initial response to the hero of his tale. We are
likely to share his hero-worshiping admiration. And we are likely
to heed the narrator's self-abnegating gestures and regard the
hero of his tale as the central figure of the fiction as a whole.
But in adopting initially the narrator's hero-worshiping attitude
in this way, we must eventually also undergo with him a change
in that attitude. We must begin to see that insofar as the narrator's tale makes it seem as if the narrator's hero is the central
figure in the fiction as a whole, the narrator's tale is, to adapt
Stanley Fish's phrase, self-consuming. Each elegiac romance examines from its own distinct point of view its narrator's strenuous
attempt, in most cases a mostly successful attempt, to overcome
the tendency to hero-worship. Elegiac romance is the drama of
an obsessive hero-*maker* struggling to become his own person.
Elegiac romances are stories about how to quit the quest, or at
any rate how to quit being a squire on someone else's quest: how

to live no longer as merely the appendage of another person's being.

From this point of view, then, the principal characteristic of nineteenth-century heroism is its appeal to self-delusion. The exemplary nature of the elegiac romance narrator is based on careful, conscious, voluntary disillusionment. Mark Harris has made one of the most succinct statements of this theme. The only heroes today, a character in Harris's elegiac romance *Bang the Drum Slowly* sagaciously remarks, are those who have learned to live without heroes.[45] The person living without heroes—or rather, striving to live without them—is the distinctively modern figure given to the twentieth century in the narrator of elegiac romance.

Psychological and Epistemological Fiction

Elegiac romance may sometimes, therefore, be painful to read. The action of the narrator's tale involves loss, grief, disappointment, disillusionment, and guilt. Telling the tale involves the anguish of coming to terms, literally and figuratively, with these feelings. A primary motive in examining elegiac romance in this book is to try to get to the bottom of that anguish, because elegiac romance represents a neglected resource for understanding "modernism." A class of fiction roughly contemporaneous with the psychological novel and a counterpart to it, elegiac romance is at least its equal in its coherence as a genre and in its historical significance.

There is no pat answer, of course, to the question, What is the source of the narrator's anguish in elegiac romance? Any answer we offer must be complex and have broad cultural ramifications. As the narrator's anguish is, presumably, our own as well, our generalizations will be subject to endless modification and misunderstanding. Still, it helps to see that the narrator's travail in elegiac romance has two related sources, which I will call "epistemological" and "psychological."[46] These aspects of

45. *Bang the Drum Slowly* (New York: Dell, 1973), p. 262.
46. For further discussion of the sense in which I use the term "epistemological" in this book, see the beginning of Chapter Five.

mental experience are what, in *Science and the Modern World*, Alfred North Whitehead calls "the two great preoccupations of modern philosophy." We might assume that these preoccupations underlie many problematic aspects of modern life. Whitehead defines the terms respectively as interest in how the mind gains "knowledge of a common objective world" and interest in "mental functionings in themselves and their mutual relations . . . as passions of the mind."[47]

Whitehead's distinction is admittedly somewhat arbitrary. He calls it an "uneasy" distinction giving rise to a host of perplexities. It is nevertheless useful for the purposes of this book because it leads us to observe that to date only one of these two preoccupations, the psychological, has been widely identified as a major theme in modern literature. The "psychological novel" appears in modern fiction with the work of James, Woolf, Joyce, and Dorothy Richardson. It seeks to convey mental processes directly ("the atoms that fall on the mind," in Virginia Woolf's well-known phrase), often through stream-of-consciousness techniques. About the time psychological novels first appear on the scene at the turn of the century, elegiac romances also first appear in the early novels of Joseph Conrad. Elegiac romances likewise attempt to examine the nature of mental experience. Yet the two genres differ radically in their formal conventions and thematic concerns. Elegiac romances do not render mental processes directly. They render instead, as I have been arguing, the process of understanding that the narrator undergoes through the symbolic act of telling his tale, as he tries to reveal a mental burden he has not yet recognized or perhaps is only just beginning to recognize.

That this effort to understand as-yet-unrevealed knowledge is central to elegiac romance means that elegiac romances often use images that represent the deepest levels of the symbol-maker's—that is, the narrator's—emotional life. The most important of these images is the adventurous hero of the narrator's tale. To the extent that elegiac romances reveal hidden levels of the narrator's emotional life, they too are decidedly psychological novels. But generally speaking, elegiac romance narrators do not

47. *Science and the Modern World* (New York: Free Press, 1967), pp. 146-47.

use imagery in a direct, associative way imitative of conscious thought—the "stream of consciousness." Even in novels where the narrator claims to be making up his tale as he goes along (a frequent claim in elegiac romance), he belies the claim with a strong penchant for talking shop. If he is making it up as he goes along, he is also exceedingly self-conscious about narrative technique. He complains about difficulties involved in getting across his meaning, about narrative problems inherent in his material, about the ineffectiveness of his transitions, the length of his chapters, the incoherence of his narrative sequences, and so on. In most elegiac romances, we are continually made aware that both the symbol-making impulse and the story-teller's art shape how the narrator remembers his inner experience and how he perceives the objective world, in particular the most important element in that world, the hero of his tale. Hence one of the most important larger issues in elegiac romance is epistemological: the nature of learning and knowledge, the way the mind apprehends itself and the world outside it.

Certainly psychological novels have their epistemological dimension too, although critics have rarely examined it. If we were to ask what is suggested in the psychological novel about how we gain knowledge of an objective world, we could do worse than cite the doctrine of the symbolist movement, a movement that Leon Edel taught us is intimately related to the development of the psychological novel.[48] Symbolist literature is based on the premise, Richard Ellmann suggests, that "human imagination actively constructs the world we perceive or at least meets it more than halfway."[49] It would not be difficult to construct from a study of *Ulysses*, for example, a distinctly Joycean associative-emotional theory of knowledge involving a process of imaginative construction in this sense. Virginia Woolf's *To the Lighthouse* begins with a young child engaged in an imaginative apprehension of his surroundings. James Ramsay cutting out "the picture of a refrigerator" endows it, when told of the im-

48. *The Modern Psychological Novel: 1900-1950* (New York: Lippincott, 1955).
49. Richard Ellmann and Charles Feidelson, Jr., eds., *The Modern Tradition: Backgrounds of Modern Literature* (New York: Oxford University Press, 1965), p. 7.

pending expedition, "with heavenly bliss."[50] Woolf's novel proceeds then to examine the possibilities and limitations of several varieties of epistemological experience. Even Faulkner's *The Sound and the Fury* might be read with some profit as a set of four exercises in the relative failure of understanding.

Understanding is always at issue in the psychological novel because the way the mind apprehends the objective world inevitably affects "the passions of the mind." But understanding usually is a progressive process, not an instantaneous one. It takes time. Time is at a premium in psychological novels. They tend to render the rich complexity of conscious mental processes during relatively short periods: three days, one day, several hours, or even just a few minutes. Furthermore, time is perceived in the psychological novel not as a series of periods of change, but (to use Bergson's term) as *dure*, the gathering by association of many moments, consciously and unconsciously remembered, consciously and unconsciously apprehended, and fused into a many-layered, ever-immediate present. As a result of this concept of time, while consciousness may be a continuously changing "stream," the change represented in psychological novels is not necessarily progressive. Although the "passions of the mind" are in a continual stir, they do not necessarily involve mental growth; often the "passions of the mind" are repetitive, circular, and obsessive, as for the most part Mrs. Ramsay's and Leopold Bloom's are.

Understanding by definition involves mental growth. It is a process of developmental change that may of course sometimes be desultory and incoherent, but is also often punctuated by clearly definable stages of insight marked by shifts in feeling toward ourselves and the world around us. One of the important ways elegiac romance differs from the psychological novel is that it dramatizes this process of long-term mental development.

Elegiac romance may be seen from this point of view, therefore, as representing a response to the needs of its times that differs somewhat from the response represented by the psychological novel. Both types of fiction in effect contradict what Richard Ellmann has called "the central miracle for the Edwardians

50. *To the Lighthouse* (New York: Harcourt, Brace, 1927), p. 9.

. . . the sudden alteration of the self," miraculous rebirth, the possibility of rapid change in one's fundamental constitution that could be profound, thorough, recognizable, dramatic, permanent, and welcome.[51] The psychological novel challenges this belief and affirms the coherence and integrity of the self by representing mental processes in overwhelmingly complex detail. It shows us the conscious mind much as time-stop photography shows us an opening flower or a bird in flight. But the psychological novel also seems to imply that, given a process that complex and subtle, fundamental constitutional change is unlikely. In the selves represented to us as Mrs. Ramsay and Mrs. Dalloway, we are meant neither to see nor to hope for sudden profound alteration.

Elegiac romance challenges belief in sudden alteration of the self in quite another way. Unlike the psychological novel, it is optimistic about the human potential for inner change. But it implies that change of that order occurs infrequently and is likely to be slow, painful, inconspicuous, partial, often difficult to recognize, and not always entirely welcome: what one becomes may take some getting used to. Elegiac romance also implies that inner change involves understanding. It occurs only with disillusionment, as a result of insight into the nature and effects of the illusions one has held.

The effort in elegiac romance to dramatize inner change as a difficult, long-term process implies, furthermore, a considerable difference in range of subject matter and reference to political and social contexts between it and the psychological novel. In the first place, psychological novels, with their attention directed inward toward the momentary intensities of the "passions of the mind," appear not to address their audience directly but to represent action as existing in self-contained, private, mental worlds hermetically sealed off from the interests and responses of their readers. Reading a psychological novel is an intrusive, almost voyeuristic act. We peep surreptitiously for a few fleeting moments or hours through the half-ajar shutters of someone else's mind. Elegiac romance, in contrast, dramatizes an active relationship

51. "Two Faces of Edward," in *Edwardians and Late Victorians*, English Institute Essays, 1959 (New York: Columbia University Press, 1960), p. 198.

between narrator and audience, and that dramatic relationship is structurally and thematically integral to the fiction. Reading elegiac romance is a gregarious act. We are met at the door by an entrepreneurial host, and while we are shown the labyrinthine hallways and dim rooms of the narrator's memory we are variously regaled, nagged, bullied, and conned.

Unlike elegiac romances, furthermore, psychological novels tend not to give special prominence or in some cases much reality at all to the broader, worldly context of their characters' lives. The cultural, intellectual, social, political, and material context of the world within which the mental action occurs enter the fiction, if at all, as incoherent fragments, flotsam and jetsam swept along in the rushing stream of consciousness of the fiction's focal character. Psychological fiction tends, that is, to be closet, household, or at most neighborhood fiction. Its setting is near a small vacation village, within a quiet house on a quiet London square, or in the bedrooms, pubs, side streets, and environs of a small, out of the way European capital city. Elegiac romance, in contrast, tends to be cosmopolitan. It ranges over jungles and the high seas; visits great cities and fashionable spas; experiences celebrity; does business; makes deals; drives, flies, and takes trains the length and breadth of Europe and America. The scope of action in the life of the narrator's hero, furthermore, creates a clearly evident, although seldom unequivocal, thematic relationship between the world of affairs and the narrator's inner quest.

Loosening the Grip of the Past

Indeed, one of the most remarkable aspects of elegiac romance is that it explores how, in the context of the larger world of affairs, change might, possibly, come about in the private world of the inner self and of intimate personal relations.[52] Ways of accomplishing change at this inner level of human experience are important to discover in the modern world because one of

52. In the early twentieth century, "for its vast army of readers, fiction was the most familiar means of learning to cope with change." Jefferson Hunter, *Edwardian Fiction* (Cambridge, Mass.: Harvard University Press, 1982), p. 10.

the most salient traits of modern life is rapid cultural, intellectual, social, political, and material change. Change of this kind began to accelerate in the West during a period of about forty years, from about 1890 into the early 1930s, the period in which elegiac romance emerged as a viable formal option. A mere catalogue of people at work in those years suggests the magnitude and depth of change in thought and material life that began during this extraordinary epoch: Curie, Edison, Einstein, Ford, Freud, Joyce, Lenin, Marconi, Pankhurst, Picasso, Schoenberg, Wittgenstein. Each was responsible for a dramatic change in what we know or in the way we live, think, or perceive ourselves. World War I itself in four years (and some might argue in a single month, August, 1914) radically altered the political, social, and material values and expectations of the Western world forever.

The natural response to this profound and rapid change in the complexion of the world was shock. Barbara Tuchman quotes the dismay of one diarist at the rapidity of change as he experienced it: "all the old buoys which have marked the channel of our lives," he said, "seem to have been swept away."[53] Stefan Zweig was moved to write, "I sometimes feel as if I had lived not one but several existences, each one different from the others."[54] This rapid change in orientation and way of life was in large measure the result of developments in what Marlow somewhat glibly but conveniently calls in *Lord Jim* the "European mind" (*LJ* 188). Many of these developments had a common conceptual base and direction. To try to summarize briefly the common elements in this profound change inevitably incurs the danger of trivializing them. Fortunately, the cultural historian H. Stuart Hughes provides, with appropriate reservations, an admirable schematic outline. From the many conceptual changes that occurred during this period, Hughes selects four:

    1. Most basic, perhaps, and the key to all the others was the new interest in the problem of consciousness and the role of the unconscious. . . .

    2. Closely related to the problem of consciousness was the ques-

53. *The Guns of August* (New York: Macmillan, 1962), p. 14.
54. *The World of Yesterday* (New York: Viking, 1943), p. vi.

tion of the meaning of time and duration in psychology, philosophy, literature, and history, . . . an effort to define the nature of subjective existence as opposed to the schematic order that the natural sciences had imposed on the external world. . . .

3. The problem of the nature of knowledge, [accounting for] some kind of internal comprehension [as distinguished from] the realm of external and purely conventional symbols devised by natural science, . . . [so as to] penetrate beneath the surface of human experience. . . .

4. [The attempt] to penetrate behind the fictions of political action . . . to the manipulation of half-conscious sentiments.

Most of all, Hughes stresses, the period was one "in which the subjective attitude of the observer of society first thrust itself forward in peremptory fashion" until it seemed evident that the emotional involvement of the observer, "far from being merely extraneous, might . . . be the central element in the story."[55]

As my comparison of elegiac romance and the psychological novel has suggested, these two forms together address in depth the first two conceptual issues on Hughes's list. Each in its way renders the complexity of human consciousness and implies levels of mental process existing beneath that consciousness. Each explores in its own way the human experience of time. But for the most part elegiac romance alone, through its unique structure and the cosmopolitan range of its material, addresses the third and fourth points in Hughes's summary. Point 3, the problem of knowledge, treated briefly in this chapter, is discussed in greater detail in Chapter Five. It remains here only to suggest the potential of elegiac romance for addressing Hughes's fourth point, exposing "the fictions of political action" and the "half-conscious sentiments" that lie beneath them.[56]

To explore, however briefly, some aspects of the political and social significance of elegiac romance we must return to the question of the hero in modern fiction. I suggested earlier in

55. *Consciousness and Society: The Reorientation of European Thought, 1890-1930* (New York: Knopf, 1958), pp. 63-66, 15.

56. See also the discussion of *All the King's Men* in Chapter Five, and Patricia Merivale's argument about the potential in elegiac romance for the clarification and "affirmation of national identity." "The Biographical Compulsion: Elegiac Romances in Canadian Fiction," *Journal of Modern Literature*, 8 (1980), 139-52.

this chapter that nineteenth-century heroism involves an appeal to self-delusion. I now suggest that in the twentieth century that appeal took on a social and political dimension as protection against rapid change.

It is perhaps not too much of an overgeneralization to say that the most important social and political changes of the early twentieth century challenged what Stefan Zweig called "faith in the infallibility of the authority to which we had been trained to over-submissiveness in our . . . youth."[57] This faith sharply limited life, but it had the advantage of offering the illusion of security provided by an ideally powerful force or person, or simply by a person seemingly more powerful, more knowing, more forceful than oneself. Loss of this faith made suddenly obsolete the belief in such a person and at the same time destroyed the possibility of security based on that belief.

Yet at just this moment when reliance on a secure authority was being challenged, Zweig wrote further, "this feeling of security was the most eagerly sought-after possession of millions, the common ideal of life."[58] In short, rapid change in the cultural, intellectual, social, political, and material world that people found themselves living in was not matched by corresponding changes in the private world of the inner self and of intimate personal relations. Surrounded by threatening change, people tended privately to hang on tight to institutions, beliefs, and feelings that could provide the measure of security they craved. As Adrienne Rich has observed, in our public and private lives alike all of us carry with us "the influence of failed institutions . . . when we set out to create anything new."[59] What this tended to mean in social and political life at the turn of the century (and to a large extent still means) is that people continued to try to meet new needs with old intellectual concepts and with old institutional structures of social class, racial and sexual division, and governmental and economic organization all inherited from the past. What it tended to mean emotionally was that people carried with them into their adult inner lives and into their

57. *World of Yesterday*, p. 297.
58. Page 2.
59. "The Case for a Drop-Out School," *New York Review of Books*, June 15, 1972, p. 35.

intimate personal relations the needs and illusions of childhood and the influence of archaic fantasies, feelings, and values. And people projected this residue of childhood and the past on public figures who seemed to promise help in bearing the insecurity that the situation fostered. People created heroes.

Furthermore, this parallel between the effect of the past on our public and private lives is not a simple analogy. The two processes are complexly interrelated. Many of the institutions that failed in the early years of the twentieth century—social hierarchies, oppressive and arbitrary governmental structures, oppressive and arbitrary racial and sexual conventions—seem in retrospect to have been created in the first place to serve needs generated in our earliest experiences of life. They provided an illusion of security by allowing reliance on what Marlow calls in *Lord Jim* the "familiar emotions," but at the price of deep-seated, tenacious resistance to change.

The political implications of elegiac romance arise from the fact that the genre provides an imaginative means of understanding the relationship between forces at work in private, personal life and forces at work in the social and political world. Confronted by a complexly rooted resistance to change in himself and by a surrounding cultural, social, and political milieu undergoing profound, irresistible change, the narrator in elegiac romance sets out to create something new, a self adaptable to new needs of a new world, a self that can live without heroes. To change himself in this way he must undermine the influence of failed institutions that he carries within him. He must find in himself "the will or the capacity to look consciously under the surface of familiar emotions" (*LJ* 159).

But elegiac romance narrators are all, like their prototype, Conrad's Marlow, people with "European minds." And like their contemporaries, they are subject to the insecurity that leads to creating heroes. One reason the "European mind" creates heroes, is that it is, as Marlow observes, "so often concerned with mere surfaces" (*LJ* 188). As a prototypical elegiac romance narrator and prototypical exemplary figure in modern literature, Marlow's most salient virtue is his willingness to penetrate that surface and confront the hidden but potentially explosive force of the past. It is from this confrontation that these narrators derive knowledge of themselves as they tell their tale. They discover that the past remains what Conrad calls a powerful "inner truth" in their lives, a force that affects present thought, feeling, and action. One way of reading the political implications of elegiac romances such as *All the King's Men* and *Doctor Faustus* is to see there the capacity of the genre to suggest ways the self may move toward understanding, and thus possibly bring about a political world independent of the deleterious effects of hero-worship. As we shall see in Chapters Four and Five, elegiac romance provides this direction by illuminating the source of these deleterious political effects of hero-worship in the "inner truth" of the "European mind."

The form and content of this "inner truth" is not of course accessible directly, being by definition unconscious.[60] Fiction can

---

60. The term "unconscious" is widely misunderstood and misused. Anyone who sets out to use it with some degree of appropriateness, as I try to do in this book, does well to read Norman N. Holland's cautionary essay, "A Polemical Epilogue and Brief Guide to Further Reading," in *Poems in Persons: An Introduction to the Psychoanalysis of Literature* (New York: Norton, 1973), pp. 164-76. Another helpful guide is David J. Gordon, *Literary Art and the Unconscious* (Baton Rouge, La.: Louisiana State University Press, 1976). Gordon points out that literary critics tend to use the term in a "less strict sense"—less strictly, of course, than Freud and psychoanalysts use it. In this less strict sense, Gordon says, the unconscious denotes "mental events that are merely removed rather than barred from awareness, that are not fully conscious but capable of becoming so without much resistance . . . (*i.e.*, preconscious)." "The basic Freudian sense" of the term refers, in contrast, to "the repressed or repressing, which sometimes thrusts towards consciousness but becomes conscious 'only [with] considerable expenditure of energy or possibly never at all'" (pp. xiv, xiii). Gordon is quoting Freud, *New Introductory Lectures on Psychoanalysis* (New York: Norton, 1965), p. 71.

In the present book, not by any means a "psychoanalysis of literature," I have used the term *unconscious* in two senses. One is the "less strict sense" of "preconscious," referring to forgotten material that is accessible to consciousness through, in this particular case, the act of narration. The elegiac romance narrator taps the "forgotten" experience of his relationship with his hero in order to fabricate his tale and to reach the dramatized insights it leads him to. In using the term in this less strict sense I am following, for example, Nabokov's narrator, who speaks of "unconscious cerebration" (*SK* 183) and of human "souls . . . unconscious of their interchangeable burden" of the past (*SK* 204-05); and also John Knowles's narrator, who speaks of his hero having "unconsciously invented a game" (*SP* 31).

The second way I use the term is in discussing human character and certain events in the lives rendered in these novels. Here I approach, I believe, the stricter sense of the term: in discussing Conrad's notion of "inner truth" (*HD* 34), and Marlow's "impulse of unconscious loyalty" to Kurtz (*HD* 74) and his reveal it at best only indirectly and implicitly. But unlike other genres of fiction, which may represent only inadvertantly an unconscious level of thought and feeling, elegiac romance seems devoted as a genre to representing it. Elegiac romance represents the form and content of "inner truth" by symbolic projection. The narrator's hero as the narrator describes him—Gatsby, Leverkühn, Willie Stark, Kurtz, Jim—is a creature of the narrator's memory and imagination. The narrator's hero represents to us, therefore, a level of unconscious reality of great importance in the narrator's life. The narrator—Nick, Zeitblom, Jack Burden, Marlow—symbolically renders in his hero his dream-self, an unconscious fantasy that underlies and informs much of the narrator's conscious feeling, thought, and perception. The narrator projects this fantasy in his tale in order to see it, understand it, and outgrow it. Thus in elegiac romance the reader may glimpse a level of a fictional character's unconscious mind represented in a more nearly explicit way than it is represented in most other literary genres. What is more, the reader may also perceive, in a relatively unthreatening form, a model of the human mind that accounts for potentially threatening aspects of the reader's own interior world.

In short, every elegiac romance, major or minor, reveals a level of unconscious reality in its very structure. A few major elegiac romances take a further step. They attempt to pursue

reference in *Lord Jim* to "the Irrational that lurks at the bottom of any thought, sensation, sentiment, emotion" (*LJ* 88-89); Ford's reference to "that mysterious and unconscious self that underlies most people" (*GS* 104); and Mann's narrator's discovery that "unconsciously (*unterderhand*)" he had "formed quite decided opinions" (*DF*, Ch. 40), and his reference to a life of the unconscious (*Unbewusstsein*) (*DF*, Ch. 30).

By "inner truth" Conrad seems, sometimes at least, to mean the sort of unconscious force that "drives" Marlow to Africa and compels his slip of the tongue when he advertently tells Kurtz's Intended that he heard Kurtz's last words. "Inner truth" in this sense refers to a force unaccountable by any conscious means. Marlow concludes that such a force has a "logic," but he forbears trying to define it, because by his lights it cannot be defined. In "Conrad's View of Primitive Peoples in *Lord Jim* and *Heart of Darkness*," *Modern Fiction Studies*, 16 (1970), John E. Saveson identifies in Marlow a change in "moral assumptions" as a result of becoming "educated to the fact of [a distinctly pre-Freudian] Unconscious" (pp. 163, 185). See also Chapter Four. Mann is of course more specific and knowledgeable on this issue. In *Doctor Faustus* "underhanded" forces, forces of the unconscious compelling otherwise unaccountable actions, are given their full due (see Chapter Five).

more explicitly the essential nature of this unconscious "inner truth." In Conrad's *Heart of Darkness*, for example, Marlow infers from his experience that unconscious reality is a sort of Jungian "collective unconscious." Marlow calls it the memory of a prehistoric "unrecorded" "night of first ages" of humankind in general (*HD* 36, 37). A Jungian unconscious mind of this sort is suggested, in passing, in several elegiac romances through static images of antiquity: reference in *The Good Soldier* to feudalism and the provençal poets, Bunyanesque imagery in *All the King's Men* (*AKM* 28), the Byronism of *The Great Gatsby* and *The Real Life of Sebastian Knight*, and the catalogues of objects preserved intact from the past in *Doctor Faustus*, such as the "roomful of crude instruments of torture" on view in the Kaisersaschern municipal museum (*DF*, Ch. 6).

More prevalent in elegiac romance than these images of a persisting unconscious memory of a collective past, however, are images of a more "Freudian" type, the persisting unconscious memory of personal history. In *All the King's Men*, Warren's narrator Jack Burden infers from his experience a "clammy, sad little foetus you carry around inside youself" (*AKM* 9). Jack's image seems to refer to a private past remembered unconsciously by each individual person. This conception of "inner truth" tends to emerge in dynamic imagery of the sort I explore in Chapter Five. Furthermore, the triangular tensions that turn up in many elegiac romances, tensions formed on a matrix of the primary Oedipal relationship, also seem to be traces of early personal history, as is imagery reflecting stages of emotional growth in infancy and childhood, such as Zeitblom's desire to "cling" to Leverkühn and "mother" him (*DF*, Ch. 16), Jack Burden's "sad, clammy little foetus," Dowell's reference to Ashburnham as a "large elder brother" (*GS* 253), and Marlow's reference to Jim as "my very young brother" (*LJ* 160).

The greater prevalence of this "Freudian" imagery and its more dynamic nature suggest that, of the two conceptions of the root and nature of unconscious memory implied in elegiac romance, unconscious personal history is the more indigenous to the genre. In several later elegiac romances, in Warren and Mann, and in Nabokov as well, as we shall see in Chapter Six (in spite of Nabokov's outspoken criticism of Freud and Freudian thought), the Freudian conception of the unconscious clearly prevails. Something like it prevails also, implicitly, as we shall see in Chapter Four, in Conrad's prototypical elegiac romances.

What this prevalence seems to mean is that, owing to the nature of the genre, in every elegiac romance the narrator reaches back, by means of the events of his tale and especially through the dynamic image of his hero, not to a putative collective past but to forgotten passages in his own emotional past, even to feelings experienced in the earliest years of life. We are led, therefore to the conclusion that an unconsciously remembered emotional past is the true source of the "inner truth" that the elegiac romance narrator is able to grasp, and that this complex "inner truth" has great significance not only for the narrator's personal life but also for the "European mind." The ability to become as aware as possible of "inner truth" is what constitutes the rare exemplary character peculiar to twentieth-century literature, the narrator of elegiac romance.

Inevitably, elegiac romances render "inner truth" and "surface-truth" in quite different ways. They render "surface-truth" or conscious reality in the everyday details of the narrator's present and past experience. The single most significant fact of "surface-truth," indeed, the crucial fact in the dramatic situation of elegiac romance, is the death of the narrator's hero. In contrast to this rendering of "surface-truth," elegiac romances render "inner truth" or unconscious reality in the mythic structure of the narrator's tale and in his insights dramatized as he tells the tale. The single most significant fact of "inner truth" is that the influence of the narrator's hero is far from dead in the narrator's memory. In the fictional present, the power that the memory of his hero has over the "surface-truth" of the narrator's day-to-day existence is as great as the power that hero-worship had over the narrator's day-to-day existence in the fictional past, when his hero was still alive.

Conscious reality and unconscious reality together affect the narrator's life, furthermore, both positively and negatively. Their principal negative and potentially most destructive effect is to generate in the first place the problem that the narrator must deal with by telling his tale. The narrator remembers his hero consciously in a positive and worshipful way. But in the narrator's unconscious mind, the burdensome emotional dependence on which his feeling for his hero was based remains alive. This unconscious residue of dependence has prevented the narrator from resolving the state of arrested development induced by that dependence, even when his hero died.[61] As a result of his hero's death, the narrator has remained emotionally fixed, unable to mature beyond a phase of development typical of a period in childhood when hero-worship naturally occurs. Elegiac romance dramatizes these negative influences of unconscious reality on conscious reality mainly in the narrator's discomfort as he begins to tell his tale: in Dowell's desperate need to get the experience out of his head, in Charlie Citrine's obsessive guilt, in Buddy Glass's ill health, in Gene Forrester's fear and estrangement, in Zeitblom's anguished feelings of oppression, conflict, and inadequacy. But elegiac romance dramatizes these negative influences of the unconscious also in the otherwise difficult-to-account-for acts and traits of many other characters in the tale, such as Jim's jumping ship, Gatsby's obsession with Daisy, Nancy Rufford's breakdown in *The Good Soldier*, Gene Forrester's treacherous act in *A Separate Peace*, Jack Burden's dropping out of school in *All the King's Men*, and, in *Doctor Faustus*, Leverkühn's organizing role in the murder of Rudi Schwerdtfeger by Inez Institoris.

Along with these negative influences of unconscious and conscious reality on the narrator's life, elegiac romance also dramatizes their potentially positive and constructive effects. The first of these positive effects appears mainly in the narrator's insight into his plight: for example, John Dowell's discovery of two "selves" in *The Good Soldier* (*GS* 103) and Zeitblom's discovery in *Doctor Faustus* of the fact that unconscious thought may break through to articulate expression (*DF*, Ch. 40). Both of these examples reveal the positive effect that "inner truth" may have on "surface-truth." And in every elegiac romance the telling of

---

61. I have borrowed the notion that the elegiac romance narrator suffers from arrested development from Carol Ohmann, *Ford Madox Ford: From Apprentice to Craftsman* (Middletown, Conn.: Wesleyan University Press, 1964). Ohmann calls "the quality of [Dowell's] pleasure . . . curiously childlike. . . . Dowell, unknown to himself, desires to live not in an adult world but in an illusory world" (p. 79). Some readers may prefer to apply another term such as "repression."

the tale itself also reveals how the unconscious self may affect the conscious self positively. By bringing unconscious memory to the surface in his tale, the narrator manages to escape the state of arrested development and the attendant guilt that holds him captive, thus freeing himself to seek further "his own mature powers," to move on, in the words of "Lycidas," to "fresh Woods, and Pastures new."

CHAPTER 2

Formal and Thematic Genesis
in Conrad's Early Fiction

Conrad's early stories and novels, those written before *Heart of Darkness* and *Lord Jim,* may be read as a more or less conscious attempt to create fiction in a distinctively new form. In these works, most of them relatively unknown, the characteristic elements of the new form grow in bits and pieces out of more familiar, more conventional forms of narrative. In this developing form there is more at issue, however, than narrative technique. Conrad sought a new fictional form, it appears, in order to try to define an exemplary virtue adequate to modern life as he perceived it. In *Lord Jim* Marlow observes that "the human heart is vast enough to bear the burden." What requires a special measure of courage is to cast that burden off (*LJ* 232). Conrad's difficulties with narrative form and technique early in his career can be read in part as the price of making the effort to discover and render in fiction that special measure of courage.

As a beginning writer of fiction, Conrad ran immediately into a number of technical difficulties. One of the most significant and readily apparent of these difficulties is narrative focus. From work to work in Conrad's early fiction the narrative focus shifts. Toward the beginning, Conrad tends to write about active, adventurous, if somewhat self-destructive men. Gradually his interest shifts to men who are more reflective. As this happens, the narrative focus of his stories shifts, at first somewhat erratically, to a dramatized narrator. The dramatized narrator emerges eventually as a distinctive character, and becomes finally Conrad's most thoroughly developed, most interesting, and most important figure: Marlow.

This emergence of a dramatized narrator as central character corresponds to two more developments. One is de-emphasis of action. Of course, action remains important throughout Conrad's fiction.[1] But from work to work we see a tendency to make active characters static in personality. They become unchanging, representative, "flat" figures. Increasingly, Conrad's "round" characters, those in whom we witness development of character as the story goes on, tend to be reflective, relatively inactive people. In particular they tend to be the narrators of these stories, who meditate on action they have witnessed rather than on action they have participated in directly themselves.

Second, as he becomes more important in the fiction, Conrad's reflective, relatively inactive narrator tends to become increasingly self-conscious *as* a narrator. Narration itself tends to take on the quality of action, as the narrator talks about what he is doing, or trying to do, in telling the tale. And the narrator also manifests a growing interest in what might be called the irreducible substance of fiction. He becomes interested in the irrecoverable past and its effects on the present: both how the past once affected the life of the hero of his tale, and how the past now affects the narrator's own fictional present.

Narrator and Narrative Focus: Tapping the Spring-Flood of Memory

Conrad's first four narratives are two novels, *Almayer's Folly* and *An Outcast of the Islands*, followed by two short stories, "The Idiots" and "An Outpost of Progress."[2] Each of these has a clear

---

1. A persuasive discussion of the importance of action in Conrad's fiction is David Thorburn, *Conrad's Romanticism* (New Haven: Yale University Press, 1974). See also "Conrad and Adventure," in Jefferson Hunter, *Edwardian Fiction*, pp. 124-52.

2. Conrad completed the first draft of *Almayer's Folly* in April, 1894, and the final draft in May; *An Outcast of the Islands*, fall, 1895; "The Idiots," April or May

focus. That is, in each work, no question arises in the reader's mind as to which character the story is "about." In addition, three of the four, excepting "The Idiots," are narrated from a third-person point of view by an undramatized voice indistinguishable from that of the author.

Each novel focuses, furthermore, on a single rather hopeless figure. In one, Almayer is a failed trader who rests all his hopes on his daughter Nina. Nina fails to fulfill these hopes, because she opts for the world of her Malayan mother and falls in love with a young Maylayan trader, Dain. In the other novel, Willems, the outcast of the islands, gets caught purloining funds from his employer and flees to an obscure trading station. There, the native Malayans manipulate him, using his love for a native woman, Aïssa, as leverage. To keep Aïssa's love, Willems betrays Lingard, the man who twice rescued him from himself, and in the end Willems betrays Aïssa too, and she kills him.

Almayer and Willems, the focal characters in these two novels, are cut from the same cloth. Each is a white colonist, "a man possessed by the masterful consciousness of his individuality with its desires and rights; by the immovable conviction of his own importance, of an importance so indisputable and final that it clothes all his wishes, endeavors, and mistakes with the dignity of unavoidable fate." Each is also a man "deceived by the emotional estimate of his motives, unable to see the crookedness of his ways, the unreality of his aims, the futility of his regrets."[3]

1896; "An Outpost of Progress," July, 1896. Dates of composition and completion given here and in the following notes are based on information provided in Frederick R. Karl, *Joseph Conrad: The Three Lives* (New York: Farrar, Straus and Giroux, 1979), supplemented by Jocelyn Baines, *Joseph Conrad: A Critical Biography* (New York: McGraw-Hill, 1960).

I have for the most part ignored *The Rescue* (see, however, note 21), which was not completed until 1919, even though a large portion was written during the earliest period in Conrad's career, beginning in February-March, 1896. It is hard to determine in the sequence of Conrad's early narratives the place of such a work-in-progress, and to consider it here in detail would not alter the argument appreciably. Also, because of the difficulty of attributing crucial decisions as to form and content, I have not referred to the two novels Conrad wrote in collaboration with Ford Madox Ford, *The Inheritors* (1898-1900) and *Romance* (1898-1902).

3. *An Outcast of the Islands*, p. 296; *Almayer's Folly*, p. 102. For all of Conrad's

In contrast to the single focus of these first two novels, the narrative focus in Conrad's first short story is divided between two equally important characters. In "An Outpost of Progress," two incompetents, Kayerts and Carlier, left alone in an isolated trading station, decline rapidly, stumble into selling friendly natives as slaves for ivory, and wind up killing each other. Through it all, they act out their comic disaster as a complementary pair. Similarly, in "The Idiots," Jean-Pierre and Susan Bacadon, demoralized by their inability to conceive normal children, act out as a complementary pair their inexorable tragedy of marital failure.

Although, in contrast to the novels, the narrative focus doubles in these two stories, the narrator's identity does not change appreciably. The narrator is almost equally obscure in all four works. Only in "The Idiots" does the narrator achieve a trace of character in his own right, identifying himself at the beginning of the story as a kind of reporter. Yet even here he disclaims responsibility for the content of his tale, except to piece together fragments of it collected "in my wandering about the country."[4]

Conrad's next story, "The Lagoon,"[5] returns to undramatized third-person narration, although this story again has a divided narrative focus: it has two central characters rather than one. But "The Lagoon" departs formally in an important way from the technique of the first four stories. Instead of presenting two characters on the same narrative plane and engaged together in the same significant action, Conrad joins them here only in dialogue. The significant action occurs in a tale that one character tells the other. In short, "The Lagoon" is Conrad's first tale-within-a-tale.

The story involves Arsat, a native settler, and a white trader who visits him. In the frame tale, the unnamed trader arrives at Arsat's isolated cabin by river-canoe on the evening Arsat's wife dies of fever. Her death occasions Arsat's story of their dangerous escape from tribal forces who threatened them, an escape

fiction other than *Heart of Darkness* and *Lord Jim* I have used the collected edition (Garden City, N.Y.: Doubleday Page, 1924).
  4. *Tales of Unrest*, p. 97.
  5. "The Lagoon" was written during 1896-1897.

that required Arsat to leave his brother behind to die covering their flight. The story as a whole (in contrast to Arsat's tale) remains ambivalent in focus. Conrad devotes half of it to the frame, the trader's visit and conversation with Arsat, and half to Arsat's tale. Which of the two men Conrad intended to be the story's main character is not clear. We may speculate, in tracing Conrad's early development as a narrative artist, that he had at this time not quite made up his mind where his own priority lay: whether he was more interested in the man who participates in the action, Arsat, or the man who experiences the action vicariously and who meditates upon it.

That this is not merely a technical distinction, and not thus of minor importance in Conrad's development, is suggested by the fact that it seriously affects our understanding of the story. Are we meant to see the point of "The Lagoon" in Arsat's sacrifice, all for love, which has now reached its crisis with the death of his beloved? Or is the point of the story contained in the trader's second-hand experience of his friend's grief in the context of the exotic, ominous, melancholy jungle river scene?

To answer these questions we might ask one more: Within which of the two characters does some sort of inner action seem to occur—which of the two undergoes demonstrable inner change in the course of the story? That is, for which character is the emotional experience underlying the story dynamic? This question is not a matter of perspective. The story as a whole is certainly told from the trader's perspective. And he is the character we see first and are left with as the story ends. Yet the trader apparently undergoes no change or development of character, and he gains no insight into himself or his friend. Hearing Arsat's tale only seems to confirm the feeling of gloom he suffers as the story begins.

Arsat, on the other hand, undergoes considerable change as he tells the tale, and possibly even because he tells it. Grief over his wife's illness and death has induced, or magnified, a state of emotional paralysis. In the course of telling his tale, he overcomes this paralysis and resolves to revenge his brother's death. By the measure of inner action or character development, then, "The Lagoon" is a story about a man who frees himself to act and to make a new life for himself by telling the story of an experience,

77

the memory of which burdens him. In this respect, "The Lagoon" is a turning point in Conrad's early fiction. It is the first
of three stories in which a story-teller emerges as thematically
significant in his own right.

The other two stories, written immediately after "The Lagoon," are The Nigger of the "Narcissus" and "Karain: A Memory."
Conrad handles the point of view in The Nigger of the "Narcissus"[6]
much more awkwardly than in "The Lagoon." This story is somewhat flawed in its narrative structure, however effective it may be
otherwise. It is about conflict fomented among a ship's crew driven
to self-indulgent cantankerousness by one unscrupulous rabble
rouser, Donkin, who takes advantage of the crew's ambivalence
over a slowly dying crewmate, the "nigger," James Wait.[7] Nothing in Conrad's earlier stories anticipates the revelation of obscure, troubling emotions that occurs in this story. More important
for our immediate purposes, there is nothing in Conrad's earlier
stories to suggest the degree of what appears to be technical
deficiency that the story displays. Conrad's uncertainty of direction, or perhaps ambivalence toward his material, causes him to
tell the story from one point of view after another, each apparently as inadequate as the others to convey the material as he
would have it conveyed.

That the story's point of view is unsettled is clear in a brief
summary of these changes of direction. As it begins, the story
is told in third-person. For twenty pages or so an undramatized
narrator refers to the crew of the "Narcissus" as "they." Following
this, for forty-five pages the narrator emerges as one of the crew,
whom he now refers to as "we." This first-person plural point
of view yields again to about twenty pages more of third-person
narration, in which the reader steps into the minds of several
individual crew members, and witnesses a secret conversation

---

6. The Nigger of the "Narcissus" was begun in June, 1896, and completed in
January-February, 1897. "Karain: A Memory" was completed April 1, 1897.

7. "Conrad's 1914 Preface to the American edition [of The Nigger of the
"Narcissus"] makes clear that he meant the tale's focus to be on the crew's response
to Wait: 'In the book [Wait] is nothing; he is merely the centre of the ship's
collective psychology and the pivot of the action' " (Daniel R. Schwarz, Conrad:
"Almayer's Folly" to "Under Western Eyes" [Ithaca, N.Y.: Cornell University Press,
1980], p. 41).

between Donkin and Wait. Then, once again for twenty pages, the collective "we" takes over, and the novel ends with two pages written in sharply restricted first-person singular. Thus the narrator at the very end emerges at last in his own person as "I."

It seems that this confusion in point of view was inadvertent on Conrad's part. Possibly he was at this time not yet fully aware of the value of controlling point of view, although he was by this point in his career already fully aware of, and impressed by, the fiction of Henry James.[8] And we must admit that the wandering point of view in *The Nigger of the "Narcissus"* has some significance, both thematic and historical. First, like the issue of priority in "The Lagoon," in *The Nigger of the "Narcissus"* the issue of point of view affects our interpretation of the story. Conrad may have committed the fallacy of imitative form inadvertently, but it seems to work. The novel passes around with such alacrity the responsibility for what we are told, that we ourselves are left as puzzled and uncertain about where the story's center of value lies as the crew of the "Narcissus" were puzzled and uncertain about their attitude toward Donkin and James Wait.

Second, the novel's restless point of view suggests something about the trend of Conrad's interest in narrative form in this phase of his development as a writer. The way Conrad's struggle with point of view ends in the last two pages of *The Nigger of the "Narcissus"* indicates (in retrospect) the direction his most important fiction will take. *The Nigger of the "Narcissus"* seems to be evidence of a difficult formal transition Conrad was making from the ambiguous narrative focus of the "Lagoon" to the secure narrative focus of his next story, "Karain: A Memory." At the end of *The Nigger of the "Narcissus,"* Conrad suddenly and sharply distinguishes his first-person narrator from the rest of the crew. "From afar I saw them discoursing," the narrator says. "They appeared to be

8. Conrad and James exchanged complementary copies of their recent publications and met in October, 1896 (Karl, *Joseph Conrad*, p. 382). On James's influence on Conrad, see Karl, pp. 397-99, and Elsa Nettels, "James and Conrad on the Art of Fiction," *Texas Studies in Literature and Language*, 14 (1972), 529-54. Nettels argues that "the question of influence does not arise" between James and Conrad. "There is no indication that . . . Conrad consciously set about to follow James's example, although he expressed in many letters his admiration of James's work" (p. 529).

creatures of another kind." In the same breath, Conrad stresses his narrator's deep sympathy for his fellow man. "Good-by brothers!" the narrator exclaims, "You were a good crowd."[9]

The story ends with this reflection on loss. It seems an appropriate ending for a story about a crew's response to the death of one of its members. Oddly enough, however, all of the crew but two, the narrator and one other, have already forgotten James Wait. And the subject of the narrator's reflection on loss is not his loss of Wait in particular, but his loss of the crew as a whole. It is as if with the crew dispersed, the narrator feels free to distinguish himself at last as a discrete individual with feelings and perspective different from those of the collective group. Brought out finally into relief against that receding collective background the narrator admits to us and to himself the importance of his own imaginative resources, "the spring-flood of memory."[10]

By emphasizing the perspective of a narrator in this way, Conrad effectively shifts the story's focus, if only at the very last minute, from its ostensible, titular hero and the crew, of which he was a member, to the narrator's memory of hero and crew. To speak more generally, the narrator's self-assertion at the end of The Nigger of the "Narcissus" changes the story's focus from characters in action to a meditative narrator's imaginative confrontation with and reflection upon characters in action; from characters whose dominant trait is their ability (or compulsion) to act, to a character whose dominant trait is a reflective turn of mind, a tenacious memory, and an ability (or compulsion) to tell the tale.

That this last-minute shift of focus in The Nigger of the "Narcissus" is an important event in Conrad's development is confirmed by his next story. Narrative focus in "Karain: A Memory" is much better controlled. But whereas in The Nigger of the "Narcissus" Contrad does not seem to know quite what he wants to do formally, in "Karain" he seeems to know what he wants to do but cannot yet quite bring it off.

"Karain" is short and relatively simple. A group of gun-run-

9. Page 190.
10. Page 190.

ning young Englishmen encounter a "petty chief of a conveniently isolated corner of Mindanao," Karain, who tells them his
story of overmastering guilt. Like Arsat, Karain was responsible
for the death of a friend, and now he is obsessed by memory
and plagued by hallucinatory sights and sounds: he is haunted
by the man he killed. The narrator brings Karain to the center
of the stage dramatically, and then lets him tell his own tale.
Technically, this story, like "The Lagoon," is a tale-within-a-tale.
Yet it is so with important differences.

The first difference is that here the narrator is firmly and
clearly dramatized right from the beginning of the story. He
identifies himself immediately as a member of a select group:
"the few who survive," for whom "a strange name wakes up
memories."[11] Throughout the story, he is evidently more concerned with the implications to himself and to people like himself
of the events he narrates, than with the implications of those
events to the man who took active part in them. At issue, as the
title implies, is not Karain so much as the narrator's memory of
Karain. And the title, "Karain: A Memory," has a double meaning. Karain is insidious memory personified.

This dramatized narrator, unlike the trader in "The Lagoon,"
is not half-indifferent to his friend's fate. He claims a special
relationship with him. He tells us that he was Karain's confidant,
and he appears to be the person to whom his shipmates defer
in dealing with Karain. At the same time, the narrator poses a
clear contrast, with his rather solemn, cautious, somewhat pe-
destrian character and manner, not only to Karain's glamorous
façade but also to the more forward personalities of the other
Englishmen. And for the first time in Conrad's stories, the narrator here speaks self-consciously about the task he is engaged
in—telling a tale. He expresses curiosity about "what the reader
thinks," and he confesses to feeling inadequate "to convey the
effect of [Karain's] story" and fears that the "vividness" of his
own memory "cannot be made clear to another mind."[12]

Perhaps the most striking new feature of this story is the nature
of the central character in the narrator's tale. For the first time

11. *Tales of Unrest*, p. 3.
12. *Tales of Unrest*, pp. 85, 42.

in Conrad's fiction we find traits in the title character that are substantially similar to those of the narrator's hero in elegiac romance. Karain seems to be the rudimentary model on which Kurtz and Jim are drawn. He seems to be the model also for characters as diverse as Ashburnham, Gatsby, Willie Stark, Adrian Leverkühn, and Sebastian Knight. The peculiar, common characteristics of these figures emerge in the quick strokes that the "Karain" narrator uses to sketch his hero. He is "an adventurer . . . an outcast, a ruler—and my very good friend." This "friend," the narrator says, was

> dressed splendidly for his part, . . . [was] incomparably dignified, [and was] made important by the power he had to awaken an absurd expectation of something heroic going to take place. He was ornate and disturbing, for one could not imagine what depth of horrible void such an elaborate front could be worthy to hide. He was not masked—there was too much life in him, and a mask is a lifeless thing; but he presented himself essentially as an actor, a human being aggressively disguised.[13]

This intricate, impenetrable defense against intimacy and self-knowledge is the essence of Karain's legacy to the narrators' heroes of elegiac romance.

"Karain: A Memory" is not a strong story, and it is further weakened in the end by the narrator's lack of clarity about his attitude toward his hero and toward his memory of him. The final conversation, between the narrator and his one-time shipmate Jackson on a busy London sidewalk, does not convey—to me at any rate—how deeply the narrator had been affected by his experience, if he was affected by it at all. Despite this ambiguity in resolution, however, the theme of the story as a whole remains clear, and it is a theme that looks forward to the central theme of elegiac romance. More than in any of Conrad's other early fiction, that theme is integrally related to the story's structure and focus. The theme of "Karain: A Memory" is the tenacity of the past. The narrator cannot forget a man who could not forget a man who would not forget. And the narrator assures us that he wants above all to tell his tale unforgetably.

13. *Tales of Unrest, pp. 12, 8-9.*

This resolution of Conrad's struggle with narrative form, centering on the intelligent narrator reflecting on his own past and in effect merging two figures, protagonist and narrator, led within a year to the first of Conrad's most effective stories, "Youth."[14] In this story for the first time Conrad gives his narrator a distinct and clearly dramatized personality and a name. "Youth" is Marlow's bemused exercise in autobiographical self-regard. It is Conrad's first romance in Northrop Frye's sense of that term, an adventurous "search for some kind of imaginative golden age in time or space," and is a pure example of what Frye calls the *penseroso* phase of romance, or "contemplative adventure." "A characteristic of this phase" of romance, Frye says, "is the tale in quotation marks, where we have an opening setting with a small group of congenial people, and then the real story told by one of the members."[15] In "Youth," a frame narrator speaks for "we" who "were sitting around a mahogany table that reflected the bottle, the claret-glasses, and our faces as we leaned on our elbows." In this setting, the frame narrator says, "Marlow . . . told the story, or rather the chronicle, of a voyage."[16] The chronicle turns out to be an attenuated, sophisticated joke that Marlow tells at his own expense.

Heart of Darkness and *Lord Jim* are similarly tales Marlow tells at his own expense. In these stories, Conrad amalgamates the two types of tale-within-a-tale I have described. As in "Karain," but not in "Youth," Conrad's narrator seems in these novels to be telling a tale about another person. As in both "Youth" and "Karain," he is really telling a tale about himself. In *Heart of Darkness* and *Lord Jim*, however, Conrad finds an indirect way to reveal deeper levels of his narrator's nature than he can render directly when the narrator tells a tale about himself as he does in "The Lagoon" and "Youth." This is accomplished through a narrator more subtle and courageous than the callow narrator of "Karain," a narrator who reflects these deeper levels of his own

---

14. "Youth" was begun early in spring, 1898, and completed by the beginning of June the same year.

15. *Anatomy of Criticism* (Princeton, N.J.: Princeton University Press, 1957), pp. 186, 202.

16. *Youth and Two Other Stories*, p. 3.

nature in the mirror of the heroic figure whom he describes in his tale.

Narrator and Plot: Coming to Terms with the Past

This discussion of narrative focus and point of view in Conrad's early fiction leads us to consider now two more aspects of his early fiction that look forward to elegiac romance: plot and character. As for character, two types are at issue: the new kind of narrator Conrad created and the heroic figure that suited his new formal and thematic demands. I examine these character-types in the next section. In this section I examine the kind of "plot" that required them.

By "plot" I mean something fairly simple and traditional in concept—a coherent action beginning with tension that increases through a sequence of conflicts and resolves through significant change. Arsat's tale in "The Lagoon" has plot in this sense: it begins with the young people's desire and the family's opposition, increases in tension with their flight, and resolves in their escape through the brother's sacrifice. But these elements of plot in "The Lagoon" are external. Conrad's goal, if my understanding of his early fiction is correct, was to create "contemplative adventure" out of the materials of exotic tales and the literature of the sea. To do this, he had to transform external action into an internal process so as to render the human experience of being affected by the past.

To achieve a narrative form that would reveal from the inside how the past affects the present, Conrad needed a plot in which the central character would confront the influence of the past, understand it, and overcome it. In this "contemplative adventure" the central character would *come to terms* with the past, in both the literal and figurative sense of that phrase. The central character could not simply feel guilty or nostalgic about a past action when he fought a battle or sought a Shangri-la. The central character must be fighting now, in the fictional present, with the grip of the past alive within him. He must be seeking now, in the fictional present, a state of mind in which the grip of the past is weakened and made of less consequence to his present and future life.

For all its limitations, Arsat's tale in "The Lagoon" was the closest Conrad had yet come to such a plot. The immediate occasion of Arsat's tale is his wife's death. But her death only leads him to recall his brother's much earlier death, a memory which disturbs him still more deeply. Arsat's brother is the *apparent* hero of Arsat's tale. He is the man whose devotion and courage enabled Arsat to escape with the woman he loved. But despite the heroic stature of Arsat's brother, or rather because of it, our view of him is superficial. It is enhanced and simplified by the selective memory of the admiring, indebted, and guilty-feeling narrator. Arsat tells his visitor, "There was no braver or stronger man in our country than my brother."[17]

The reason we hear little more than this about the ostensible hero of Arsat's tale is that the tale is actually about the unheroic Arsat himself. Arsat's real purpose in telling the tale is to prepare himself to resolve to return to his country. His tale puts him into a state of mind which allows him to "see clear enough to strike."[18] We therefore infer, as Arsat tells the tale, that he undergoes significant change. When he begins talking, he is resigned and passive before death. By the time he concludes he is a man who sees his future clearly.

This type of significant change is inner action of the sort Conrad sought. The theater of the action is the narrator's mind and feelings. The contest, if we may call it that, involves the narrator's creative imagination and a memory of the past that robs him of self-possession and drains him of energy and hope. Arsat resolves this contest by expressing it symbolically in telling the tale. The trouble with this kind of action in fiction, however, is clear. The important incidents go on behind the scenes, within the narrator's mind. What really happened? Is there any way a reading audience might share the process directly?

To answer these questions positively, Conrad needed a new cast of characters. More precisely, he had most of the traits of character and types of action he needed in the stories he had

17. *Tales of Unrest*, p. 339.
18. *Tales of Unrest*, p. 347.

written so far, but they were insufficiently developed and, so to speak, ineffectually combined. It was as if he had chosen the script correctly, cast it well, and designed an appropriate set of costumes, but the actors so far had appeared on stage wearing the wrong garments and reading the wrong lines. In the next section we will look at these confusions in character more closely, and try to see how the tangle would have to be unravelled before *Heart of Darkness* and *Lord Jim* could be written.

Narrator and Character Type: Delusion and Self-Mastery

Conrad's first four narrative works concern characters defeated by delusions they cannot control and inadequacies they cannot overcome. But these characters—Almayer, Willems, Kayerts and Carlier, Jean-Pierre and Susan Bacadon—are too ignorant or too unintelligent to understand what happens to them. Following these first four works, Conrad began to populate his fiction with more intelligent and sophisticated characters who are no less baffled than the earlier set, but are more capable of self-knowledge. They are more likely to feel the pain of confusion, and have also at least a fighting chance of overcoming it.

Arsat, in "The Lagoon," for example, seems neither ignorant nor dull. Within his own society he was born an aristocrat and a potential leader. His failure to understand himself and his situation at the beginning of the story results from his grief and feelings of guilt. James Wait is articulate and discerning. He seems capable of understanding both his own condition and the disturbance he causes in the crew of the "Narcissus." But he remains mute. We can say only that he acts sometimes as if he understood. Karain seems mentally alert too. But his presuppositions, represented in his request for a magic talisman to control his hallucinations, defeat understanding from the start.

Conrad's creation of these vivid, assertive, intelligent characters would be hard to predict from his first four narratives. A second development hard to foresee from Conrad's earliest work is his interest in characters who are masters of men and in other traditional ways heroic. Lingard is a stock masterful, swaggering man of the sea, but he is merely a prop in Conrad's first two novels. The central characters in the fiction written before "The Lagoon" are self-destructively dependent and unheroic. Almayer, Willems, Kayerts, and Carlier are conspicuous for their helplessly subordinate status in the management hierarchy. They maintain the illusion that they are pursuing their own lives and their own goals, but in reality they serve the convenience, egoistic satisfaction, and material needs of more powerful, more apparently self-possessed men.

The illusion these early characters share is that in spite of living and working at the obscure ends of the countless tributaries of empire, thousands of miles from the centers of commercial power, they are certain to become rich and successful. Their strategy for success is to attach themselves to the coattails of another man—a Hudig or Lingard—whose success seems assured if not already evident. Each tries in his own fashion to emulate an aloof, masterful character whom he admires and serves, and upon whom he becomes both economically and emotionally dependent. The ignorance and foolishness of these born losers nevertheless undermine their presumption and eventually destroy their lives.

Conrad develops only sketchily most of the truly (or at least successfully) masterful figures in his early fiction. Hudig ("the Master" of a trading company) and the anonymous "director" of the trading company remain in the background, consistently vague in character. Hudig appears briefly in *Almayer's Folly* and *An Outcast of the Islands* as Willems's wrathful, self-interested, unscrupulous, and merciless superior. "The director" is described in "An Outpost of Progress" as "a man ruthless and efficient" who passes from view smiling sardonically at the two men he has left behind to be swallowed up by the jungle.[19]

Lingard alone, the independent owner and captain of a trading ship, is not totally heartless. In fact, he is developed as a character in some detail. And he alone among Conrad's early masterful figures is more generous to Willems than Willems deserves, picking up the pieces when Willems makes himself the outcast of the islands by embezzling funds from Hudig. He is

19. *Tales of Unrest*, pp. 147-49.

the best example of Conrad's successful masterful character to appear in these early narratives:

> Tom Lingard was a master, a lover, a servant of the sea. The sea took him young, fashioned him body and soul; gave him his fierce aspect, his loud voice, his fearless eyes, his stupidly guileless heart. Generously it gave him his absurd faith in himself, his universal love of creation, his wide indulgence, his contemptuous severity, his straightforward simplicity of motive and honesty of aim. . . . He loved [the sea] with the ardent affection of a lover, he made light of it with the assurance of perfect mastery, he feared it with the wise fear of a brave man, and he took liberties with it as a spoiled child might do with a paternal and good-natured ogre. . . . [H]e soon became known to the Malays, and by his successful recklessness in several encounters with pirates, established the terror of his name. Those white men with whom he had business, and who naturally were on the look-out for his weaknesses, could easily see that it was enough to give him his Malay title to flatter him greatly. So when there was anything to be gained by it, and sometimes out of pure and unprofitable good nature, they would drop the ceremonious "Captain Lingard" and address him half seriously as Rajah Laut—the King of the Sea.[20]

Conrad develops Lingard's character on a framework of simple, basic contradictions. He is generous and fatherly in manner, yet he in effect buys Almayer as a husband for his adopted Malayan daughter. He is fiercely independent himself but he likes to meddle in other people's lives. He is physically attractive and gregarious, but he is "dead to the subtle voices and blind to the mysterious aspects of the world." He is "ready for the obvious, no matter how startling, how terrible, how menacing, yet defenceless as a child before the shadowy impulses of his own heart." Because he is "simple in himself—all things [are] simple" to him. He is "only angry with things he could not understand, but for the weaknesses of humanity he could find a contemptuous tolerance."[21]

---

20. *An Outcast of the Islands*, pp. 10-11.

21. The sketch of Lingard in this paragraph is a composite, with elements drawn from *An Outcast of the Islands* and from early chapters of *The Rescue*. In *Conrad: "Almayer's Folly" to "Under Western Eyes,"* Daniel R. Schwarz acknowledges Lingard's importance in the development of key figures in Conrad's fiction: "Lingard anticipates Kurtz in the Congo, Jim on Patusan, and Gould in Costaguana as men who are finally unable to conquer themselves by means of conquering their environment" (p. 7).

The successfully masterful character-type represented in Lingard appears fully developed for the first time in the central character of *The Nigger of the "Narcissus."* James Wait is "calm, cool, towering, superb," and manifests Lingard's benign condescension toward his fellow man:

> He overtopped the tallest by half a head. . . . He enunciated distinctly, with soft precision. The deep, rolling tones of his voice filled the deck without effort. He was naturally scornful, unaffectedly condescending, as if from his height of six foot three he had surveyed all the vastness of human folly and made up his mind not to be too hard on it.

As the biggest man aboard the "Narcissus," Wait attracts respect and admiration, and yet he is also a dying man whose face is "pathetic and brutal." Because this contradiction sustains a doubt in the crew about Wait's true nature, he soon commands the concern and the "weird servitude" of almost everyone aboard ship. Doubt is maintained by Wait's masterful opacity. "He fascinates us," the narrator says:

> He would never let doubt die. He overshadowed the ship. . . . Had we been a miserable gang of wretched immortals, unhallowed alike by hope and fear, he could not have lorded it over us with a more pitiless assertion of his sublime privilege.[22]

Wait's inner life and motivation, however, like those of Hudig and Arsat's brother in "The Lagoon," remain unanalyzed, and Conrad reveals Lingard's inner life in only the most general terms. In "Karain: A Memory" for the first time, however, there are signs of an important new development leading, as I have already suggested, to the creation of the two types of character required by Conrad's new fictional form. In "Karain" Conrad treats his masterful figure in depth. The narrator synthesizes details of Karain's past picked up during earlier conversation

---

Lingard's importance in the development of key figures in Conrad's fiction: "Lingard anticipates Kurtz in the Congo, Jim on Patusan, and Gould in Costaguana as men who are finally unable to conquer themselves by means of conquering their environment" (p. 7).

22. Pages 59, 32.

aboard the schooner, and describes Karain's distraught state of mind sympathetically. When we finally hear Karain's own story, we have a fairly comprehensive understanding of his public character, and we understand the details of his private past in that public context. Karain has made himself a master of men only by struggling with inner forces which eventually prove beyond mastery. In Karain, that is, Conrad has begun the redistribution of character traits that will result eventually in the two central figures of his most important fiction, on one hand the narrator's hero, Kurtz and Jim, and on the other the narrator, Marlow.

For his new narrator's hero, Conrad draws on his early masterful figures' glamorous, attractive, but impermeable surface, their appearance of self-possession and success, their benign condescension, and their inner simplicity and childlike defenselessness before the "shadowy impulses" of their own inner lives. He adds to these characters' heroic traits several traits found in his early subordinate characters: their tendency to model themselves on an idealized image of manhood, their ambition, their ultimate failure, and their situation—immobilized in an obscure corner of the European trade empire. In short, Conrad's new heroic figure builds his public mastery out of the same material he builds his public defeat, a "masterful consciousness of his individuality . . . the immovable conviction of his own importance . . . so indisputable and final that it clothes all his wishes, endeavors, and mistakes with the dignity of unavoidable fate."[23] Finally, like his early subordinate characters, Conrad's new heroic, masterful characters commit a "breach of faith with the community of mankind" (*LJ* 113), and then, to help them escape their confusion and guilt, seek the aid and complicity of another person.

The second of Conrad's two new character types, his new narrator, is an even more complex figure who, because it is he who experiences the sort of inner action we observed earlier in "The Lagoon," becomes the true protagonist of Conrad's new narrative form. To create this character, Conrad again draws traits from both of his earlier character-types. From his early masterful characters, he draws the significant public role—in

23. *An Outcast of the Islands*, p. 296.

particular, Lingard's position as ship captain. This role allows the narrator freedom of action, breadth of experience, and a degree of sophistication that makes him knowledgeable, gregarious, and intelligent. Conrad also draws, of course, on the reputation of men of the sea as tellers of tales.

But this masterful surface of Conrad's new narrator is relatively thin. Strangely enough, Marlow seems to be more closely modeled at a deeper level on several fundamental traits of Conrad's earlier unmasterful characters. Like them, he has a tendency to identify easily with seemingly stronger, more masterful-seeming men who appear to be illustrious specimens of heroic manhood. Marlow tends to be rather easily drawn into another man's life, to want to become another man's ally and his accomplice, as for example, Almayer does (and as, one must also point out, Lingard does too). Marlow inherits several rather unattractive traits from Conrad's earlier subordinate figures as well. He suffers from an admitted tendency to self-deception (throughout "Youth" and in part of *Lord Jim* where he rationalizes his attendance at Jim's trial). He is willing in spite of himself to deceive others (lying to Kurtz's Intended despite his claim to detest lies), and to be a bit of a bully (toward his listening audience especially). And when sorely pressed, he practices a sort of servile manipulation (in getting a job in *Heart of Darkness* and in "handling" both Kurtz and Jim). Marlow also exhibits a compellingly attractive trait that even Almayer enjoys but for which he is seldom given credit—the capacity for forming an abiding, deeply felt, affectionate commitment to another human being.

Finally, Conrad endows Marlow with two traits found in none of his earlier characters. They are traits that more than any other distinguish Marlow as a representative twentieth-century character type. Conrad transforms the apparent self-mastery of his early masterful characters into the honest self-doubt that leads Marlow to a "contemplative adventure," an inner quest for authentic self-mastery gained through self-knowledge. That is, Conrad gives Marlow the courage to look into "the Irrational that lurks at the bottom of every thought, sentiment, sensation, emotion," into the "illusions" and other "artful dodges" that we use "to escape from the grim shadow of self-knowledge" (*LJ* 89, 59), and into the other "shadowy Impulses" of men's inner lives, including his own. And he also gives Marlow the fortitude to bear the stress of inner change in response to what he finds there.

The Mind of Men

How the central characters of Conrad's mature work differ from those in his earlier fiction remains to be developed and completed in the discussion of *Heart of Darkness* and *Lord Jim* in Chapters Three and Four. One important aspect of the change in his central characters from apprenticeship to mature fiction, however, is still to be dealt with here. Throughout his fiction, Conrad's witness-narrators are white Europeans. In the early fiction up to and including "Karain," with the single exception of Lingard, Conrad's active, heroic figures are not white, not European. In Conrad's earliest work, that is, the heroic character upon whom the narrator focuses his attention and concern is one of "them." In both *Heart of Darkness* and *Lord Jim* the focal character is "one of us."

This change does not mean that Conrad ultimately believed that white European colonists are inherently superior to or more interesting than black or brown men subject to white rule. Conrad's Malayan characters frequently express their resentment of whites taking over their lands and lives. In *An Outcast of the Islands*, for example, Lakamba's advisor Babalatchi, a character of subtle political and social intelligence, confronts Lingard with a classic statement of colonialism from the point of view of the colonized. Lingard voices "with great earnestness" the glib, paternalistic colonist line, "If I ever spoke to Patalolo, like an elder brother, it was for your good—for the good of all." Babalatchi uncompromisingly labels the remark for what it is:

> "This is a white man's talk," exclaimed Babalatchi, with bitter exultation. "I know you. That is how you all talk while you load your guns and sharpen your swords; and when you are ready, then to those who are weak you say: 'Obey me and be happy, or die!' You are strange, you white men. You think it is only your wisdom and your virtue and your happiness that are true. You are stronger

than the wild beasts, but not so wise. A black tiger knows when he is not hungry—you do not. He knows the difference between himself and those that can speak; you do not understand the difference between yourselves and us—who are men. You are wise and great—and you shall always be fools.[24]

The significance of Conrad's shift from nonwhite to white heroic figures is not that he found the oppressed uninteresting, but that he found the core of the problem where Babalatchi found it, in the minds of men who believe that only their own wisdom, virtue, and happiness are true and of value. Conrad was troubled primarily by a tendency to self-delusion among his own people, among white people of, broadly speaking, Western culture. He seems to have observed that colonialism did not create this troubling characteristic but was one of several symptoms of it. Colonialism, a product of a Western tendency to self-delusion, only exacerbated that self-delusion, perpetuated it, and exposed it mercilessly to view.

The evidence for this interpretation, that Conrad's main concern was not "the mind of man" but the mind of Western white men, lies in Conrad's second attempt, following "The Idiots," to write domestic fiction. "The Return"[25] is Conrad's last attempt in his early work to render characters' mental processes directly through a third-person omniscient point of view. Referring to the story's central character, Alvan Hervey, Conrad told his publisher, "I wanted the reader to *see him think* and then to hear him speak—and shudder."[26] Hervey is a middle-class Englishman who comes home from work one evening to find that his wife has run off with another man. While he broods over this event, his wife unaccountably returns. She has discovered that she lacks the courage and integrity to leave her husband. But Hervey discovers in turn that he cannot bear to live with a woman who wanted to leave him. So he leaves her, never to return.

The story is not, as most critics have seen it, about an inadequate man who is inferior to his wife. It is about a man confronted by the fact that his wife too is inadequate, and in every

24. Pages 200-21.
25. "The Return" was written May to September, 1897.
26. Baines, *Joseph Conrad*, p. 192.

dreadful detail his equal. In the course of the story, Conrad dissects an important formative element of Western culture, the ethos of masculinity founded on a belief in mastery—self-control, control of the conditions of one's life, virtues that make one superior, presumably, to those who lack this control. The theme of the story, as Conrad expressed it, is "the fabulous untruth of that man's convictions—of his idea of life."[27] Western men, Conrad implies, tend to confirm and maintain this idea of life by the simple expedient of regarding people who are not male or not white as not quite human. Lingard says that nonwhite colonials are "beasts." Willems feels that women are charming creatures who respond to "gradual taming" by words of love.

"The Return" renders in great detail, although somewhat heavy-handedly, the action of an ordinary Western male mind when confronted by persistent, incontrovertible evidence that its idea of its own superiority is an illusion. Faced with this reality, Hervey scrambles desperately to refabricate the "fabulous untruth" of his "idea of life" out of memory and sheer fantasy. Like Jim, Hervey tries to "save from the fire his idea of what his moral identity should be" (*LJ* 60), and to do that, again like Jim, he tries to put "out of sight all the reminders of [his] folly" (*LJ* 125) by substituting heroic fantasies and daydreams for realistic perception and accurate memory. In "The Return," this process takes the form of a series of visions "quick and distinct as a dream."[28] These visions are escape fantasies which Hervey wills and needs, and yet at the same time finds himself afflicted with and imprisoned by.

The story is a glimpse, in short, of the inner experience of neurosis. Each of Hervey's defensive daydreams is provoked by a feeling of anger or fear, and each ends abruptly as soon as Hervey's fear or anger dissipates and he feels reassured. The story ends when Hervey's daydreams no longer succeed in turning off reality and reestablishing his equilibrium. When this happens, he must either cast his whole conception of life "into the flame of a new belief," or let "the habit of years affirm itself."[29]

27. Baines, *Joseph Conrad*, p. 192.
28. *Tales of Unrest*, p. 222.
29. *Tales of Unrest*, p. 313.

He chooses the latter and runs away. In *Heart of Darkness*, Marlow is faced with similar alternatives. He achieves an important victory over his racial presuppositions, realizing that Africans are not "brutes" but human beings like himself. But toward women, Marlow's attitudes change no more than Hervey's do. Lying to Kurtz's Intended to keep in her own "beautiful world," Marlow confirms and protects his traditional presuppositions of male superiority.[30]

The new narrative form Conrad strove to create had to represent the mind of a Western man—in the person of the narrator—contemplating not the minds of men of other cultures, but the minds of men culturally very much like himself. Conrad's central concern, one taken up also by later authors of elegiac romance, was a fabric of delusion with which he was intimately familiar. The greatest virtue of his new narrator, and a virtue that is new to the West, is his courage to rend that fabric of delusion. Conrad's new exemplary figure has the ability to face conscious, voluntary disillusionment. He has the courage to see the bitter untruth of his own convictions and of his own idea of life vividly and uncompromisingly represented in the mirror of another man's "heroic" life and mind. And he has the courage to bear the agony involved in changing the mental "habit of years" so as to cast his life "into the flame of a new belief."

30. For a bibliography of current views of the "mind of men" see Eugene R. August, " 'Modern Men,' or, Men's Studies in the 80's," *College English*, 44 (October, 1982), 583-97.

CHAPTER 3

"Understand the Effect of It on Me"
A Lesson in Reading Elegiac Romance

Conrad's experimentation with a new narrative form did not end with "Karain." In *Heart of Darkness* and *Lord Jim*, he was still refining it. As in the earlier fiction, some structural elements in these more mature novels still seem unpolished and less than fully integrated into the whole. The most apparent of these unassimilated elements is frame narration. In *Heart of Darkness*, a friend of Marlow's retells Marlow's tale as it was told to him on a yacht in the Thames estuary while waiting for the tide. *Lord Jim* begins with a third-person account of Jim's youth by an anonymous narrator, leading to the courtroom scene where Marlow and Jim first exchange glances, and then to the after-dinner scene where Marlow tells his tale. The novel ends with a letter, written years later to the most attentive of Marlow's after-dinner listeners. In both novels this superstructure is for the most part redundant. It helps to focus attention on Marlow and his tale, which are in themselves sufficiently demanding of our attention.

This structural redundancy is one element of Conrad's new form avoided by those who have taken up the form from him and reshaped it for their own use. In *The Good Soldier*, Ford Madox Ford drops the frame narrator altogether, although Ford's "Marlow," the narrator of the tale, John Dowell, does keep up the fiction of an imaginary conversation by "the fireplace of a country cottage." But here this structural element has already become integrated thematically with the narrator's tale. In Con-

rad's elegiac romances, this thematic integration has not yet occurred. The setting in which Marlow tells the tale is significant
("And this also . . . has been one of the dark places of the earth"),
but there is little irony in the way the setting is represented. The
Thames estuary at dusk is described as exactly that. In Ford,
there is a starkly significant difference between where Dowell
says he is as he begins the tale and where he really is. He says
he is at the fireside of a cosy country cottage. In fact, we discover
later, he is sitting in Edward Ashburnham's empty gun-room
alone, "all day and all day in a house that is absolutely quiet"
(*GS* 254). Dowell has to imagine that he is engaged in a com-
fortable, friendly fireside chat under a moon nearly as bright as
in Provence, because he requires the feeling of security such a
fantasy gives him. The content of the fantasy of cosy friendliness
suggests, furthermore, the depth of Dowell's emotional insecurity. And his reference to Provence and its poetry of adulterous
liaison suggests the source of his insecurity. It is the knowledge
he becomes aware of only as he tells the tale, that his wife and
Ashburnham were lovers.

After Ford, even the fiction of an imagined conversational
setting with imagined listers tends to disappear from elegiac
romance. Most elegiac romance narrators simply address intended or hoped for readers. In effect, the frame situation atro-
phies and disappears from the form, a natural enough process
since the conventions of elegiac romance have their own integrity
to which fireside chats are not essential. In the major elegiac
romances of Fitzgerald, Warren, Nabokov, and Mann, the occasion of the narrator's tale is represented as entirely a function
of the narrator's emotional need, the need, as Dowell puts it, to
get the sight out of his head, to disencumber himself of the
memory of his hero and its influence on his present life by telling
the story.

Since a fictional frame audience gathered for a social occasion
has played a part historically in the development of elegiac romance, however, one way to look at the narrative form of elegiac
romance is to see how it emerges in part from the social conventions appropriate to such an occasion. In both *Heart of Darkness* and *Lord Jim* the narrator guides his listeners' attention
tactfully toward the point he intends to make. He does this as a

matter of social graciousness. But he does it also in order to gain
a useful rhetorical end. In *Heart of Darkness* especially, Conrad
uses this device of dramatized narrative self-consciousness as an
opportunity to explain his new form and to give us a lesson in
how to read it. The explanation is brief, but it is explicit and
precise.

To grasp the import of Conrad's lesson we should remind
ourselves, in reading elegiac romances, that the story of the
narrator's hero—the story about Kurtz, Jim, Ashburnham,
Gatsby, and so on—represents the narrator's recollection of who
his hero was and what he did. The action in the story about the
narrator's hero occurs in the novel's completed fictional past,
not in its dramatized fictional present. It is what has happened,
not what is happening. The narrator's hero looms large in the
novel because he loomed large in the narrator's life. His importance to us is wholly contingent upon his importance to the
narrator. We never see the hero "as he was." We never know
for sure what he was "really" like, what he "really" did, or what
"really" happened to him. We must take the narrator's account
of the hero, even his very existence, on faith. Although there is
little need to press the point here, the narrator's hero may never
have existed at all. For all we know in fact, he could be a total
fabrication. In short, it is axiomatic in elegiac romance that the
narrator's hero exists, as Marlow says of Jim, "for me, and after
all it is only through me that he exists for you" (*LJ* 161). The
inevitable corollary of this axiom is that what we can know, and
must strive to know as best we can, is the medium through which
an account of the heroic figure reaches us—the narrator himself
and his tale.

On this fundamental point Conrad is helpfully clear. His explanation in *Heart of Darkness* begins with the frame narrator's
attempt to classify Marlow's stories by type: it is a somewhat
vague but simple and straightforward exercise in genre criticism.
One type of story, "the yarns of seamen," the frame narrator
tells us,

> have a direct simplicity the whole meaning of which lies within the
> shell of a cracked nut. But Marlow was not typical . . ., and to him
> the meaning of an episode was not inside like a kernel but outside,

enveloping the tale which brought it out as a glow brings out a haze (*HD* 5).

As we might expect, Marlow's own explanation of his type of tale is more exact and informative. To introduce his listeners to his story he tells them just where to focus their attention:

> I don't want to bother you much about what happened to me personally . . . yet to understand the effect of it on me you ought to know how I got out there, what I saw, how I went up that river to the place where I first met the poor chap. It was the farthest point of navigation and the culminating point of my experience. It seemed somehow to throw a kind of light on everything about me—and into my thoughts. [*HD* 7]

Several things are notable in this explanation. The first is that although Marlow mentions Kurtz, he does so only in passing. Kurtz and what happened to him do not seem to be of primary importance to Marlow. Nor are the events of the adventure themselves, which Marlow calls "what happened to me," of primary importance. To be sure, neither of these aspects of the tale is meaningless. The meaning of each is the sort the frame narrator has spoken of, meaning "inside like a kernel." The events of the adventure are meaningful, furthermore, because without them we cannot understand and evaluate what, to Marlow, is important in the tale. What is important to Marlow, and on his urging should be important to us, is not the adventure, "what happened to me," but its impact, "the effect of it on me." What Marlow tells us to attend to in reading this kind of fiction, in short, is its rendering of a culminating moment in the narrator's own emotional and intellectual life—the "kind of light" his experience throws on "everything" about the narrator, and especially "into" his "thoughts."

Marlow's instructions for reading Conrad's new form of fiction have several implications, three of which are especially worth exploring. To read fiction of this sort properly, the instructions imply, we should first of all restrain our natural interest in the more glamorous of its two central characters, the narrator's hero; but we should nevertheless try to understand the nature of that hero as a reflection of the narrator's inner life. Second, in looking closely at the narrator we should direct our efforts principally to identifying and understanding why exactly he is telling the tale. Third, if Marlow does claim not to want to "bother" his audience much about what happened to him "personally," an implication nevertheless remains that he does want to "bother" us a good deal about some other, impersonal aspect of what happened to him. The narrator's response to what happened during his extraordinary experience should bother us because it is a troubling reflection of our own response to perhaps less sensational but nonetheless analogous events in our own more mundane lives.

With these implications in mind, therefore, let us look closely at these three thematic elements central to elegiac romance as they emerge in *Heart of Darkness* and *Lord Jim*: the ambiguity of the narrator's relationship with his hero, the narrator's insight dramatized as he tells the tale, and the narrator's rhetorical manipulation of his readers.

Poor Chap: Kurtz as Sympathetic Hero

When Marlow instructs his audience, his one reference to the ostensible hero of his tale is brief but revealing. Marlow regards Kurtz as a "poor chap." We tend first to read this phrase as heavily ironic. It is a striking way of referring to the Kurtz who used the miracle of a Winchester rifle to bully Africans into subjection, forced people to ravage their own land, executed men who refused to "crawl to him," and proposed as an ultimate solution to the problem of "savage customs" to "exterminate all the brutes!" On the surface, indeed, the irony of the phrase is so obvious and heavy-handed as to seem out of character for a teller of tales who, the frame narrator has just assured us, is unusually subtle and elusive. Could it be that the phrase is not ironic at all? Is it possible that Marlow does indeed regard Kurtz sympathetically? Or, more likely, could it be that the irony of the phrase is more intricate than we might at first suppose? In just what sense *was* Kurtz a "poor chap"?[1]

I think we can discern at least two senses. First of all, as Marlow sees him, Kurtz is desperately poor in spirit. He is the type of character whom Conrad sketched as the central figure in "Karain," carried to a hideous extreme. Kurtz is "poor" because his "elaborate front," like Karain's, hides a "horrible void." As the "Karain" narrator points out, this front is not a mask. A mask is artificial, lifeless, and unintegrated with the personality behind it, a self-conscious pretense of the sort George Eliot observes in *Middlemarch* when she says of Casaubon, "Doubtless some ancient Greek has observed that behind the big mask and the speaking-trumpet, there must always be our poor little eyes peeping as usual and our timorous lips more or less under anxious control."[2] Kurtz, as Marlow perceives him, is no self-conscious pretender in this sense. No poor little eyes peep from behind Kurtz's emaciated façade. He does not posture in order to impress or delude. Like Karain, Kurtz appears essentially as an actor who lives his part, entirely lacking in self-doubt. Until the last moments of his life, he remains profoundly convinced of his ultimate self-importance and of the universal significance of his life. As T. S. Eliot implied, Kurtz is the ultimate "hollow man."

When Marlow refers to Kurtz as a "poor chap," then, the phrase suggests that Marlow recognizes that he himself had been taken in by Kurtz's performance. Kurtz's poverty of spirit as Marlow's tale renders it is in part a reflection of the fact that, in spite of the gruesome details of Kurtz's life, Marlow sympathizes with Kurtz as he perceived him, and upon this sympathy Marlow's "unconscious loyalty" to Kurtz is based (*HD* 74). By his own admission, Marlow has identified with Kurtz. Toward the end

1. V. J. Emmett, Jr., also has observed that Marlow's identification with Kurtz and loyalty to him requires explanation: "By confronting Marlow in *Heart of Darkness* with the charismatic villain Kurtz, Conrad offers a critique of the widespread nineteenth-century phenomenon of hero worship. . . . Internal evidence suggests that . . . it is almost as though Conrad offers Marlow's yarn as a rebuttal to the views expressed by Carlyle in the six lectures that make up *On Heroes*" ("Carlyle, Conrad, and the Politics of Charisma: Another Perspective on *Heart of Darkness*," *Conradiana*, 7 [1975], 145). But Emmett does not work out the most interesting implication of this insight. He concentrates on the hero worship of "primitive man," i.e. native Africans, in "adoring the 'universal genius' Kurtz," whereas the principal and by far the most problematical hero worshiper in *Heart of Darkness* is Marlow himself.
2. *Middlemarch*, ed. Gordon S. Haight (Boston: Houghton Mifflin, 1958), p. 207.

of the tale he tells us explicitly that he feels it is Kurtz's "extremity that I seem to have lived through" (*HD* 72). Marlow feels Kurtz's poverty of spirit so deeply because through Kurtz he recognizes his own. Thus, it is no accident that Marlow reduces Kurtz to a passing reference in introducing the tale. Kurtz functions in Marlow's tale as every other narrator's hero in elegiac romance functions, as a reflecting surface representing a dream-self created by the narrator's own inner life, to suit the ends and fulfill the desires of that inner life. Everything an elegiac romance narrator, including Marlow, says about his hero should be read primarily, therefore, as suggesting something about the narrator himself.

This conclusion makes it easier to recognize the second reason Kurtz is a "poor chap" in Marlow's eyes. It leads us to ask how Marlow did in fact "read" Kurtz. The answer is that Marlow's view of Kurtz was informed by two persuasive literary conventions. First, Marlow had "seemed to see" Kurtz, long before he met him, cast in the conventional romantic role of the courageous, solitary explorer of popular fiction, a daydream of "the lone white man turning his back suddenly on the headquarters, on relief, on thoughts of home—perhaps; setting his face towards the depths of the wilderness, towards his empty and desolate station" (*HD* 32). Later, in telling the tale, the conventions that inform Marlow's view of Kurtz change from those of literal explorer to those of a figurative one. Marlow vests Kurtz with the conventions of the Faust tradition. Kurtz gained "forbidden knowledge" in the wilderness of the self; he allowed "forgotten and brutal instincts" to beguile "his unlawful soul beyond the bounds of permitted aspirations"; and he "made a bargain for his soul with the devil."[3]

These conventions of traditional literary figures allow Marlow to distance Kurtz, to perceive him as not quite human. This distance provides the margin of ambiguity in their relationship that allows a sensitive, perceptive man to sympathize with one whose atrocities would otherwise revolt him. Marlow softens and

3. I have developed this point further in "The Lesser Nightmare: Marlow's Lie in *Heart of Darkness*," *Modern Language Quarterly*, 25 (1964), 322-39; reprinted in *Joseph Conrad: Heart of Darkness*, ed. Robert Kimbrough (New York: Norton, 1971), 233-40.

blurs the facts of Kurtz's life by casting him as a mythic character of heroic stature. He fabricates Kurtz in the mold of traditionally sympathetic figures of the Western literary tradition. For Marlow, Kurtz adds up to an extreme version of the Byronic hero. Like Childe Harold, the Corsair, and Manfred, Kurtz is drawn romantically larger than life. He is a man who seems, as Marlow describes Jim, "overwhelmed by his own personality," mysteriously corrupted, attractively glamorous, self-possessed, condescending, inaccessible, and capable therefore of awakening "an absurd expectation of something heroic going to take place." Like Jim, and like Ashburnham, Gatsby, Willie Stark, and Leverkühn, indeed like the narrator's hero in every elegiac romance, Kurtz is a person whose specious appeal to us is attributable to the fact that his "attitude got ahold" of the narrator *"as though* he had been an individual in the forefront of his kind, *as if* the obscure truth involved were momentous enough to affect mankind's conception of itself" (*LJ* 69, emphasis added).

One of the deepest ironies of *Heart of Darkness* lies, therefore, in Marlow's helpless admiration and sympathy for Kurtz juxtaposed to the appalling facts he meticulously parades before us as he tells his tale. It is quite as if we were being asked to sympathize with the inner problems and emotional stresses of a Hitler (poor chap). One of the most remarkable features of Conrad's new fictional form is that its narrator can seduce us into feeling sympathy for this type of hero, or at least can confuse and temper our revulsion against him. The narrator of elegiac romance speaks to us with the persuasive passion of a convert to a cult of insidious belief who has only just begun to doubt the grounds of his conversion.

A similar ambivalence to the narrator's hero is to be found in the most sophisticated, complex, and painful of all Conrad's descendants, Mann's *Doctor Faustus*. There too we are taken in by a narrator, Serenus Zeitblom, who had been taken in by the person who becomes the hero of his tale, the composer Adrian Leverkühn. The crucial difference in this respect between *Heart of Darkness* and *Doctor Faustus* is that in reading Mann's novel (as in reading most elegiac romances after *Heart of Darkness*) the narrator leads us out of this emotional quandary. He perceives his error through insights dramatized in the very course of telling the tale.

A Kind of Light: Dramatized Insight

We must observe, therefore, that *Heart of Darkness* is an incomplete elegiac romance in this respect. There is no evidence that by telling the tale Marlow works his way through his obsession with Kurtz. *Heart of Darkness* contains no dramatized insights. One reason Marlow's language in this novel becomes frequently abstruse and turgid, as many critics have complained, might be that Conrad was still trying to make his narrator express through a mode of narrative exposition native to the nineteenth-century novel a human concern and a level of response that demand quite another mode of expression. The stylistic limitations of Marlow's tale themselves become a convention of elegiac romance, however, even when the narrator's awkward effort to explain the past directly and explicitly is overridden by the insights he gains in the fictional present as he tells the tale. The apparently amateurish, awkward, inconsistent narrative manner of Ford's John Dowell, Fitzgerald's Nick Carraway, Salinger's Buddy Glass, and Mann's Serenus Zeitblom, seems traceable ultimately to the precedent set by Marlow.

It is perhaps not surprising, however, to find Conrad still continuing to depend so heavily in *Heart of Darkness* on the mode of direct narrative exposition that he was about to leave behind and when he had already invented the new mode that made such dependence unnecessary. This sort of hybridization is not unusual during transitional phases in the emergence of new styles and genres in every medium. Conrad's attempt to deal thus directly with human emotional reaction to loss and change does not disappear entirely even in *Lord Jim*. But in this last effort to clarify his new fictional form, Conrad did resolve the central structural issue. Unlike *Heart of Darkness*, the narrator in *Lord Jim* does gain insight as he tells his tale.

Marlow's dramatized insight in *Lord Jim* occurs early. In the fifth chapter of the novel, Marlow raises the novel's central issue explicitly and admits he hasn't yet resolved it: "Why I longed to go grubbing into the deplorable details of an occurrence which, after all, concerned me no more than as a member of an obscure body of men held together by a community of inglorious toil and by fidelity to a certain standard of conduct, I can't explain." As he continues to talk, however, Marlow debates the issue with himself, reasoning his way methodically toward a solution. He establishes first that his longing was a genuine quest, not idleness or morbidity: "You may call it an unhealthy curiosity if you like; but I have a distinct notion I wished to find something." What did he hope to find? "Perhaps, unconsciously, I hoped I would find . . . some profound and redeeming cause, some merciful explanation, some convincing shadow of an excuse," an excuse, that is, for Jim's crime, some way to exonerate Jim. But this goal was illusory. Marlow did not know then that his goal was illusory, but he knows it now: "I hoped," he says, "for the impossible."

But realizing now that hoping to find an excuse for Jim's crime was to desire "a miracle" does not settle the matter. It only leads to the true, underlying issue, Marlow's own motive: why then did he "desire it so ardently?" Here at last Marlow takes the final step in his self-examination. "Was it for my own sake that I wished to find some shadow of an excuse for that young fellow whom I had never seen before . . .?" Marlow's affirmative answer to this question constitutes the novel's central dramatized insight: "I fear that such was the secret of my prying" (*LJ* 38-39).

Marlow sheds "a kind of light" on "everything about me, and into my thoughts" in *Lord Jim*, therefore, by acknowledging that he sought to rationalize Jim's life not for Jim's sake but to satisfy some need of his own. This dramatized insight is the context, the definitive frame of reference, for everything else Marlow says in the novel. His tale so far leads up to this insight. He continues telling the tale in order to work out its implications. Thus significant change in the narrator and his world is an important theme in *Lord Jim*.

This is not the case in *Heart of Darkness*. There, significant change is almost entirely absent. True, the experience Marlow records in *Heart of Darkness* did affect some change in his racial attitudes toward the black men he encountered in Africa. But as for the African colonial trading enterprise as a whole, Marlow seems as skeptical about its motives and goals at the beginning of the novel as he is at the end. His attitude toward women certainly does not change. He patronizes Kurtz's Intended at the end of the novel as he patronizes his aunt toward the beginning. Most important, Marlow's attitude toward Kurtz, although certainly better informed after his journey than before, and perhaps somewhat more coherent after telling his tale, remains substantially unchanged also, except of course that he no longer considers Kurtz "mad." By the end of *Heart of Darkness*, Marlow has merely transformed the obsessive impulse that "drove" him to Africa into an equally obsessive memory of Kurtz. Although he "wanted" to give up that memory, he now claims he cannot do so: "I can't choose. He won't be forgotten" (*HD* 51). Finally, even the world Marlow returned to, the sepulchral city, remains substantially unchanged.

In contrast, *Lord Jim* assumes that the narrator's world is a world of change, and that change is the main difference between the narrator's world and the world of his hero. When Marlow left Jim for the last time, he recalls, Jim became in his memory a static figure in a static world, whereas the world Marlow returned to was a world of vitality and flux:

> Next morning . . . all this dropped out of my sight bodily. . . . It remains in the memory motionless, unfaded, with its life arrested, in an unchanging light. These are the ambitions, the fears, the hate, the hopes, and they remain in my mind just as I had seen them—intense and as if forever suspended in their expression. I had turned away from the picture and was going back to the world where events move, men change, light flickers, life flows in a clear stream, no matter whether over mud or over stones. I wasn't going to dive into it; I would have enough to do to keep my head above the surface. But as to what I was leaving behind, I cannot imagine any alteration. . . . They exist as if under an enchanter's wand. [*LJ* 237]

In short, in *Lord Jim* the narrator's world is living; his hero's world is dead. Jim is not of course, literally dead before Marlow begins telling his tale. In this respect *Lord Jim* too, historically speaking, lacks the structural refinement of later elegiac romances. Later elegiac romance writers clarify the form by making their narrators declare or imply broadly at the outset of the tale that their hero is dead, and thus establish loss and change unequivocally as the condition and one of the central themes of the fiction. In placing Jim in a changeless world, Conrad nevertheless establishes the condition that before the narrator begins to tell his tale, his hero must be irretrievably lost.

A second, and equally important, implication of Marlow's dramatized insight in *Lord Jim* is to show even more powerfully than in *Heart of Darkness* how pernicious is our conventional way of dealing with the past. In *Heart of Darkness*, Marlow calls this conventional response the tendency to "bury dead hippo" (*HD* 50) so as to get the stench out of our nostrils. In *Lord Jim* he is more explicit. Our conventional response to the past, "the wisdom of life, . . . consists in putting out of sight all the reminders of our folly, of our weakness, of our mortality; all that makes against our efficiency—the memory of our failures, the hints of our undying fears, the bodies of our dead friends" (*LJ* 125).

This conventional wisdom of life assumes, furthermore, that what gets buried stays buried. But Marlow has discovered, as we shall see in Chapter Four, that although we may put out of sight the reminders of folly, weakness, mortality, failure, and fear, we continue carrying the burden within us in the "secret" memory of "inner truth"—unconscious memory—where "the human heart," Marlow observes in *Heart of Darkness*, "is vast enough to contain all the world."[4] Moreover, Marlow has found that what gets buried there remains troublingly alive: "you wake up at night and think of it—years after—and go hot and cold all over" (*HD* 35). Marlow's heroic act in these two novels is voluntarily to exhume the past buried within himself and look steadily and unblinkingly at it.

I have suggested that the courage required by the character who undertakes this task of digging up the past and discovering its significance is of a particular kind. The elegiac romance narrator must be more than "valiant enough to bear the burden" of the past. He must also have "the courage that would cast it off." This kind of courage, however, is not flamboyant. The modern virtue exemplified in the Marlows, Dowells, Nicks, Jack Burdens, and Serenus Zeitbloms of twentieth-century fiction is ironic,

4. On the use of the term "unconscious" in this book, see Chapter One, note 60.

unpretentious, modest, and accessible. It lies in their willingness to tap "the spring-flood of memory" and thereby do what Alvain Hervey failed to do—overcome the habit of years and thrust their conception of life "into the flame of a new belief."

Our Common Fate: Narrator, Reader, and Rhetorical Judo

Although the elegiac romance narrator's courage is modest in kind, it is not modest in magnitude. The effort to tap "the spring flood of memory" requires the courage to tolerate the painful memory of what can wake you up at night and make you go hot and cold all over. This pain is exacerbated by the fact that beneath both the narrator's acknowledgeable loss of his hero by death and the impoverishment of spirit in the larger cultural sense that that loss represents lies another void. This void is the vaguely remembered, archaic, and radical condition that Marlow calls "our common fate." "For where is the man," he asks, "—I mean a real sentient man—who does not remember vaguely having been deserted in the fullness of possession by someone or something more precious than life?" (*LJ* 198-99).

The effect of this profound underlying vulnerability is to intensify the grief we may feel for loss experienced later in life. Radical vulnerability reinforces and magnifies to overwhelming proportions Marlow's reaction, for example, to learning only that Kurtz *may* have died before Marlow had yet had the chance to meet him. Marlow's "sorrow," even at that moment of merely imagined loss, he tells us, "had a startling extravagance of emotion. . . . I couldn't have felt more of lonely desolation somehow, had I been robbed of my destiny in life" (*HD* 48). When Kurtz did die, furthermore, Marlow felt as if he was passing "through some inconceivable world that had no hope in it and no desire" (*HD* 72). Marlow feels something of this extreme "lonely desolation" over the loss of Jim, too, although he expresses it more subtly: Jim "confided so much in me," Marlow says, "that at times it seems as though he must come in presently and tell the story in his own words. . . . It's difficult to believe that he will never come. I shall never hear his voice again" (*LJ* 246-47).

The impact of any elegiac romance depends in large measure

on the narrator's ability to arouse and play upon the reader's own vaguely remembered radical loss "in the fullness of possession [of] someone or something more precious than life." But because this sense of radical loss is one of those things all of us would like to "bury" and "put out of sight," no elegiac romance narrator can be content to let his dramatized theme—to exhume and reexamine the past—work on his audience unaided. The success of his effort requires undermining our resistance. The narrator sets out to do this by drawing us into complicity with himself in admiring his hero, poor chap, so that we will, first, share the narrator's insight into the causes and implications of his hero-worship.

The narrator engages us this way by a species of rhetorical judo. His principal gesture is a tease. He dangles before us a fascinating character described in figures drawn from traditional literary conventions: Faust (Kurtz, Leverkühn), the Chevalier Bayard (Ashburnham), the Byronic hero (Jim, Gatsby, Sebastian Knight). Well imbued as we are with the traditions of Western culture, we tend to respond to these conventions conventionally. Our conventional response blurs our vision of the hero's character as the flawed human being he presumably was. We take him as given to us, as "heroic."

While the narrator is performing this trick with his right hand, with his left he performs another. He seems to protest the utter unimportance and irrelevance of himself and his own interests and concerns to what happens in the tale.[5] In some cases he does this stylistically by affecting carelessness and lack of self-concern, as in Ford's *The Good Soldier* and Nabokov's *The Real Life of Sebastian Knight.*[6] In other cases he is quite explicit. In *Heart of Darkness*, Marlow slips in his real agenda (that we should "understand the effect of it on me") as a subordinate phrase in a sentence that begins "I don't want to bother you much about what happened to me personally." In Mann's *Doctor Faustus*, Zeitblom insists, "I have no wish to bring my own personality

5. See for example Henry Hatfield's remark on Mann's narrator in *Doctor Faustus*: "Throughout the first part of the book the narrator, Serenus Zeitblom, strikes one as a bore" (*From The Magic Mountain: Mann's Later Masterpieces* [Ithaca, N.Y.: Cornell University Press, 1979], p. 116).

6. See also Chapter One, note 34.

into the foreground." In spite of these protests, however, what the elegiac romance narrator does in fact is saturate his description of his hero with his own personality, his own values, and above all his own deepest emotional problems. Jim represents, Marlow tells us, "the illusions" of Marlow's own "beginnings." Our image of Gatsby is suffused with Nick's feelings about his own unglamorous "beginnings" in the American Midwest. Zeitblom's hero, Leverkühn, represents Zeitblom's own wish for artistic "genius."

Sensitive readers will be taken in by this treatment. We will be snared by the narrator's delusions about the grandeur and cosmic importance of the narrator's hero. We will take for granted unquestioningly that the narrator's hero is the central figure in the fiction as a whole. And (much as the *Heart of Darkness* frame narrator responds to Marlow) we will patronize and make generous allowances for this bumbling amateur who has so much trouble telling his tale and who seems so naively "unaware of what [his] audience would best like to hear" (*HD* 7). Dazzled by the narrator's hero and frustrated by the narrator's apparent incompetence and self-abnegation, we pitch in to help him out, poor chap. We become the narrator's ally, his helper, his accomplice. That is, our relationship to the elegiac romance narrator becomes analogous to what his relationship once was to the hero of his tale. Once we have lost our own bearings as the narrator lost his in the past, we have accumulated as he did too much of an emotional stake in the game to withdraw. The narrator's gesture of rhetorical judo is thus complete. He has thrown us with the latent weight and momentum of our own deepest feelings and unquestioned cultural assumptions.

To be thrown by the narrator's effects is as it should be. To be defeated by them is another matter entirely. Readers so defeated are in danger of missing the point that the elegiac romance narrator desperately hopes we will not miss. The point will be missed (as it has been missed in most critical studies of most major elegiac romances to date)[7] if we accept the narrator's rep-

7. Readings of major elegiac romances misinformed by a mistaken notion of their genre are numerous. They are mainly of the type that Norton R. Girault identifies in critical studies of *All the King's Men*, readings assuming that the narrator's hero can be understood whether the narrator is understood or not ("The Narrator's Mind as Symbol: An Analysis of *All the King's Men*," *Accent*, 7

resentation of his hero and himself as our own. To do so, leads us to misinterpret the central issue in elegiac romance as some variation on the perennial nineteenth- and twentieth-century enterprise of defining "the modern hero."

Readers who are sensitive but also careful and persistent, however, perceive that we are being asked to share not only the narrator's illusions but also his disillusionment; we see through the static figure of the narrator's hero, dead and gone, and through the narrator's pretense of dishing up in his tale "the modern hero," to the fundamental issue—hero-worship. We recognize that in elegiac romance what conveys the *author's* insight into an aspect of our "common fate" is what happens to the narrator in the course of telling the tale. And we share the narrator's quest for what in *Heart of Darkness* Marlow calls "inner truth" contained in what he calls in *Lord Jim* half-consciously evolved illusion—truth contained in involuntary fantasy, in dreams, in symbolic recreation, in the art of narration.

This truth, in particular as it is contained in the art of narration, is the import of a curious passage that occurs as Marlow draws near the end of his after-dinner tale in *Lord Jim*. He recalls there the feeling of "utter solitude" he felt during his last evening in Patusan. To feel "as though I had been the last of mankind," he says,

> was a strange and melancholy illusion, evolved half-consciously like all our illusions, which I suspect only to be visions of remote unattainable truth, seen dimly. This was, indeed, one of the lost, forgotten, unknown places of the earth; I had looked under its obscure surface; and I felt that when to-morrow I had left it for ever, it would slip out of existence, to live only in my memory till I myself passed into oblivion. I have that feeling about me now; perhaps it is that feeling which had incited me to tell you the story, to try to hand over to you, as it were, its very existence, its reality— the truth disclosed in a moment of illusion. [*LJ* 232]

Here, explicitly, Marlow connects his profound feeling of loss to the act of telling the tale. His narration is an effort in effect to create a community of readers who share vicariously both his

[1947], 220-34)—see Chapter Five, note 8. For some readings that make the appropriate genre assumptions, see Prologue, note 10.

illusions and his disillusionment. Here Marlow takes a position very much like the one expressed in the epigram Conrad chose for *Lord Jim*, drawn from Novalis: "It is certain my conviction gains infinitely, the moment another soul will believe in it."

The narrator's gesture in elegiac romance, then, is to wean himself from dependence on hero-worship and affect his audience similarly. The narrator asks us to see reflected in his feeling of loss the regret we feel as our own lives slip away, the grief we feel for the loss of the illusions of our own beginnings, the pain we feel in recalling something or someone more precious than life torn from us in the fullness of possession. If we can admit to identifying with this "inner truth" in the life of the elegiac romance narrator, then we are prepared to reaffirm with the narrator the coherence of life, our "common fate," through the vicarious experience he offers.

CHAPTER 4 /

"Under the Surface of Familiar Emotions": Some Psychological Assumptions of Elegiac Romance Prefigured in Conrad

In *Joseph Conrad: The Three Lives*, Frederick Karl remarks that Conrad and Freud were "exact contemporaries."[1] He goes on to say: "Conrad more than most recognized that the individual does not escape from his past; just as Freud—whose ideas Conrad considered a kind of magic show—instructed generations that the unconscious is part of everyman's baggage and not something to be rationalized and purged. Freud's theory of the unconscious for the individual was roughly analogous to Conrad's sense of history for the race, and for himself."[2] The word "roughly" here must be read with heavy emphasis. Freud's conception of the human inner self is precise and systematic. Conrad's is loose, fragmentary, and highly generalized. Still, similarities between the two do exist, and Conrad's exploration in *Heart of Darkness* and *Lord Jim* of the differences and complex relationships between what he calls "inner truth" and "surface-truth" provides an important psychological foundation for further development in the hands of future writers of elegiac romance. Some of these writers, most notably Thomas Mann, were to understand the human inner self in a way profoundly influenced by Freud. This understanding would be more precise than Conrad's intuitive, rough-and-ready one. But the basic premises

1. Page xiv.
2. Page 657.

involved would not be materially different. These premises are expressed in elegiac romances figuratively, as a past relationship between two characters, the narrator and the narrator's hero, carried into the present by the narrator's recollection of that relationship.

In Conrad's two elegiac romances, the same narrator recollects two apparently quite different past relationships with two apparently quite different men. For the purposes of discussion in this chapter, however, similarities between Kurtz and Jim far outweigh differences, as do similarities in Marlow's relationship with them. The basic similarity between Kurtz and Jim as Marlow saw them is that they were both heroes of Western imperialism; and, as he saw them, both were also among its victims. Both sought distinction by committing their lives to "trade" in the imperial possessions of the West. Both were destroyed by that commitment. Marlow saw Kurtz as the archetypal "lone white man" facing the wilderness (*HD* 32). Jim bore comparison in Marlow's eyes to "an individual in the forefront of his kind" who was nevertheless "one of us" (*LJ* 69, 33, and *passim*).

The similarity in Marlow's relationship with Kurtz and with Jim was that neither relationship could be accurately described as friendship. There was too much personal distance involved in both for the interdependent intimacy of friendship to take root. True, the distance between Marlow and Kurtz was quite different in type and origin from the distance between Marlow and Jim. Marlow knew Kurtz only briefly and adulated him as "a gifted creature," somehow much superior to himself (*HD* 48). He knew Jim considerably longer and more familiarly, but the gap in age and experience between the two led Marlow to patronize Jim affectionately as "my very young brother" (*LJ* 160). Despite this difference in what caused the personal distance between the men in these two relationships, however, the result was the same. Marlow experienced each relationship not as intimacy but as an obsessive attachment that he could not escape, an "unconscious loyalty" (*HD* 74) that involved him with both men as their "ally" and "accomplice" (*LJ* 69).

Marlow's attachment to both Kurtz and Jim is best described as a kind of identification or feeling of kinship based on deep, complex cultural and personal resonance. Culturally, Marlow is the quintessential worldly European, and his worldliness is reflected in his heroes. To the "making" of Kurtz, Marlow says, "all Europe contributed" (*HD* 50). Jim has what Marlow calls "a European mind" (*LJ* 188). He was "the sort you like to imagine yourself to have been." In both Kurtz and Jim, Marlow felt "the fellowship" of "illusions you had thought gone out, extinct, cold, and which, as if rekindled at the approach of another flame, give a flutter deep, deep down somewhere, give a flutter of light . . . of heat!" (*LJ* 93).

This deep cultural and personal response also reveals, however, a sinister underside to Marlow's identification with Kurtz and Jim. In the course of his acquaintance with them, Marlow discovered that both men suffered from a "subtle unsoundness" (*LJ*, 66). Each maintained an unquestioned belief in his own superiority and in the inevitability of his own heroic role in an "impossible world of romantic achievements" (*LJ* 62). Kurtz was "avid of lying fame, of sham distinction, of all the appearances of success and power" (*HD* 69). Jim aspired to become "an example of devotion to duty, and unflinching as a hero in a book" (*LJ* 7). Because so much in Marlow resonated culturally and personally with Kurtz and Jim in positive ways, Marlow's glimpse of this "subtle unsoundness" beneath their romantic façades inevitably raised "the ghost of doubt" in his mind about his own personal integrity and the integrity of Western humanity in general (*LJ* 39). Just possibly, Marlow began to feel, he too might unknowingly suffer the limitations he had discovered in these men, admirable in so many ways and similar in so many ways to himself. Thus, as he begins his narrative in both novels Marlow has begun to lose confidence in the coherence, propriety, and rectitude of his own cultural background and inner life. Marlow's experiences with Kurtz and Jim each in its own way revealed to Marlow what wilderness solitude had revealed to Kurtz and what jumping ship had revealed to Jim: "things about himself which he did not know" (*HD* 59).

To have such things revealed to oneself is one issue. To accept and understand them is quite another. Neither Kurtz nor Jim assimilate their self-revelation. Marlow does. But in order to do so he must evolve psychologically in a way that radically changes his view of himself and his world. He must learn to accept an element in both himself and his cultural background that earlier in his life he had explicitly rejected.

To see this psychological evolution in Marlow requires us to read *Heart of Darkness* and *Lord Jim* almost as if they were a single work, or at least as if they were closely complementary works. Such a reading is justified because Conrad wrote these two novels in a closely complementary way. Shortly after beginning *Lord Jim*, Conrad put the manuscript aside to write *Heart of Darkness*. Then, with that done, he returned immediately to writing *Lord Jim*. The result was a tandem set of formally similar novels that address different aspects of the same problem and approach the problem at different stages in its solution. *Heart of Darkness* explores the psychological implications of Marlow's disillusionment at an early stage. *Lord Jim* extends this psychological exploration while also suggesting some related cultural implications.

Together, then, the two novels sketch a process of psychological change in Marlow that is typical of the change that occurs in the narrators of most elegiac romances. This change is not so much a change in what or how much the narrator sees. The depth and complexity of the narrator's insight varies widely from work to work in the genre as a function of the novel's situation and perhaps the narrator's experience and intelligence. For example, the insight of the young, mid-American, college-educated stock-broker, Nick Carraway, in *The Great Gatsby*, is in content relatively simple and plain, whereas the insight of the middle-aged, well-read, intellectually highly trained and sophisticated European academic, Serenus Zeitblom, in *Doctor Faustus*, is relatively intricate and profound.

What is at issue instead in the change elegiac romance narrators undergo as they tell their tale is not what they see, but what they are emotionally capable of seeing. Here, situation, experience, and intelligence signify less; sensibility and courage signify a good deal more. In this respect, Nick Carraway and Serenus Zeitblom are peers. Both experience, as Marlow does, a change that stretches their conception of what "reality" may encompass. In *Heart of Darkness* and *Lord Jim*, Marlow implicitly defines this sort of change in prototypical form. During the experiences Marlow narrates and while he narrates them, the boundaries of his early, narrow conception of reality expand. In the end, his sense of reality includes much of what he had previously rejected as "unreal." He also illuminates and in part overcomes the "subtle unsoundness" he saw in his heroes and feared in himself.[3]

In tracing here the course of the psychological evolution that Marlow undergoes in *Heart of Darkness* and *Lord Jim*, I will be pointing to evidence that suggests not only what Marlow thinks reality is, but more importantly how much reality he can bear to acknowledge. I will be observing in this prototypical narrator of elegiac romance the growth of the very virtue Marlow believes he identified in Jim, "the will or the capacity to look under the surface of familiar emotions" (*LJ* 59).

Stretching the Limits of Reality

Before the period of Marlow's psychological evolution began, before he met Kurtz and Jim, Marlow's views would be most simply and accurately described as nineteenth-century bourgeois. His conception of existence was governed by the narrow,

3. Paul S. Bruss argues that Marlow undergoes a "subtle maturation," defined as a new "access to flexibility of perspective" (*Lord Jim*: The Maturing of Marlow," *Conradiana*, 8 [1976], 13-26, pp. 15, 25). The substance of my argument with respect to the change in Marlow is similar to Bruss's, but I have tried to clarify the issue by being somewhat more precise and specific. Eloise Knapp Hay calls Marlow "a detective of the human soul" engaged in an investigation that results in his suffering "a mental crisis." Hay's position is that the Marlow in *Heart of Darkness* and the Marlow in *Lord Jim* are two quite different characters, so she does not suggest the evolution in character within the two novels taken together that I sketch here. She does observe, however, that in *Heart of Darkness* Marlow "believes . . . that dangerous knowledge must be suppressed," whereas in *Lord Jim* he "believes that even dangerous knowledge is worthy of examination" (*The Political Novels of Joseph Conrad* [Chicago, Ill.: University of Chicago Press, 1963], p. 129). See also Chapter One, note 60, John E. Saveson, "Conrad's View of Primitive Peoples in *Lord Jim* and *Heart of Darkness*." Only in a late revision of the present chapter did I begin to see some parallels also between the way I describe the path of Marlow's development and William G. Perry's description of higher cognitive development in *Forms of Intellectual and Ethical Development in the College Years: A Scheme* (New York: Holt, Rinehart and Winston, 1970). I must acknowledge a possible influence here, since I have been familiar with Perry's book for nearly a decade. In another frame of reference entirely, that of Thomas Kuhn and Richard Rorty, Marlow's development might be described in terms of a "paradigm shift."

conventional, middle-class, European, male values of his time. He made his living sailing ships of the Western commercial empire. He felt himself "tingle with enthusiasm" when he read Kurtz's report to the Society for the Suppression of Savage Customs (*HD* 51). He accepted unquestioningly the "fixed standard of conduct" that governed his life as a seaman (*LJ* 39). He classified his world, furthermore, into two exclusive categories: what he called "reality"—what was common, recognizable, and conventionally unexceptionable—and what he called "unreal"—what was unusual, bizarre, enigmatic, unconventional. Reality encompassed everything accountable by traditional Western thought (*HD* 13, 23). Unreality lay outside that compass and could therefore be dismissed from thought. In short, Marlow could bear to acknowledge, to begin with, only a thin slice of the reality he could later perceive. He could grant at first only the value of "efficiency," "the world of straight-forward facts," "the truth of things . . . that had its reason, that had meaning," the "redeeming facts of life" determined within the same "Providence and . . . established order of the universe" trusted in by Jim's parson father (*HD* 6, 14, 13, 23; *LJ* 245).

Marlow's tales are heavily populated with characters who share with him these conventional values. Kurtz's original intentions in going to Africa were largely those expressed by Marlow's aunt. He set out to claim the wilderness and its native population for Western civilization. His report on the Suppression of Savage Customs was intended for the "future guidance" of the established Western order. The Agents of his company were Europeans of a more ordinary sort who rationalized exploitation in more ordinary but no less conventional ways: their goal was to make "no end of coin by trade" (*HD* 10). Marlow especially admired people like Brierly who seemed supremely confident of their righteousness according to the prevailing standards of accomplishment and virtue. Marlow even found himself attracted by the dignified appearance of the *Patna's* hospitalized Chief Engineer, who in spite of a brutal case of delirium tremens looked "fine and calm" (*LJ* 38).

The first phase of Marlow's psychological evolution away from absolute, unquestioning dependence on these conventional values occurred at the beginning of the experience he narrates in

Heart of Darkness. At that time he became gradually aware of another set of facts that lay hidden behind this orderly everyday appearance, that contradicted it, and that seemed unaccountable by its light. Marlow's aunt, despite Marlow's insistence that African exploration was undertaken for profit, continued unaccountably to rationalize imperialistic ventures as "weaning those ignorant millions from their horrid ways" (*HD* 12). Marlow himself felt that to take a job as master of an African river steamboat was a "notion" that, unaccountably, "drove me" (*HD* 8). He discovered that in the Congo a Danish shipmaster, "the gentlest, quietest creature that ever walked on two legs," had killed a village chief over "a misunderstanding about . . . two black hens (*HD* 9). He found a note, "Exterminate all the brutes!" appended to Kurtz's idealistic report on "savage customs" (*HD* 51). He met a trustworthy-appearing young man, Jim, who had unaccountably jumped ship. The ideal ship captain, Brierly, committed suicide. The *Patna's* Chief Engineer claimed to see pink toads under his hospital bed—and, unaccountably, Marlow "stooped instantly" to see for himself (*LJ* 40).

At first Marlow discounted these experiences as anomalies in the reality he unquestioningly accepted. They were meaningless aberrations, exceptions that proved the rule. He dismissed his own feeling of being driven to Africa as a "senseless delusion" (*HD* 13). His aunt was a woman, and women "live in a world of their own, and there never had been anything like it" (*HD* 12). The company's Agents were "bewitched" (*HD* 23). Brierly thought too much of himself. Jim was haunted by the "ghost of a fact" (*LJ* 141). Kurtz was "mad" (*HD* 57).

By the end of the tale told in *Heart of Darkness* and the beginning of the experience narrated in *Lord Jim*, however, Marlow has begun to believe that the established order he had complacently accepted is only a partial reality. Accordingly, the language he uses to describe reality changes. Experience he once rejected as unreal, bewitched, ghostly, egotistical, feminine, delusory, and mad, he begins to see as evidence of a larger reality, an "inner truth," a "truth stripped of its cloak of time" (*HD* 37). He begins also to distrust the "straight-forward facts" that had once constituted his whole reality. These now seem "mere incidents of the surface" (*HD* 34), given more credence than they warrant by the accident of temporal immediacy and superficial coherence.

This new willingness to classify as in some sense real what he had before discounted out of hand as altogether unreal is what Marlow gains in the first phase of his psychological evolution. His new awareness marked the beginning of his disillusionment and resulted in several remarkable changes in attitude. It led him to acknowledge implicitly, for example, a similarity between his own inner life and that of the "savages" who worked for him. They too had "creepy thoughts," "impulses, motives, capacities, weaknesses" (*HD* 42). They too, just like white men, were capable of exercising restraint. As Marlow recognized this "distant kinship" between himself and native Africans, he also for the first time reevaluated the coherence of his own actions. Although he had once felt driven to Africa, he had not then questioned the inherent value or validity of the voyage. It somehow implicitly made sense. Gradually, however, he lost confidence in this belief that whatever he did implicitly made sense. He continued to feel driven to meet Kurtz, at any cost, but he also began to perceive that in striving to meet Kurtz he was "striving after something altogether without a substance" (*HD* 48). Worse, he began to feel that under these conditions no conscious act of the will would be effectual. "My speech or my silence," he says, "indeed any action of mine, would be a mere futility" (*HD* 39).

With this disillusionment and the resulting self-doubt came the first explicit acknowledgment of a reality beyond "any action of mine." Marlow began to grant that "the essentials" of his experience "lay deep under the surface, beyond my reach, and beyond my power of meddling" (*HD* 39). Whereas once Marlow could only classify Kurtz as "mad," later he could allow that Kurtz had not been just a "lunatic" but had acted with an intelligence that Marlow began to perceive as "perfectly clear" (*HD* 67). This first phase in Marlow's psychological evolution ends, then, with Marlow wondering if underlying the unaccountable elements in the behavior of Kurtz and Jim—and underlying his own behavior as well—there might be "some sort of method." The task ahead was to try to discover the "thread of logic" (*LJ* 42) that Marlow suspected at this juncture might exist even in delusion.

In this first phase of Marlow's psychological evolution, then, he observed that a larger reality exists than is recognizable by conventional Western thought and values. In the second phase he condemned those conventions for their seductive narrowness, corruptibility, and superficiality. He reached this conclusion in *Lord Jim* by trying to understand the "inner truth" of another person, Jim, who seemed, in all respects but one, perfectly normal, reliable, and admirable. Marlow first responded to Jim therefore, as he first responded to Kurtz, out of the conventional ideas and values of his past. To respond conventionally to Kurtz meant dismissing him as "mad," because what Marlow first saw of Kurtz lay wholly beyond the scope of those conventions—an emaciated skeleton of a man shouting and gesticulating wildly, his hut ringed by severed heads stuck on poles. In contrast, what Marlow first saw of Jim was wholly comprehensible within the scope of conventional Western ideas and values. Jim seemed to be "an upstanding, broad-shouldered youth . . . clean-limbed, clean-faced, firm on his feet, as promising a boy as the sun ever shone on" (*LJ* 31). Even under the pressure of the trial, Jim seemed composed, youthfully energetic, attractive. Thus, just exactly the ready-made categories Marlow depended upon in dismissing Kurtz as "mad" prevented him from dismissing Jim; and yet not one of those conventions helped Marlow understand Jim. Marlow was totally at a loss to know whether Jim's appearance was "the outcome of manly self-control, of impudence, of callousness, of a colossal unconsciousness, of a gigantic deception" (*LJ* 58).

In the face of the failure of these categories and of the conventions that underlay them, to help him understand Jim, Marlow exclaims with dismay, "Who can tell!" Like Jack Burden's question in *All the King's Men*, "How was I to know?" (*AKM* 13), however, Marlow's cry can be read not as a gesture of hopelessness but as the beginning of genuine inquiry. Read this way, it implies a critique of the means of knowing. Thus, in the second phase of Marlow's psychological evolution the issue became in part what is the central issue in several later elegiac romances, a problem of knowledge.

For Marlow, the problem of knowledge is a very personal problem. The kind of knowledge that interests him most results from getting under the surface of experience, a surface shaped by conventional Western ideas and values, and grasping the "thread of logic" there. Each of Marlow's tales records an experience in which such knowledge failed him. In each case he jeopardized his understanding of himself and of others by identifying emotionally with—that is, becoming the willing "accomplice" and "ally" of—men whom he admits he "could not see" (*LJ* 69). Marlow misjudged people by reading them conventionally and thus failed to gain knowledge of what lay under the surface. Misjudgment of this sort occurs in both novels under several guises. Marlow misjudged Kurtz's erstwhile companion, the Russian youth, for example, and he misjudged the ideal sea captain, Brierly. Jim too fatally misjudged the character and goals of Gentleman Brown.

To Marlow the problem of knowledge is considerably more than a general interest in what makes other people tick. Marlow prides himself rather too conspicuously on his perspicacity, his "confounded democratic quality of vision." "I have met so many men, and in each case," he says smugly, "all I could see was merely the human being" (*LJ* 69). Yet despite this flourish of self-congratulation, Marlow is forced to admit that the "inner truth" of human character is beyond him. With regard to everyone he has known, including Jim, "the envelope of flesh and blood on which our eyes are fixed melts" as Marlow reaches out "to grapple with another man's intimate need," "and there remains only the capricious, inconsolable, and elusive spirit that no eye can follow, no hand can grasp" (*LJ* 129).

The elusiveness of the inner person challenges both Marlow's perspicacity and the soundness and realiability of his upbringing, the cultural frame of reference within which he makes judgments and perceives reality. Marlow says he felt "aggrieved against" Jim "as though he had cheated me—me!—of a splendid opportunity to keep up the illusion of my beginnings" (*LJ* 95). An illusion of this sort is also the origin of Jim's difficulty judging Gentleman Brown. Both Marlow and Jim assumed unquestioningly the superiority of people of their own culture and race. Because the person both men attempted to evaluate was "one of us"—presumably culturally identical—both men assumed that that person must therefore be trustworthy and above reproach. Marlow confesses that he relies on "the right kind of looks" (*LJ* 35). Jim relied on them too, and fell for Brown's "subtle reference to their common blood, an assumption of common experience" (*LJ* 279).[4]

The illusion of cultural superiority destroyed Jim. Marlow, more fortunate, was able to destroy the illusion. Wounded by his association with Kurtz, Marlow's assumption of cultural superiority had received a mortal blow by the time he admits in *Lord Jim* that being deluded by "mere surfaces" is not only a personal failing of his own but a characteristic of "the Western eye" in general (*LJ* 188). Disillusionment with Jim helps disillusion Marlow in turn about "the established order" of Western thought and values that Jim represents.

The second phase of Marlow's psychological evolution culminates, therefore, when he concludes that the premises and assumptions of Western culture are merely "haggard utilitarian lies" (*LJ* 202). Given Marlow's hatred of lies, this is stark condemnation. It is a measure of how much more inclusive Marlow's conception of reality has now become. He had of course seen conventional values revealed as deceptive in his aunt's delusions

---

4. Avrom Fleishman rejects "racial prejudice" as a factor in Jim's crucial actions (*Conrad's Politics* [Baltimore: Johns Hopkins Press, 1967], p. 109). Perhaps for Fleishman the term implies something too superficial to seem adequate to the case. The motive at issue may be more accurately described as unequivocal, uncompromising ethnocentrism. Whatever the appropriate term, Jim's experience in the novel from this point of view is decidedly symmetrical. He makes two "mistakes," one on the *Patna* and the other in Patusan. In both instances he betrays conspicuously trusting, peaceful, serious people whose skins are brown and whose culture is non-Western, to throw in his lot with conspicuously irresponsible, disreputable, hostile people whose skins are white and whose culture is European.

That the dimensions and tenacity of the state of mind Jim's actions reveal remain undiminished among at least some Western peoples today is suggested, furthermore, by a front-page article in *The New York Times* a mere decade ago, April 16, 1973. Entitled "Mastery Over World Oil Supply Shifts to Producing Countries," the article quotes the Saudi Arabian Minister of Petroleum Affairs, Ahmed Zaki al-Yamani, making a prediction that, until very recently, has proven accurate to a fault: "We are in a position to dictate prices," said Mr. al-Yamani, "and we are going to be very rich." In response to the aspect of the contemporary world economic situation revealed in Mr. al-Yamani's prediction, an unnamed "European oil-company official" is quoted in the same article as having made the following comment, one that exposes more perhaps than he quite intended about the contemporary world cultural situation. "When a million little Bedouins in Libya," the official said, "have the power, by denying their oil, to paralyze the economy of a modern European nation of 50 million people such as Italy, that is a ridiculous situation."

about the purpose of European imperialism. He had then seen them mercilessly exposed in the addendum to Kurtz's report on the Suppression of Savage Customs: "Exterminate all the brutes!" (*HD* 51). But now he had seen these values indicted by the brutal fact of Gentleman Brown's gratuitous murder of Dain Waris. What Marlow wants us particularly to "notice" in this act, in fact, is what it reveals about the presumptuous, self-deceptive nature of the "utilitarian lies" of Western culture. There was in Brown's attack on Dain, Marlow says, "a superiority as of a man who carries right—the abstract thing—within the envelope of his common desires. It was not a vulgar and treacherous massacre; it was a lesson, a retribution—a demonstration of some obscure and awful attribute of our nature which, I am afraid, is not so very far under the surface as we like to think" (*LJ* 291).

Involuntary Memory, Involuntary Acts

In the second phase of Marlow's psychological evolution he arrives at a point where he can see and condemn this conventional Western self-righteousness, "the abstract thing." In the third and last phase, the field of reality that Marlow is emotionally capable of acknowledging expands still further to include conscious, cautious acceptance of the necessity of a culture's "utilitarian lies" in one form or another. This phase begins with an implicit analysis of the Western world's "obscure and awful attribute of self-righteousness," and concludes with an attempt at a somewhat more explicit analysis.

Marlow's implicit analysis of that "obscure and awful atttribute" of our nature occurs in the imagery of his tale in *Heart of Darkness*. This imagery reveals first that the "vast and dismal aspect of disorder" that constitutes "inner truth" coexists in us simultaneously with "sheltering conception of light and order," "the utilitarian lies of our civilization" that we construct to avoid confronting inner chaos (*LJ* 225, 202). And secondly, this imagery reveals that, paradoxically, these two simultaneously coexisting levels of reality are dynamically related in time. The dark, chaotic reality of "inner truth" is composed of past personal history which, remaining alive in involuntary memory, profoundly influences present feelings, responses, and actions. This influence is the underlying "thread of logic" that explains the many unaccountable acts of the men Marlow observes, and many of his own acts as well, acts unaccountable according to the conventional Western "sheltering conception of light and order." In revealing implicitly this temporal relationship between "inner truth" and "surface-truth," Marlow prefigures the psychological principle that underlies the narrator's development in many elegiac romances.

Marlow's journey in *Heart of Darkness* involves otherwise unaccountable involuntary responses, involuntary memories, and involuntary acts from start to finish. His journey into the Congo began, indeed, with an involuntary response. When he looked by chance into a store window at a map of Africa that showed a river "resembling an immense snake uncoiled," he tells us, "it fascinated me as a snake would a bird—a silly little bird. . . . I went on along Fleet Street, but could not shake off the idea. The snake had charmed me" (*HD* 8).

Under the influence of this obsession, Marlow continued to act contrary to his ordinary pattern of behavior in a way, he implies, that still embarrasses him. First, he immediately and impulsively placed himself in an unaccustomed relationship of childlike dependence upon women:

> I am sorry to own I began to worry [my relations]. This was already a fresh departure for me. I was not used to get things that way, you know. I always went my own road and on my own legs where I had a mind to go. I wouldn't have believed it of myself; but, then—you see—I felt somehow I must get there by hook or by crook. So I worried them. The men said "My dear fellow," and did nothing. Then—would you believe it?—I tried the women. I, Charlie Marlow, set the women to work—to get a job. Heavens! Well, you see, the notion drove me. [*HD* 8]

Having begun with this one pattern of involuntary action, Marlow's African experience ended with yet another. Once again he placed himself in a disadvantageous position with regard to a woman. Having returned to Europe, on impulse he visited Kurtz's fiancée. He says he had then "no clear perception of what it was I really wanted" in seeing her (*HD* 74), and he professes now in telling the tale that he still cannot fully explain it. Marlow does speculate illuminatingly, however, about the "inner truth" of the visit. It occurs to him that he visited Kurtz's Intended in order to fulfill "one of those ironic necessities that lurk in the facts of human existence" (*HD* 74).

But if so, the demands made by those "necessities" were not fulfilled solely by the impulse to make the visit. Compulsion compounded itself. One involuntary act occasioned another in a sequence that ended only at the moment that becomes the climax of Marlow's tale. Driven involuntarily to visit Kurtz's Intended, when Marlow arrived at her door he experienced a vivid, involuntary memory of Kurtz, "opening his mouth voraciously, as if to devour all the earth with all its mankind" (*HD* 74). Then as Marlow ended his visit he made a momentous verbal slip by which he revealed the fact that he had heard Kurtz's last words. Through this slip, Marlow in effect offered involuntarily to provide information that he had had no conscious intention of giving up. He was then forced to cover his slip by lying, itself an act he claims to detest (*HD* 27):

"You were with him—to the last? . . ."
"To the very end," I said, shakily. "I heard his very last words. . . ."
I stopped in a fright.
"Repeat them," she murmured in a heart-broken tone. "I want—I want—something—something—to—to live with."
I was on the point of crying at her, "Don't you hear them?" The dusk was repeating them. . . . "The horror! The horror! . . .
I pulled myself together and spoke slowly.
"The last word he pronounced was—your name." [*HD* 79]

These two involuntary acts framing the experience Marlow narrates in *Heart of Darkness*—a compulsive response to the chance sight of a map and a nearly disastrous verbal slip—have an important element in common. They both seem related to an extremely early stage in Marlow's emotional development, as early, indeed, as childhood. In both cases, in the midst of living and acting as a mature adult Marlow for a brief period (a few weeks, a few seconds) acted as if he were suddenly once again the child, the "little chap" he once had been (*HD* 8). In the first instance he was overcome by the threateningly phallic image of an "immense snake uncoiled, with its head in the sea." This experience left him feeling powerless as a "silly little bird," with the result that he placed himself dependently into the protective, motherly hands of his aunt. In the second instance, he stood before the door of a woman's house and felt the threat of annihilation by a force female in nature, when he experienced the hallucination of a "mouth" opening "voraciously, as if to devour all the earth with all its mankind." This experience too incapacitated Marlow. It deprived him of self-control so that he blurted out a guilty secret as a child might who feels he cannot contain the awful knowledge of an evil act performed by a playmate. As such, Marlow's involuntary confession was peculiarly appropriate to his recollection of his experience with Kurtz, part of which had struck him as being "like a boyish game" (*HD* 66).

"The Secret Sensibility of My Egoism"

Having established implicitly in *Heart of Darkness* the influence of past personal history on the present, the third phase of Marlow's psychological evolution culminates in *Lord Jim* with an attempt to account explicitly in terms of this influence for the failure of Western thought and values. This analysis is telescoped and incomplete. But its effect on Marlow is to allow him to make peace on his own terms, finally, with the "utilitarian lies of our civilization."

To arrive at this reconciliation, Marlow observes first that these "lies," the conventional thought and values of civilized Western life, although they begin as honest attempts to make sense of the world, become in the end in many cases a way of avoiding understanding, responsibility, and change. This happens because what we like to think of as a "conception of light and order" is really little more than "an arrangement of small conveniences" that provides the "shelter that each of us makes for himself to creep under in moments of danger" (*LJ* 225).

In *Lord Jim*, Marlow offers examples of these sheltering values in the conventional advice of Jim's pastor-father (*LJ* 245), but even more tellingly, because more seductively, in the "charming" but "deceptive" platitudes of Marlow's friend Stein. The terms of Stein's explanation of Jim's conduct reveal values and a sense of reality as narrow as the nineteenth-century bourgeois world view Marlow began with. Stein thought in terms of traditional Western aesthetic categories ("I understand very well. He is romantic."), in terms of static states of being ("the destructive element"), and in terms of moral absolutes ("There is only one remedy!") (*LJ* 152-53).

Marlow found Stein's advice unsatisfactory because Marlow was already aware that to understand Jim he had to account for too much that Stein's easy categories did not include. What Marlow must face in *Lord Jim* is the realization that under the glittering surface of conventional values lies the dismaying fact that anyone, at least any European man of the kind Marlow knows, may be vulnerable to the sort of self-made disaster that befell Jim. "The commonest sort of fortitude," he remarks, "prevents us from becoming criminals in a legal sense; it is from weakness unknown, but perhaps suspected, as in some parts of the world you suspect a deadly snake in every bush—from weakness that may lie hidden, watched or unwatched, prayed against or manfully scorned, repressed or maybe ignored more than half a lifetime, not one of us is safe" (*LJ* 33).

"The truth," Marlow says grimly, "can be wrung out of us only by some cruel, little, awful catastrophe" (*LJ* 233), because "our imagination alone" can "set loose upon us the might of an overwhelming destiny" (*LJ* 246). This insight is what makes Jim's example so threatening. Jim's jump from the *Patna* dramatized the challenge he explicitly threw down before Marlow later: "What would you have done? What? You can't tell—nobody can tell" (*LJ* 68).

Marlow comes closest to generalizing explicitly a psychological principle to explain this potential "weakness unknown" in each of us when he is taking pains to deny his capacity to provide just such a generalization. Marlow realizes during Jim's trial that he would like to "spare him the mere detail of a formal execution." But, he says, "I don't pretend to explain the reasons of my desire—I don't think I could; but if . . . he had not enlisted my sympathies he had done better for himself—he had gone to the very fount and origin of that sentiment, he had reached the secret sensibility of my egoism" (*LJ* 110). Vague as it is, this passage read in context does express the rudimentary psychological concept on which Conrad's view of "inner truth" is based.[5]

The key word in the passage is "egoism." Marlow's "sympathies" originate, he says, in a "secret" susceptibility to impression and to the effect of this "egoism" on his "desire." In the context of discussing Marlow's fear of a potential, unknown inner weakness, "egoism" would seem to refer to an instinct for protecting oneself against such a weakness, an instinct for self-preservation, for maintaining intact the fragile existence and integrity of the deepest self we know in the face of every threat to it. Thus Marlow's "egoism" in this passage refers to the instinctive, spontaneous, ultimately unscrupulous and amoral necessity at the base of human life, the necessity to survive. If so, then by Marlow's own account this self-protective level of his own emotional life is what responded to Jim "secretly"—that is, responded unconsciously or with the unaccountable will of "inner truth."

In Marlow's acknowledgment of this unscrupulous, amoral pre-emptive instinct for self-preservation lies a large measure of his importance as a prototypical narrator of elegiac romance. Much of that narrator's anguish can be traced to his fear, stated or implied, of "losing [his] footing in the midst of waters, a sudden dread, the dread of unknown depths" (*LJ* 224). Some such unknown depth of weakness and the narrator's emotional capacity to come to terms with it at least tacitly appear, as we shall see in Chapter Five, in Jack Burden's "clammy, sad little foetus you carry around inside yourself" (*AKM* 9), in Nick Carraway's identification of "some deficiency . . . which made us subtly unadaptable to Eastern life" (*GG* 177), in John Dowell's violent second self in love with Edward Ashburnham (*GS* 253), and in Serenus Zeitblom's "fearful love" of Leverkühn's arrogance (*DF*, Ch.8). And it exists also in the Oedipal guilt, real or imagined, that many of these and other elegiac romance narrators feel with regard to the death of their heroes. Knowles's

5. John E. Saveson attributes the operative terms in this passage to Conrad's acquaintance, through H. G. Wells, with the psychological writings of James Sully ("Marlow's Psychological Vocabulary in *Lord Jim*," *Texas Studies in Literature and Language*, 12 [1970], 457-70). See also Allan O. McIntyre, "Conrad on Conscience and the Passions," *University Review*, 31 (1964), 69-74, and "Conrad on the Functions of the Mind," *Modern Language Quarterly*, 25 (1964), 187-97.

Gene Forrester is directly responsible for the death of Phinny. Dowell is indirectly responsible for Ashburnham's suicide. Jack Burden acknowledges his indirect complicity in the assassination of Willie Stark. Harris's Henry Wiggen and Bellow's Charlie Citrine express guilt for failing to make the last days of their heroes' lives easier and Citrine in particular for "patting down" his hero's grave "with my shovel."[6]

Marlow's acknowledgment of a preemptive instinct for self-preservation implies, however, a reaffirmation on his own terms of the necessity for cultural and social constraints to keep this instinct in check. What Marlow says of Jim's "crime" might be said as well of the behavior of the narrator's heroes of a number of later elegiac romances. The significance of Jim's crime, as of Kurtz's, Ashburnham's, Willie Stark's, and Leverkühn's, is "in its being a breach of faith with the community of mankind" (*LJ* 113). That necessary faith includes, for example, values such as the "restraint" demonstrated by the cannibal workmen on Marlow's riverboat in *Heart of Darkness* (*HD* 43) and the momentary intimacy Marlow felt as Jim left for Patusan (*LJ* 173). The medium in which that faith with the community of mankind is kept and expressed, and the framework that gives it for any one of us strength and integrity, are the "lies" of civilization, our sheltering conceptions of light and order.

In the collapse of his faith in conventional values and his subsequent reaffirmation of them on some such terms as these, Marlow is also therefore prototypical of later elegiac romance narrators. Samuel Hynes argues, for example, that for John Dowell, Ford's narrator in *The Good Soldier*,

society . . . depends on the arbitrary and unquestioning acceptance of "the whole collection of rules." Dowell is, at the beginning of his action, entirely conventional in this sense; conventions provide him with a way of existing in the world—they are alternatives to the true reality which man cannot know, or which he cannot bear to know. From conventions he gets a spurious sense of permanence and stability and human intimacy, and the illusion of knowledge. When they collapse, he is left with nothing. . . . In the action of

6. Saul Bellow, *Humboldt's Gift* (New York: Viking, 1973), p. 116.

Dowell's knowing, he learns the reality of Passion, but he also acknowledges that Convention will triumph, because it must.[7]

The elegiac romance narrator's explicit or implicit reaffirmation of conventional expressions of faith in the community of mankind suggests, then, that, although the model of human inner life prefigured in Conrad and followed with appropriate variations by later writers of elegiac romance is in many respects a dark one, it is by no means totally lacking in potential for attaining some sort of modern, secular version of salvation and grace. As a prototype of the elegiac romance narrator, Marlow represents also the possibility that "inner truth" may be capable of generating constructive, salutary forces. Although Kurtz and Jim, living at the outposts of Western imperialism, where the "haggard utilitarian lies of our civilization wither and die," were governed by "pure exercises of the imagination," and although Marlow himself was once "driven by a dream" to undertake an all-but-fatal upriver African voyage, the bizarre fantasy-lives men such as these led in the wilderness had, Marlow observes, "the futility, often the charm, sometimes the deep hidden truthfulness, of works of art" (*LJ* 202).

The parallel between ungoverned fantasy and artistic invention that Marlow draws in this observation is crucial to our understanding of elegiac romance. Marlow perceives that the same imaginative power that destroyed the likes of Kurtz and Jim can also serve to counteract and forestall the threat of "an overwhelming destiny." This understanding too is part of the larger field of reality that Marlow's psychological evolution gives him the emotional capacity to acknowledge. We can harness our "dreams," Marlow suggests, through narrative art. And the effort to put fantasy to productive, ameliorative work is precisely the remedy for a malfunctioning imagination that every elegiac romance narrator prescribes for himself. The exercise of imaginative transformation through literary art, the symbolic projection in a heroic figure of the inner, unconscious self, helps this narrator understand something of that inner self and escape a measure of its deleterious influence. It also helps him to regen-

7. "The Epistemology of *The Good Soldier*," *Sewanee Review*, 69 (1961), 232-34.

erate the faith that binds mankind by creating a community of sympathetic readers. Kurtz and Jim exemplify what can happen when this symbolic transformation does not or cannot occur. Marlow exemplifies what can happen when it does.

CHAPTER 5

"I See Now": Elegiac Romance as Epistemological Fiction

In the language of literary history and criticism, the phrase "psychological fiction" stands as a useful "term of art." It is a phrase not to be taken too strictly or literally. The fiction we call "psychological" has little to do with psychology as a systematic study or as an academic or therapeutic discipline. If in a literary context we mean by the term "psychological" a general interest in the inner life, however, then the term is aptly applied. The novels of James, Woolf, and Joyce render inner processes, processes of feeling and thought, in persuasive, realistic detail. For the sake of convenient reference, literary critics adopt the term "psychological," displaced from its normal scientific context and meaning, to suggest an important general characteristic of a coherent category of modern literary works.

I use the term "epistemological" in a similarly displaced sense. The proper sphere of the term "epistemology" is the philosophical study, from Descartes through Locke and Kant to Russell and Wittgenstein, of how we think and know. Epistemology is theory of knowledge. The novels I examine in this chapter no more analyze knowledge systematically than *To the Lighthouse* analyzes feeling and the "stream of consciousness" systematically. Yet these novels are "epistemological" in the same sense that Woolf's novel is "psychological": they render inner processes, in this case processes of *knowing*, the search for truth, in persuasively realistic detail. Their goal is in part that of all elegiac literature, to provide "a skeptical, revelatory vision for its own sake."[1]

Because elegiac romances are fiction, not philosophical analysis, they differ from systematic epistemology in quite another, more substantive way. Historically, epistemologists have mainly been concerned with conscious knowledge. But in the period contemporaneous with the growth of elegiac romance, sources of knowledge other than consciousness tend to be recognized as epistemologically relevant. Elegiac romance is interesting epistemologically because it treats the process of understanding in a way that assumes our apprehension of the world begins in part as an unconscious—or preconscious—process, not a fully conscious one.[2] We learn, in effect, by becoming aware, most often through language, of what we have already unconsciously or preconsciously grasped.

Elegiac romance is also interesting epistemologically because it implies that emotional adjustment to the past plays a role in knowing. We might say loosely that the problem faced by elegiac romance narrators is to recall the past and understand it, to make it part of their conscious knowledge, in order to free themselves of its influence, or at least to place that influence under a measure of conscious control. To put the matter in oversimplified Freudian terms, it is as if the narrator had been traumatized before he begins to tell his tale, had been the captive of unresolved unconscious pain and conflict. By revealing and understanding the trauma, through telling his tale, he resolves the neurosis.

In this way elegiac romance is involved with one of the conceptual changes that occurred at the beginning of the twentieth century—the new search for "some kind of internal comprehension" that would "penetrate beneath the surface of human experience" (Hughes, p. 65). The narrator's penetration beneath "surface-truth" through the imaginative symbolic act of telling the tale effects the change in himself which results in the dramatized narrative insights that punctuate the tale.

1. Potts, *Elegiac Mode*, p. 37.
2. My use of the term "unconscious" in this chapter follows conventions and limitations discussed in Chapter One, note 60.

In most cases, gaining this new understanding requires challenging and dismantling the conventions by which the narrator has in the past perceived his world. These constructions of reality are the sort that in *Lord Jim* Marlow calls variously "the established order" of Western thought and values, our "sheltering conception of light and order," and the "haggard utilitarian lies of our civilization." They include as well—indeed, in elegiac romance they are largely represented by—the traditional heroic stance of the narrator's hero: the conventions of the Faust tradition in terms of which Marlow sees Kurtz and Zeitblom sees Leverkühn; the conventions of boys' adventure fiction, cheap romantic fiction, and Byronic heroism in terms of which Jim, Ashburnham, and Gatsby respectively see themselves; and the conventions of the courtly love tradition in terms of which Dowell and others in *The Good Soldier* see Ashburnham. Elegiac romance implies that these conventions have outlived their usefulness. They perform, therefore, not as means by which to perceive the world realistically but as illusions. Dismantling them is therefore a process of disillusionment. This disillusionment is necessary, elegiac romance implies, because otherwise these outworn conventions, these illusions, serve as barriers to new understanding, to new knowledge, to the search for truth.

The ultimate subject of elegiac romance is the "thread of logic" underlying this new understanding. Cloaked in the shadows of memory, this underlying coherence is available to consciousness only when driven into the open by severe emotional strain of the sort occasioned by the narrator's loss of his hero. It is what the narrator tells his tale to expose and what he reveals in the insight he gains as he tells the tale. In earlier chapters, I have suggested reading elegiac romance as dramatizing the sentient narrator's recovery from the state of emotional paralysis he suffers as he begins his tale, a recovery accomplished through an imaginative, symbolic act giving rise to a new understanding of himself and his world. In this chapter I suggest ways in which four elegiac romances, *The Great Gatsby*, *The Good Soldier*, *All the King's Men*, and *Doctor Faustus*, dramatize the sentient narrator's new understanding of himself and his world, understanding gained through an imaginative, symbolic act generating a new emotional vitality. The epistemological message of elegiac romance might be expressed most concisely in the time-honored notion that those who don't know the past are doomed to repeat it, or, in more modern terms, those who don't recover the past are doomed to regress to it.

"A Story of the West After All": *The Great Gatsby*

The elegiac romance narrator's recovery through fuller understanding of himself and his world is dramatized most simply and clearly in F. Scott Fitzgerald's *The Great Gatsby*. In this novel the narrator, Nick Carraway, appears to have undergone some change already before he begins telling his tale. But his state of mind and his attitude toward his hero, Gatsby, as he begins telling the tale suggest that this recovery from the dependent state of hero-worship is not yet complete. His recovery continues in the dramatized fictional present of the novel as he tells the tale, and concludes with a single dramatized narrative insight as the tale ends.

With this insight, Nick suddenly understands the nature both of his present enterprise, telling the story of Gatsby's life, and of an important aspect of his own character. That some sort of change occurs in Nick as he tells the tale is evident in the difference in tone between the way he describes scenes from his youth at the beginning and the way he describes them at the end of the tale. The self-mockery he begins with entirely disappears. What effects this change is a moment of detachment that Nick achieves late in the tale. "I see now," he says at that moment, "that this has been a story of the West after all." He himself played an important part in the action that gave rise to his tale, and his participation in that action has had an important effect on his life.[3]

3. E. F. Carlisle, "The Triple Vision of Nick Carraway," *Modern Fiction Studies*, 11 (1966), 351-60; and Thomas A. Hanzo, "The Theme and the Narrator of *The Great Gatsby*," *Modern Fiction Studies*, 2 (Winter, 1956-57), 183-90. On *The Great Gatsby* and the conventions of the pastoral elegiac tradition, see Chapter One, note 25.

This is not the first time that Nick steps back from his narrative to comment on it. He has done so at least twice before. In Chapter 3, for example, he says: "Reading over what I have written so far, I see I have given the impression that the events of three nights several weeks apart were all that absorbed me. On the contrary, they were merely casual events in a crowded summer, and, until much later, they absorbed me infinitely less than my personal affair" (*GG* 56).

We must grant that Nick has a degree of insight into himself here. Nick discovers that his mind tends to select and edit memory. But more conspicuously, Nick is putting his audience on notice in this passage that the process is occurring now, here, in his tale as he tells it. These two sentences are classifiable as shop talk of the kind all elegiac romance narrators are prone to: Salinger's Buddy Glass interrupts his tale to say, "One remark in this last paragraph stops me cold"; Bellow's Charlie Citrine asks, "How should I describe this phenomenon?"; Zeitblom rationalizes the length of his chapters; Marlow stops in *Lord Jim* to explain why he has told "these two episodes at length"; Dowell and Nabokov's V. discuss the random-seeming nature of their narrative style. Remarks like these are primarily intended to keep readers of elegiac romance keenly aware that it is indeed a tale, a conscious artifact, that they are reading.

When Nick steps back from narration again toward the end of his tale, however, narrative technique has become at best a subordinate issue. This time narrative disengagement yields an important insight. "I see now," Nick says, "that this has been a story of the West, after all—Tom and Gatsby, Daisy and Jordan and I, were all Westerners, and perhaps we possessed some deficiency in common which made us subtly unadaptable to Eastern life" (*GG* 177). One might quibble that this is hardly a profound observation. It seems uninformed, with little regard for the commonplaces of cultural relativity which an undergraduate of even modest talents might have picked up at Yale in the early 1920's. At issue here, however, is not the quality of Nick's insight (which is a function of his character) but its type. Whatever its degree of conceptual sophistication, Nick's insight reveals that a significant change has occurred in his understanding of the objective world. It is evidence that by formulating what he remembers symbolically in telling the tale, Nick understands better what he remembers. And it is evidence that as he has understood the past better by this means, his attitude toward the past has changed. Furthermore, Nick's insight asserts both a new view of people and events of the past ("we possessed some deficiency"), and also a new view of at least one of Nick's activities in the present, telling the tale ("this has been a story").

This change in the way Nick views the past and the present results from his achieving, as he tells the tale, a new level of self-acceptance. Beginning in Chapter 1, he is painfully ambivalent toward himself as he remembers himself in the past. His ambivalence appears in the disharmony between what he says and how he says it. In substance, Nick's introductory autobiographical notes are self-aggrandizing. He intends them, it seems, to increase his shallow reserve of self-esteem. In tone, however, he succeeds only in revealing his uncertainty about himself and his limited self-understanding.

Nick expresses his insecurity as a desperate need to keep his inner world from flying apart. He tells us that since Gatsby's death he has felt he "wanted the world to be in uniform and at a sort of moral attention forever" (GG 2). He then trots out items from his past as if they were credentials establishing the authenticity of his "advantages," his "sense of the fundamental decencies," and the authority of his "tolerance" and "judgment." Nick displays these credentials much as Gatsby displayed his photographs and medals, as if they had an unvarying inherent value and were an intrinsic part of his identity. If he can just keep his past intact, Nick seems to feel, his inner world will remain safely intact as well.

At the same time that he is revealing this desperate reliance on the past, Nick also seems at pains to reassure himself that the past actually means very little to him. Nick defends himself, as we shall see later in this chapter Jack Burden does, against genuine feeling for the past. But whereas Jack's defense is philosophical, Nick's is rhetorical. He erects a supercilious façade of ironic carelessness, presenting himself as having the sort of "personality" Gatsby had, which Nick defines as "an unbroken series of successful gestures" (*GG* 2). Nick boasts mockingly of his similarity in appearance to the "hard-boiled" great uncle who started the family firm. He obscures the horror and debasement of the First World War by referring to it cavalierly as a "delayed Teutonic invasion" followed by a "counter-raid" which he "enjoyed" . . . thoroughly." He seems to want to give the impression through this offhand tone that he values his past only for what it does to improve his public image. He deals in the past as his family for generations had dealt in hardware, as stock in trade (*GG* 3).

By the end of Nick's tale, this painful ambivalence toward the past disappears. His concluding meditation is neither self-aggrandizing nor defensive. It suggests instead the increased emotional security that Nick has gained in telling the tale. He accepts the fact that his own dreams of a grandiose future are now, just as Gatsby's were, "already behind him." He is now able to express genuine affection for the countryside he knew in his youth, describing in an undefensive tone both what he deplores, "the bored, sprawling, swollen towns beyond the Ohio," and what he loves, riding winter trains across the prairie through "the real snow, our snow," rushing past "the dim lights of small Wisconsin stations," and feeling "unutterably aware of our identity with this country for one strange hour, before we melted indistinguishably into it again" (*GG* 177).

This changed attitude toward his past has its corollary in a changed attitude toward the present. Nick's pained ambivalence toward the past as he begins the tale reflects a present insecurity, a state of mind that has changed little since the fateful day shortly after he arrived in New York when he first met Jay Gatsby. And it is not difficult to infer that Nick arrived in New York inwardly all but paralyzed with anxiety. In this state of emotional paralysis Nick reminds us once again of Jack Burden. At the age of thirty, both were still leading tentative, emotionally and materially dependent lives, homeless, aimless, and careless. Mustered out of the army in his late twenties, Nick had drifted east to evade a putative engagement to a hometown girl. Lacking initiative of his own and still depending upon his father's financial support and the approval of his aunts and uncles, he followed the crowd listlessly into "the bond of business," because "everybody I knew" was in it. Restless, he sought "rooms," settled for a house in the suburbs cut off from more challenging and communal life in the city, and filled out his alienated, desultory existence with regressive schoolboy fantasies. His perceptions are informed with the conventional imagery of sentimental popular fiction: heroic frontiersmanship ("I was a guide, a path finder, an original settler"); eternal youth (experiencing the "familiar conviction that life was beginning over again with the summer"); "romantic women" picked out of Fifth Avenue crowds; and "poor young clerks . . . in the dusk, wasting the most poignant moments of night and life" (GG 3-4, 56-57).

This state of arrested emotional development was perfectly adapted to hero-worship. In the image of Gatsby, drawn similarly from the sentimental imagery of popular fiction, Nick created a preferred alternative self. In this way he fulfilled the wish to conquer the uncertainty and ambivalence which afflicted him, by projecting onto that willing "screen" the opposite qualities: singleness of purpose and unwavering desire, absolute self-confidence, "romantic readiness," "heightened sensitivity to the promises of life" (GG 2). But Nick's hero-worship was more than a truncated personal relationship. It expressed Nick's way of viewing his world. In fact, Nick's hero-worship is evidence that he did not attempt to understand his world but instead edited and revised it by projecting on it his own fantasies. In a word, Nick apprehended the objective world in a mythical, magical, animistic way that was emotionally regressive. He viewed aspects of his present world as he viewed aspects of his past—as if objects and persons were integrally part of himself, not separate entities. The most conspicuous and successful attempt to veil the world from himself in this way, of course, was his identification with the "great" Gatsby.

In this magical revision of the world, the world fortunately did not cooperate. None of it, that is, except Gatsby. To Nick's already formidably well-developed fantasy life, Gatsby—whose own self-image, we are told, froze at the age of seventeen—contributed pseudo-autobiographical embroidery and self-dramatizing pose, both drawn from sentimental and Romantic fiction. In the latter case the principal source was Byron. The tale of Daisy's marriage has parallels with Byron's fantasy narrative, "The Dream" (*GG* 77-78). And Gatsby's claim to having "lived like a young rajah in all the capitals of Europe . . . and trying to forget something very sad that had happened to me long ago" (*GG* 66) is so transparent a travesty of the Byronic hero that even Nick could barely contain his laughter.

However he may have laughed, though, Nick was unquestionably taken in. The screen upon which he projected his own fantasies effectively contributed its own distortions. Nick gradually found he could barely distinguish himself from his hero. At the height of his confusion of identity after Gatsby's death, Nick tells us, he made arrangements for the funeral with "a feeling of defiance, of scornful solidarity between Gatsby and me against them all" (*GG* 166).

Nick remained in the grip of the arrested emotional development underlying this confusion of identity throughout the fictional past covered by his tale. He began to break out of it only well after Gatsby's death. By telling the tale he completes the task. At the end of his tale, Nick reveals implicitly a new understanding of himself and his world through a heightened awareness of his earlier identification with Gatsby, through a "certain shame" he feels for Gatsby (*GG* 170), and through a more self-accepting view of past and present. His new understanding is based on a newly integrated inner life. Nick by the end of the tale seems at peace with himself. And his new understanding is achieved through an imaginative, symbolic transformation of the past that leads to the intuitive insight dramatized in the novel's fictional present.

An Unconscious Source of Knowledge: *The Good Soldier*

The narrator of Ford Madox Ford's *The Good Soldier* similarly transforms his conception of the past.[4] Ford's narrator, John Dowell, an idle, rich, timid, overbred, and under-sexed

4. For a review of the debate about who the central figure in *The Good Soldier* is, see Lawrence Thornton, "Escaping the Impasse: Criticism and the Mitosis of *The Good Soldier*," *Modern Fiction Studies*, 21 (1975), 237-41.

American, has retired to his fireside to tell the tale of Edward Ashburnham, Dowell's friend and his wife's lover. As Dowell tells his tale, he frequently steps back from it, as Nick Carraway does, to comment on its progress. At first he rationalizes his admiration of Ashburnham by stressing similarities between his hero's cultural background and his own. It soon becomes clear to him, however, that admiration understates the case. Dowell's awareness that he identified with Ashburnham grows as he tells his tale, until in the end he arrives at the conviction that Ashburnham "was just myself" (GS 253).

This developing self-understanding suggests that knowledge might be an important theme in *The Good Soldier*. In fact, the epistemological theme of elegiac romance is a good deal more evident in this novel than it is in *The Great Gatsby*, and a good deal less abstruse than it is, as we shall see in the next section, in *All the King's Men*.[5] If the central issue in Ford's novel is the emotional integrity of its central characters, the novel develops that issue in terms of what its narrator knows and does not know, and in terms of what he learns as he tells the tale. Whereas Nick Carraway arrives at a single insight as a result of telling his tale, Dowell achieves four successive and related insights dramatized in the course of his narration. These insights progressively deepen his understanding of his world, himself, and the substance of his tale.

The Good Soldier also differs from the elegiac romances of Fitzgerald and Warren in the character of its narrator. All three narrators are of course of the same general type: depressed, troubled, self-examining men, erstwhile hero-worshipers, incipient tellers-of-tales. And all three have been, and to some degree as they begin telling their tale still are, emo-

5. Samuel Hynes argues that the central action in *The Good Soldier* is "the action of the narrator's mind as it gropes for the meaning, the reality of what has occurred, . . . Dowell's thoughts about what has happened, not the happenings themselves" ("The Epistemology of *The Good Soldier*," pp., 226, 230-31). See also Paul B. Armstrong, "The Epistemology of *The Good Soldier*: A Phenomenological Reconsideration," *Criticism*, 22 (1980), 230-51; and William P. Peirce, "The Epistemological Style of Ford's *The Good Soldier*," *Language and Style*, 8 (1975), 34-46. Peirce argues that the novel renders "Dowell's discovery of truth at the same time that it invites the reader's participation in this discovery" (p. 34).

tionally over-defended: each is an American naif suffering
from emotional paralysis. Nick's defense is provinciality, Jack's
is a sort of philosophical rationalization, and Dowell covers
with social snobbery a case of extreme sexual repression. There
can hardly be a less virile, more self-effacing, gullible dupe in
all of fiction than Dowell. Yet despite the fact that his character,
as he puts it, is "faint" (*GS* 237), he does not lack complexity.
Dowell has a violent temper, he is an engaging amateur story-
teller, and for all his ignorance and self-abnegation, he is far
from simple-minded. Sometimes he seems stupid; but his stu-
pidity is always of the emotionally defensive variety. Dowell
has refused to understand what he knew full well but could
not bear emotionally to acknowledge to himself.

Dowell tells us right away that what he knows and does not
know about himself and his surroundings plays an important
part in the tale he has to tell. He insists as he begins the tale
that he knows "nothing—nothing in the world—of the hearts
of men" (*GS* 7), and nothing about the private lives of his
acquaintances. He claims an "extreme intimacy" with the Ashburnhams, yet has to admit that "in another sense" he actually
"knew nothing at all" about them (*GS* 3). He speaks of telling
his tale as an attempt finally "to puzzle out what I know of this
sad affair" (*GS* 3), yet throughout the first third of the novel
he rings changes on the repeated refrain of his sad story, "I
don't know."[6]

Partly because knowing is such a basic problem in Dowell's
life, it is the basic problem in the lives, as he perceives them,
of every character in his tale. The nature of the problem of
knowledge in this novel is suggested by the fact that all the
characters in Dowell's tale value knowledge more for its ex-
trinsic power than for its intrinsic worth. Florence, Dowell's
wife, succeeds in using her superficial tourist's information to
seduce Edward Ashburnham, and tries also to intimidate Edward's wife Leonora with it. In the latter attempt, however,
she fails ludicrously, not because Leonora knows more than

6. Hynes calls the novel "a study of the difficulties which man's nature
and the world's put in the way of his will to know" ("The Epistemology of
The Good Soldier," p. 230).

Florence or values what she knows more highly, but because she is more skillful than Florence in wielding knowledge as a weapon.

Blackmail, the malicious misuse of knowledge for personal gain, is as central to the novel, therefore, as the sexual jealousy that in most cases motivates it. Major Basil and Florence's first lover Jimmy are, literally speaking, the novel's only black-mailers. But Florence maintains her "hold over Leonora" with her knowledge that Leonora boxed Maisie Maidan's ears. There is in fact hardly a character in the novel, with the possible exception of Dowell, who does not provide or withhold information for an emotional price. Everyone is busy withholding knowledge from Dowell. And Dowell is exceptionally busy withholding knowledge from himself, until he acts imaginatively to arrest the tendency by telling his tale.

Knowledge is of such great moment to all these people because it must serve them, as knowledge serves all of us, as a guide to life. Florence succeeds in perverting even this intrinsic value of knowledge by using her massive, accurate, but tedious Baedeker information to guide people from monument to monument, and to manipulate them in other ways to her own ends. But one crucial fact in the novel reveals the extent to which knowledge is a profound necessity. Every character in *The Good Soldier* lacks conscious knowledge of sex, "the first thing in the world," until well into early adulthood. Dowell still has no direct knowledge of sex in his mid-forties. Lacking this point of reference, not only for mature sexual relations but for "the more subtle morality of all other personal contacts, associations, and activities" (*GS* 12), the lives of these characters are fraught with anxiety and irreconcilable conflict.

Dowell's understanding of sex may be severely limited, but his understanding of why he is telling his tale is acute. As he begins his narration he already has a firmer grasp of his purpose than either Nick or Jack Burden ever have: "It is not unusual in human beings who have witnessed the sack of a city or the falling to pieces of a people to desire to set down what they have witnessed for the benefit of unknown heirs or of generations infinitely remote, or, if you please, just to get the sight out of their heads" (*GS* 5). Discovering this motive, to heal the wounds inflicted by loss, is a significant insight for the narrator of an elegiac romance, and itself justifies telling the tale. Still, through a series of four dramatized insights, Dowell accomplishes even more: he alters his mode of apprehending his world. The series of insights Dowell experiences as he tells his tale affect his mode of apprehension because they progressively develop his understanding of the power that "unconscious desires" (GS 237) exercise over conscious thought and action. Each insight prepares him to take still another step in accepting the full impact of this difficult truth, and each in turn casts more light on the meaning of the insight that preceded it.

Dowell's first dramatized insight is in degree and kind very much like Nick's insight, "I see now." It illuminates the past by characterizing one of the personal relationships important in the tale, and it illuminates the present by characterizing the narrative that Dowell has been telling. "Looking over what I have written," he says, "I see that I have unintentionally misled you when I said that Florence was never out of my sight. Yet that was the impression that I really had until just now. When I come to think of it she was out of my sight most of the time" (GS 88).

This insight differs from Nick's, however, in two ways. First of all, it occurs relatively early in Dowell's tale, not at the end. It therefore makes possible still further change in perspective as the tale goes on. Second, although Dowell's first dramatized insight covers roughly the same ground as Nick's, it is somewhat more fully developed. Nick tells us that his tale is not what he thought it was when he began to tell it, but he does not suggest why. This is just what Dowell suggests with the epithet "unintentionally" in the clause "I have unintentionally misled you." That he did something he did not consciously intend to do implies that his action had a guide he was not conscious of. A few pages later, Dowell generalizes this implication into a principle: the mind is divided into a conscious self and an unconscious self, both of which may know and therefore act independently of the other. We may draw upon a resource of understanding we are not aware of having, and this unconscious source of knowledge can have a profound effect on our lives by guiding us in directions we do not expect or consciously intend (*GS* 103).

Dowell's notion of the existence of effective knowledge we are not aware of explains why we can sometimes do something that we did not intend to do, as, for example, Dowell can "mislead" his audience "unintentionally." Dowell's notion of an unconscious source of knowledge also suggests a possible explanation of the seemingly random, seemingly absent-minded, yet always dependably self-correcting form of Dowell's narration. As we shall see in Chapter Six, Dowell's quest is like that of the narrator in Nabokov's *The Real Life of Sebastian Knight*. It follows its own "rhythmical interlacements," "its own magic and logic . . . using the pattern of reality for the weaving of its own fancies" (*SK* 137). One of the most obvious effects of Dowell's first dramatized insight, therefore, is stylistic. From this point on in the novel (roughly, the beginning of Part Three), Dowell begins to act on his new understanding. His tale becomes less random, less constrained by apology, and more fluent and coherent in a conventional narrative sense. The refrain, "I don't know," all but disappears. Dowell's understanding of other characters and their lives becomes more lucid and in some respects even profound.

By raising the issue of unconscious intention, Dowell's first dramatized insight also has another effect. It implies that Dowell may have still more to learn about himself as his tale goes on. We might expect him to discover, for instance, what motivated him to regard Ashburnham as heroic, and what guides him as he tells the tale in its peculiar random-seeming form. Dowell's second dramatized insight helps him begin to answer these questions. Commenting at the beginning of Part Four on the mazelike, rambling character of his tale, and protesting that he is trying to present events as perceived from the several points of view of the participants in them, Dowell is led to the conclusion that the villain of his tale is his wife, Florence. It was she, he says, who was really the "contaminating influence" upon their lives. She, therefore, is the person most at fault for the emotional disruption they all have suffered (*GS* 184). Florence merits this censure, but of course she is not alone to blame. All four people involved in this "middle-aged affair" bring to it the "contaminating influence" of their own ignorance and emotional inadequacy. This is the fact that Dowell is not yet fully aware of. Least of all is he fully aware yet of his own particular contribution, revealed in his hero-worship of Ashburnham.

Dowell's third dramatized insight carries him closer to this awareness. Near the end of his tale, after arriving at the conclusion that he is now "very much where I started thirteen years ago" (GS 236), Dowell demonstrates that in understanding himself he is in fact very far indeed from where he started. This insight arises from Dowell's discovery that he disapproves of Ashburnham's widow's second marriage; that he disapproves of it because he is jealous; and that only one person would have a right to be jealous—Ashburnham himself. Logically this series of observations leaves Dowell with two alternatives. Either Dowell loves Leonora, which he says he does not, or else Dowell identifies Ashburnham's emotional life with his own. Thus Dowell's reasoning leads him for the first time to assert tentatively that "in my fainter sort of way I seem to perceive myself following the lines of Edward Ashburnham." He develops this first intimation that he identifies with Ashburnham by bringing to bear on it his first insight that he has a "dual personality." And he concludes that his identification with Ashburnham is based on no superficial admiration of Ashburnham's "splendid" qualities, but is profoundly rooted "in my unconscious desires" (GS 237, 103).

Dowell's fourth and final dramatized insight occurs in the last few pages of the novel. There, Dowell finally realizes the true nature of his identification with Ashburnham, the "intimacy" with Ashburnham that he has claimed since the beginning of his tale: "I can't conceal from myself the fact that I loved Edward Ashburnham—and that I love him because he was just myself" (GS 253). Dowell's love for Ashburnham was (and, insofar as it still exists, remains) love of an idealized self. Sexually underdeveloped himself, Dowell projected a sexual fantasy onto the willing screen that Ashburnham conveniently provided. Dowell thereby became captive to the "fancy" that "if I had the courage and virility and possibly also the physique of Edward Ashburnham I should . . . have done much what he did" (GS 253). One thing Dowell means by this of course is that he wanted to be as much of a husband to Florence as, in spite of himself, he knew that Ashburnham, in Dowell's place, had in fact become. This realization verifies the novel's assumption of an unconscious source of knowledge. Dowell sensed for nine years what he struggled for those nine years not to know consciously: all that time his wife and Ashburnham had been lovers.

Dowell makes clear that his sexual "fancy" about Ashburnham was emotionally regressive, furthermore, when he says that he admired Ashburnham as "a large elder brother who took me out on several excursions and did many dashing things whilst I just watched him robbing the orchards, from a distance" (GS 253-54). Dowell's hero-worship is thus a version of the primary Oedipal relationship displaced into adult social and marital relations. The triangular relationship that so often obtains among narrator, narrator's hero, and a woman associated with the hero (Marlow, Kurtz, and Kurtz's Intended; Marlow, Jim, and Jewell; Jack Burden, Willie Stark, and Ann Stanton; Zeitblom, Leverkühn, and the Leipzig prostitute; and even—an odd twist—Zeitblom in his desire to "mother" Leverkühn, Leverkühn, and Rudiger Schildknapp) strongly suggests the possibility that the structure of elegiac romance is at some level generically a displaced version of that primary Oedipal relationship.

What Ashburnham represents to Dowell in this novel is something analogous to what Gatsby represents to Nick and, as we shall see in the next section, Willie Stark represents to Jack Burden. Ashburnham as we know him through Dowell's tale is an atavism, a projection of Dowell's own deep, unrecognized wishes for himself, formed during a stage of life now long past, frozen then and still remaining with him in the present, unchanged and powerfully effective. The narrator's hero in all three novels expresses, as a symbolic figure, latent thought and feeling buried well beneath the threshold of the narrator's conscious mind. At least until he tells his tale, and to a large extent after he completes it, Dowell's life is bound by shackles imposed upon him early in life. These are the same shackles that he now perceives were once imposed upon Ashburnham as well, shackles formed by "the quality of his youth, the nature of his mother's influence, his ignorances," as well as by all those "excellent influences upon his adolescence" that Dowell, speaking for his generation, says "we all have to put up with . . . and no doubt it is very bad for all of us" (*GS* 152).

It is not clear, however, that by telling his tale Dowell manages to free himself from these shackles. Perhaps at the age of forty-five it is too late for him to overcome influences so deeply buried in the past. It is evidently not too late, though, for him at least to understand them. And this much Dowell does accomplish. Hence the strong epistemological emphasis of the novel.

To achieve this understanding, Dowell must overcome the rigid formulas or false paradigms of knowledge informing most of those "excellent influences" that gradually distort perception in childhood and youth and that veil what Jack Burden calls "true images." Like Nick and Gatsby, Dowell, Ashburnham, and several supporting characters in Ford's novel frame their lives on the formulas of sentimental popular fiction. Ashburnham rationalizes his sexual adventures quixotically by casting them in the conventional terms found in "novels of a sentimental type—novels in which typewriter girls married marquises and governesses earls" and in which "salvation can only be found in true love, and the feudal system" (*GS* 161). Leonora, Nancy Rufford, and Dowell himself describe Ashburnham as a compound of Lohengrin, the Cid, and the Chevalier Bayard (*GS* 226). Leonora convinces Nancy to perceive him in the role of the fatally enthralled mythic lover, a delusion to which Nancy contributes "chance passages in chance books" (*GS* 223). Unexamined values drawn eclectically from the American brands of puritanism, Roman Catholic doctrine, and the courtly love tradition of the Provençal poets also narrow and filter what people are willing to know, and hence capable of knowing, throughout the novel.

Dowell reveals at the end of the tale that he fully understands the crucial effect of this formulaic knowledge on the lives of the characters in his tale when he points out that Ashburnham's "mind was compounded of indifferent poems and novels" (*GS* 255-56). In the course of the tale, furthermore, Dowell himself overcomes a series of conventional conceptions of himself and his life. He perceives first that he and Florence are in no sense a "model couple" as he had once assumed the Ashburnhams were. He also realizes that Florence is in no sense like the Provençal lady who disdained the adulterous advances of Piere Vidal. Finally, he discovers that the husband's role in that story, urging upon his wife the suit of an admired friend, however glamorous and "romantic" in a literary setting, is in real life painful and inane. But the most conclusive evidence demonstrating that Dowell understands the need to break through conventional formulas of thought, feeling, and knowledge is the form of his tale itself. It is structurally about as unformulaic as a story could be, yet it is exactly because of its unconventionality, as Dowell himself insists, that it seems "most real" (*GS* 103).

"How Was I to Know?": *All the King's Men*

Like *The Good Soldier*, Robert Penn Warren's *All the King's Men* raises the epistemological issue of the nature of knowledge overtly. Warren's novel differs in this respect from Ford's, however, in that it raises that issue in nearly traditional philosophical terms and also suggests some of the issue's political implications.[7] *All The King's Men* is the story of a graduate school drop-out, journalist, and political flunky, Jack Burden, who narrates the career of his boss, the demagogue Willie Stark.[8] Early in the tale Jack asks himself "How was I to know"

7. On Warren's philosophical background as evidenced in *All the King's Men*, see Richard G. Law, " 'The Case of the Upright Judge': The Nature of Truth in *All the King's Men*," *Studies in American Fiction*, 6 (1978), 1-19; and Cushing Strout, "*All the King's Men* and the Shadow of William James," *Southern Review*, 6 (1970), 920-34.

8. On Jack Burden's centrality in *All the King's Men* see Norton R. Girault, "The Narrator's Mind as Symbol: An Analysis of *All the King's Men*," *Accent*, 7 (1947), 220-34. Girault argues that "the story" is "a product of Jack's mind" and that the novel is seriously misread if we assume that "Willie can be understood and interpreted whether Jack is or not." "What we experience,"- Girault points out, is the story of Willie Stark "happening inside Jack Burden's head. . . . [T]he form of the novel forces the reader to take the Willie Stark story as a mystery—a mystery throughly explored in the psychological terms of Jack

that the stolid, unpromising looking country bumpkin he met in 1922 would turn out a decade later to be a man of heroic personal appeal and national political stature? (*AKM* 13). Jack reviews signs of Willie's intelligence, presence, and self-awareness that he noticed at the time but discounted because they seemed so firmly contradicted by the stereotype in which Jack initially cast Willie in "the picture of the world inside his head" (*AKM* 247).

Warren's novel asks the question, "How is one to know?" not only explicitly in this way, but also implicitly through the central action of Jack's tale. The tale is a sort of detective story. Willie orders Jack to dig up a flaw in the past of the politically independent Judge Irwin. Jack obediently goes to work. But this plunge into another man's past becomes inadvertently a search for the truth about Jack's paternity. As a result, Jack's epistemological question becomes more sophisticated in form. The question, "How is one to know?" evolves first into the question, "How is one to find 'the facts'?" and then evolves still further into, "Having found the facts, how is one to understand and accommodate oneself to them?" Jack arrives at answers to this series of questions only after reviewing, through telling the tale, a radical change in his perception of the world that occurred during and since his acquaintance with the hero of the tale, Willie Stark.

Jack's initial conception of the way we gain knowledge of the objective world is something he calls "Idealism." Until he was forced to come to terms with his own past, he believed that "if you are an Idealist it does not matter what you do or what goes on around you because it isn't real anyway" (*AKM* 30). Stated this way, Jack's youthful perspective was a sort of oversimplified and debased Berkeleyanism. Like the eighteenth-century philosopher, Jack took the position that nothing in the world exists except what our minds recognize. We

<hr>

Burden's experience." Quoted from Robert H. Chambers, ed., *Twentieth Century Interpretations of All the King's Men*, pp. 29, 47. Jonathan Baumbach argues that Jack Burden "is the novel's center" and suggests parallels with *Heart of Darkness* and *The Great Gatsby* ("The Metaphysics of Demagoguery: *All the King's Men* by Robert Penn Warren," in *The Landscape of Nightmare* (New York: New York University Press, 1965), p. 17; reprinted in Chambers, *Twentieth Century Interpretations*). See also Chapter One, note 36.

learn only what we choose to learn by a willful, singular act of conscious intelligence. Jack's "Idealism" is debased because it was merely a rationalization. Jack maintained this venerable philosophical viewpoint only to defend himself against unpleasant feelings and unwelcome knowledge. "What you don't know," he concluded, "don't hurt you" (*AKM* 30).

Stated this way, the epistemological issue in Warren's novel seems simple: Jack's "Idealism" is a case of burying his head in the sand. But Jack's oversimplified statement of one aspect of the idealist position reveals only half of his complex rationalization. The other half is his belief in what he calls "the Great Twitch" (*AKM* 435). This term represents a mechanistic-materialistic view that reduces every human being to "a peculiarly complicated piece of mechanism," a sophisticated robot (*AKM* 311). Hence, Jack's emotional retreat was a compound of seemingly incompatible philosophical elements. In order to suggest Jack's state of arrested development, self-abnegation, and emotional retreat, Warren weds seemingly disparate points of view, mentalist idealism and mechanistic materialism, into an extreme sort of positivism that we might call "mechanistic idealism." On one hand, Jack maintains that the world is nothing but a creation of his own mind; on the other, he maintains that his mind is nothing but a complex of electro-chemical neural synapses.[9]

The basic characteristics of Jack's mechanistic dream can be found in the details of his early world view. Life, Jack then believed, is lived according to a "perfectly arbitrary system of rules and values," and the context in which one lives is "simply an accumulation of odds and ends of things" (*AKM* 189). Things in this incoherent "flux" exist as more or less identical one to another in an isolated and disjunctive state, related only in immediate and trivial ways. Jack calls this view of things "the dream of our age," an illusion that the twentieth-century West

9. Warren's wedding of mechanistic philosophy and idealism is not as farfetched as it may seem at first. It reflects rather accurately the odd history of the most influential and pervasive of all modern philosophies, logical positivism. See John Passmore, *s.v.* "Logical Positivism," *The Encyclopedia of Philosophy*, ed. Paul Edwards, vol. 6 (New York: Macmillan, 1967), pp. 52-57.

takes to be "the secret source of all strength and all endurance," because seemingly it "solves all problems" (*AKM* 311).

Life according to this view is a sort of game that we have the option of sitting in on or not, as we choose. This is the way Jack once perceived his own life. For him, life seemed endlessly full of opportunities for fresh starts because events endlessly repeated themselves. Jack felt he was continually stepping into scenes that "had happened before, or had never stopped happening" (*AKM* 110). He lacked a sense of coherence with respect to the past and of intention with respect to the future, a sense of "what you've been or what you're going to be" (*AKM* 71). Every event seemed autonomous, pastless, and futureless— "an island in the middle of time" of the sort Jack's mother created for him when he went home for a visit (*AKM* 112). Jack limited his experience of life, that is, to immediate, temporally noncontextual perception. Events passed out of present immediate reality into the past without becoming part of the context shaping future experience. Like the cow beside the road, for whom the passing car is merely a "black blur," Jack perceived life with a "remote, massive, unvindictive indifference" (*AKM* 36). Each event seemed to be "an independent phenomenon unrelated to . . . anything in the whole tissue of phenomena which is the world we are lost in" (*AKM* 313).

Because it rejected or refused to perceive growth or development in others or himself, Jack's mechanistic perception of the world tended to erase any notion of identity. It seemed to him that he never acted. He only reacted with "the dark heave of blood and the twitch of the nerve" (*AKM* 311). As a result life seemed to him "a strange loveless oscillation between calculation and instinct," anonymous, irresponsible, and void of self-knowledge, knowledge of others, and "essential confidence in the world and in" himself (*AKM* 311).

Since this was Jack's state of mind in his youth, it is not surprising that he should have felt that there was some "secret" in the world he could not quite fathom. What eluded him was the secret of change. Twice in the course of his tale, Jack asks the question, "How does change occur?" Appropriately, he asks it first as a question of identity. His friend Adam Stanton told him that when a person goes through a religious conversion "you still have the same personality." You "merely exercise" that personality "in terms of a different set of values" (*AKM* 316). Thinking over this comment later, Jack asks, "If so, how does a person get that different set of values to exercise his personality in terms of?" The unexplainable course people's lives have taken around him suggests an answer: "By the time we understand the pattern we are in, the definition we are making for ourselves, it is too late to break out of the box. We can only live in terms of the definition. . . . Yet the definition we have made of ourselves is ourselves. To break out of it, we must make a new self" (*AKM* 351).

Jack sees, however, that this conclusion only turns the question on itself once again: "But how can the self make a new self," he asks, "when the selfness which it is, is the only substance from which the new self can be made?" (*AKM* 351).

So long as Jack maintained a perspective of "mechanistic idealism," these questions about change remained conundrums. But his own personal experience involved just the sort of change in identity that is the subject of these questions. By his own account, his own story is that of a man to whom "the world looked one way for a long time and then it looked another and very different way" (*AKM* 435). In order to understand this change in himself, Jack had to undergo what might be called a metaphysical revolution, a complete turnabout in his perception of human experience. The revolution in Jack's perspective allows him to look back on his past mechanistic world view as a severely crippled one and to end his tale with a strong statement of human growth and harmony. Jack's single dramatized insight while telling the tale occurs in the course of this statement when he confirms that his story of Willie Stark is after all his own story too, and not merely, as he had said evasively earlier, "in a sense" his own story (*AKM* 435, 157). Telling the tale has led him to accept "the awful responsibility of Time" by giving his own "definition" to "all those dead in the past who never lived before our definition gives them life" (*AKM* 438, 228).

This insight and Jack's view of the experience that led up to it are of interest in discussing *All the King's Men* as epistemological fiction because they are based on a somewhat unconventional set of ideas referred to by the umbrella term "organicism."[10] Organicism is a model of reality that recognizes the importance of integrated, contextual organization among the parts of living organisms, and, by extension, among organisms perceived as organically interdependent communities. Each living organism is structurally an infinitely complex "Russian doll." Each element in the structure affects all other elements that form its context, and affects all other elements of which it is the context. Nothing can be understood in isolation, because the properties and behavior of things result not only from the traits of their constituents, but also from the way the constituents are related, and from relationships among those relationships.

A conception of organic interrelationship of this sort appears in many incidental images in *All the King's Men*. It is implicit, for example, when Jack describes floating "around the bay, which is a corner of the Gulf of Mexico, which is a corner of the great, salt, unplumbed waters of the world" (*AKM* 339). And Jack implies an organic relationship among human events when he explains that his putative cousin, Cass Mastern, learned about the nature of human experience "that the world is all of one piece . . . like an enormous spider web and if you touch it, however lightly, at any point, the vibration ripples to the remotest perimeter" (*AKM* 188). Jack discovered this principle of organic relatedness in his own life when, during his investigation of Judge Irwin's past, he traced the Judge's unaccountable appointment as a judge to an unusually highly paid job with a commercial firm. The trial took Jack backwards in time through the underhanded deals of several allied corporations, to the suicide of one of their officers, a suicide for which Judge Irwin was in effect responsible. Judge Irwin's history revealed not only that he was dishonest, but also that,

10. As an interpretation of human experience, organicism and its precursors have a long and troubled history. I have based my summary of current biological organicism on Morton O. Beckner, *The Biological Way of Thought* (New York: Columbia University Press, 1959). I have also found instructive in this regard some of the later works of Whitehead, especially *Process and Reality, Modes of Thought*, and *Adventures of Ideas*.

as a result of an adulterous affair with his friend's wife, he was Jack's father.

Because human relations are so sensitively related in this organic way, Jack discovered, people must exercise care to maintain a "perilous equilibrium" of two sorts: equilibrium in everyday social relations among people and equilibrium between the known self and "the thing which is in every man in the crowd but is not himself," presumably the "clammy, sad little foetus you carry around inside yourself" (*AKM* 9). Maintaining social equilibrium requires maintaining emotional equilibrium. Jack's tale reveals this interdependence by demonstrating how easily political demagoguery exploits the latter by disrupting the former. Willie Stark called forth people's desire for political and social equilibrium by evoking in his audience fear of an unresolved disequilibrium in the self, the unresolved emotional dependency implied in the phrase "the clammy, sad little foetus you carry around inside yourself." He then manipulated this deep emotional need to his own ends by suggesting that political action could satisfy personal needs. That is, Willie first excited fear of emotional and social disequilibrium and then represented himself as the sole person who could maintain equilibrium of both sorts. By reducing adults' response to their world to the emotional level of the "clammy, sad little foetus," Willie created in his constituency an investment in his own interests and a state of abject, one-sided dependence on his will.

This suggestion that common human experience in early life can affect adult life implies that organicism has a temporal dimension as well as a structural one. Organicism in fact has two temporal dimensions. The first—intentionality—is temporal with regard to the future. It implies that change is not random, accidental, and temporally compartmentalized as mechanistic thought supposes it to be. A living being is capable of goal-directed behavior. Even though Jack could not always perceive the intentional nature of his own life, he could imagine the intentionality of Willie Stark's. He speculates that as an adolescent Willie already knew "what he was," and that his "life history was a process of discovering" the intention he seemed to have been born with (*AKM* 63). Typical of elegiac romance narrators, Jack projected on his hero an ideal trait that he could not find in himself. Eventually, however, he sees intention, which he calls "direction," in his own life as well: Reality, as Jack comes to understand it, "is not a function of the event as an event, but of the relationship of that event to past, and future, events. We seem here to have a paradox: that the reality of an event which is not real in itself, arises from other events which, likewise, in themselves are not real. This only affirms what we must affirm: that direction is all. And only as we realize this do we live, for our own identity is dependent upon this principle" (*AKM* 384).

The second temporal dimension of organicism is historicity, the view that the history of an organism determines or helps determine present structure and behavior. Jack's early mechanistic view of life rationalized a deep dread of the future. This dread was related to an equally profound and, as it turned out, legitimate fear of threatening, unknown facts in his past. On one hand, Jack clung to the past, desperately fearing change and looking "back on the past as something precious about to be snatched away from us." On the other hand, he desperately rejected the past, refusing to accept its meaning. What he had to learn in the course of his experience was to accept the past and its meaning, because "if you could accept the past you might hope for the future, for only out of the past can you make the future" (*AKM* 310, 435).

The epistemological implication of these principles of organistic thought is that human beings, perceived as organically whole creatures, cannot be understood in either temporal or physical isolation. Organisms are not states of being—things—but ongoing processes. This is why Jack is at pains to identify the person he was in the past as "Jack Burden (of whom the present Jack Burden, *Me*, is a legal, biological, and perhaps even metaphysical continuator)" (*AKM* 157). To regain the comfort that a sense of this continuity provides is the reason Jack tells his tale. In telling the tale he discovers that the world is "a great snowball rolling downhill and it never rolls uphill to unwind itself back to nothing at all and non-happening" (*AKM* 301). Thus the empty seeming moments of life are not empty at all. They are laden with memory. Because moments that seem empty are in reality laden with the detritus of the past, they can ache "like the place where the tooth was on the morning after you've been to the dentist or . . . like your heart in the bosom when you stand on the street corner waiting for the light to change and happen to recollect how things once were and how they might have been yet if what happened had not happened" (*AKM* 33).

"All those dead in the past" continue to live, Jack implies, within ourselves. They set up permanent residence inside us in the company of our own personal past, the "clammy, sad little foetus you carry around inside yourself." Knowing ourselves requires knowing all the dead of the past living inside us, others and ourselves. Jack Burden addresses himself explicitly to the task all elegiac romance narrators address themselves to at least implicitly: the effort to draw "another veil" from the truth latent in the past in order "to expose a meaning" in our lives "which we had only dimly surmised at first" (*AKM* 118).

Breakthrough: *Doctor Faustus*

The veil lifted from the past in Thomas Mann's *Doctor Faustus* exposes a dimly surmised meaning more pernicious and corrupting even than the one Jack Burden finds. But because the characters in this novel experience an extreme distortion of reality, the narrator's success in breaking through to clearer perception is profound. Since Mann was an acquaintance of Freud's,[11] it comes as no surprise that *Doctor Faustus* represents the existence and effects of an unconscious source of knowledge more forcefully and in greater detail than any other elegiac romance I discuss here. Of course, the novel's ironic complexity, the momentous nature of its social, cultural, and political background, and its sheer intellectual density make

11. "In the 1930's Thomas Mann became a frequent guest in the Freud household." (Hughes, *Consciousness and Society*, p. 380). See Ernest Jones, *The Life and Work of Sigmund Freud*, 3 vols. (New York: Basic Books, 1953), vol. 3, pp. 170, 199, 205, 247, 462-64. Also, Thomas Mann, *Essays of Three Decades*, trans. H. T. Lowe-Porter (New York: Knopf, 1947), p. 422.

the task of doing justice to it in a few pages difficult at best. Indeed, *Doctor Faustus* may seem to be one of the least likely of modern novels to be discussed in connection with *The Great Gatsby, The Good Soldier*, and *All the King's Men*. Yet comparative discussion is enlightening because the same formal structure governs the meaning of all four.[12]

In *Doctor Faustus*, Mann's narrator, the German classicist Serenus Zeitblom, has been driven from his university professorship by the Nazis several years after the death of his friend, the composer Adrian Leverkühn. Like Jack, Nick, and John Dowell, Zeitblom undertakes to tell his friend's life story. Zeitblom establishes personal and cultural identity with his hero in at least three ways. He recounts his emotional identification with Leverkühn's untoward sex life. He parrots Leverkühn's aesthetic and psychological views even though he believes they are "remote" from his own. And just as Nick felt a special "solidarity between Gatsby and me," as Jack Burden felt that "the story of Willie Stark" is "my story too," and as Dowell felt that Ashburnham was "just myself," Zeitblom states explicitly toward the middle of his tale that he felt "as though I stood here and lived for [Leverkühn], instead of him; as though I bore the burden his shoulders were spared, as though I showed my love by taking upon me living for him, living in his stead" (*DF*, Ch. 26).

12. The length of *Doctor Faustus* makes the underlying elegiac romance structure hard to discern, an issue discussed regarding Proust's *Remembrance of Things Past* in Chapter Six. One of the effects of attenuated form is that some of the material in a long novel such as *Doctor Faustus* may seem to be beyond the range of the narrator. But this material must of course be read with the convention of elegiac romance in mind, where, as Fitzgerald noted, the author may "grant [himself] the privilege, as Conrad did, of letting [the narrator] imagine the actions of the characters" (*LT* 168). Zeitblom himself addresses this issue. He asks, "may not my readers ask whence comes the detail in my narrative, so precisely known to me, even though I could not have been always present, not always at the side of the departed hero of this biography?" and he later answers, "It is a psychological fact that I was there, for whoever lived a story like this, lived it through as I have lived this one, that frightful intimacy makes him an eye- and ear-witness even to its hidden phases" (*DF*, Chs. 18, 41). The absolute tone of the passages in which Mann causes Zeitblom to make this convention explicit lends credence to the view that in elegiac romance, attempting to discover what the narrator's hero may be "really like" is not of the greatest importance in understanding the fiction, whereas understanding the narrator's character and situation is central.

This similarity and others between Mann's narrator and Warren's, Fitzgerald's, and Ford's have their counterpart, furthermore, in similarities among the narrators' heroes in these novels: Leverkühn, Willie Stark, Gatsby, and Edward Ashburnham. We are told that all four of these heroic figures pursued an active, aggressive quest in a demanding and perilous field. Leverkühn sought to overcome the limitations of nineteenth-century classical music; Willie Stark strove to stamp the politics of state government with his populist imprint; Gatsby yearned to recapture a fantasied past based on his memory of Daisy; and Ashburnham was driven "by the mad passion to find an ultimately satisfying woman" (GS 51). To succeed, each of these heroic figures somehow had to reconcile past and present. Each failed in this effort, with the result that his heroic quest ended in self-destruction. Finally, the active heroic quest of each narrator's hero, a quest occurring in the novel's fictional past, has its parallel in the narrator's own inner quest in the fictional present to understand himself better and to understand a spiritual malaise afflicting himself, his hero, and their national culture alike.

Serenus Zeitblom pursues his inner quest by narrating what appears to be a sympathetic, elegiac account of Leverkühn's life and work. Telling the tale forces him to confront Leverkühn's character, upon which the past maintained a deadly aesthetic, emotional, and physical grip, and to confront also similar traits in his own character of which he had been unaware. As he begins narrating, Zeitblom is still a bewildered, provincial pedant, convinced of the integrity of his own personality and of the value of his "Christian-Catholic tradition of a serious love of culture" and his "lively and loving sense of the beauty and dignity of reason in the human being" (DF, Ch. 2). The insights his narration leads him to are profoundly disillusioning. Mann's novel is at once an elegy for the irrecoverable loss of the residual old-German national culture that gave birth to both the narrator and his hero, and also an expression of hope that in the catastrophe of World War II the remaining vestiges of that ancient culture may at long last be buried. Only Zeitblom's final dramatized insight provides a glimmer of hope that the German people who survive, including himself, may somehow overcome their humiliation and negotiate a new personal integrity and a new relationship with the world at large.[13]

A reading of *Doctor Faustus* may therefore lead to a better understanding of these broad cultural and historical issues. But it cannot begin with them. The structure of *Doctor Faustus* requires that a reading of this novel, as of any other elegiac romance, begin with the one-way intimacy of narrator and hero that controls every aspect of the novel's meaning. Mann makes explicit the "one-way" nature of this relationship. Zeitblom tells us that Leverkühn's "absentness" of feeling for other people "was an abyss, into which one's feeling towards him dropped without a trace" (*DF*, Ch. 1). This emphasis makes clear the degree to which the character Leverkühn as he appears to us in the narrator's tale, like the character of most elegiac romance heroes, is to a large extent a product of the narrator's imagination.

This limitation puts everything about Leverkühn in doubt, including his musical "genius," even though the evidence that Leverkühn's "genius" was genuine seems impressive. Zeitblom tells us that the best European orchestras played Leverkühn's work, and that he attracted a coterie of admirers. Yet if we keep in mind the fact that we have no way of verifying the quality of the work firsthand, and also the fact that adoration influenced Zeitblom's judgment to an indeterminable degree, then the true difficulty of authenticating Leverkühn's "genius" becomes clear. One can make a strong case, indeed, for the view that, as Zeitblom hints throughout his tale, Leverkühn's mind lacked genuine vitality, feeling, or "soul." His music, perhaps only mediocre at best, was constrained and contrived, the art of a man whose "great gift" was "threatened with sterility by a combination of scepticism, intellectual reserve, and a sense of the deadly extension of the kingdom of the banal" (*DF*, Ch. 18).

To make this argument is not to deny the quality of Leverkühn's music entirely. It is to point out the likelihood that

13. Henry Hatfield observes that Zeitblom is "an evolving character, not a static one" (*From the Magic Mountain*, p. 116).

even his music may have been crabbed and distorted by the atavistic traits of his character. Although he set out to alter the course of music, to do so, he reverted to conventions of medieval music and to archaic, provincial musical forms. The parallel between this tendency and, for example, his retirement from the world to a farm that duplicates in every detail his childhood home is striking. Even in his desire to "take back" Beethoven's Ninth Symphony, Leverkühn's values are shaped perversely by a morbid sense of futile competition. To the entrepreneur Saul Fitelberg, indeed, whose view we may assume to be sophisticated and informed, Leverkühn's music evidences the conflicting traits of "arrogance and a sense of inferiority, of scorn and fear" that Zeitblom's tale reveals to be an element in German personality. "C'est 'boche,' " Fitelberg says of Leverkühn's music, "dans un degré fascinant" (*DF*, Ch. 37).

Fortunately, however, since *Doctor Faustus* is an elegiac romance, our task in understanding the relationship between narrator and hero does not depend on deciding whether or not Leverkühn's "genius" was genuine. It depends instead on our ability to determine why Zeitblom had to believe that Leverkühn's "genius" was genuine. By analogy with the three other elegiac romances we have been considering in this chapter, we could answer this question quite simply. We could observe that Zeitblom had to believe that Leverkühn was a "genius" because Leverkühn's character as we know it was a projection of Zeitblom's own obsessions. In this respect Leverkühn is much like Gatsby, Ashburnham, and Willie Stark. He is "great," "splendid," kinglike, or in this case a "genius" in the narrator's eyes (but not necessarily in the eyes of the reader) because the narrator is the type of character who needed a seemingly greater-than-human figure on whom to project self-aggrandizing fantasies.

This simple answer is made more complicated in *Doctor Faustus*, however, by the fact that the values Leverkühn represents contradict what seem to be Zeitblom's own most cherished values. A similar contradiction appears in other elegiac romances. John Dowell is a phlegmatic and sexless cypher; Ashburnham is a sportsman, a military man, and a womanizer.

Jack Burden protests Willie Stark's political use of blackmail. Nick's honest Midwestern integrity "disapproved of [Gatsby] from beginning to end" (*GG* 154). But in none of these cases does the contradiction seem as profound and absolute as it does in *Doctor Faustus*. Zeitblom is a Christian humanist to whose values Leverkühn's cold, cruel, self-centered abstraction is utterly repugnant.

Because of this extreme contradiction of values, our simple question, "Why did Zeitblom have to believe that Leverkühn's 'genius' was genuine?" becomes a more difficult, more pointed question: "Why did Zeitblom, despite his humanistic convictions, *love* Leverkühn's 'arrogance'?" Answering the question in this form is central to understanding the novel. An analysis of Zeitblom's profound ambivalence to Leverkühn reveals the novel's epistemological assumptions, its assumptions about the way the human mind apprehends both itself and the objective world.

Zeitblom expresses his ambivalence to Leverkühn very early in the novel, illuminating hidden recesses of his own inner nature. This illumination is the first of the novel's two dramatized narrative insights. The two insights (occurring in Chapters 8 and 46) frame the long central portion of Zeitblom's tale. From the point of view of Zeitblom's own metaphysical quest, his motive for continuing to tell the tale after achieving his first insight is to achieve the second. The first insight is a shocking disillusionment. The second overcomes the shock of that disillusionment by solving the problem it raises.

Zeitblom's first dramatized insight concerns the nature of his feelings for Leverkühn. It is a shocking insight because it sharply contradicts Zeitblom's consciously held convictions, his "Christian-Catholic" humanistic belief in "the beauty and dignity of reason in the human being." To reach this first insight, Zeitblom summarizes the import of his story so far. Up to now he has detailed Leverkühn's character, especially his "arrogance" (*Hochmut*), defined as "the *privilege* of keeping a distance" (*das* Vorrecht . . . *einen Abstand zu wahren*). Zeitblom has also gradually brought to light his own "disquiet" (*Ängstigende*) in the face of Leverkühn's arrogance (*DF*, Ch. 8).

Zeitblom's first insight occurs, then, when he tries to rationalize his youthful attraction to Leverkühn. In spite of his disquiet he suggests offhandedly that youthful arrogance may, of course, be "very impressive to a companion with a simpler mental constitution." Into this self-abnegating commonplace, however, an entirely different line of thought abruptly intrudes, revealing a deeply rooted trait of Zeitblom's character that he had never before been aware of:

> Of course it is also very impressive to a companion with a simpler mental constitution, and since I loved him, I loved his arrogance [*Hochmut*] as well—perhaps I loved him for its sake. Yes, that is how it was: this arrogance [*Hoffart*] was the chief motive of the fearful love [*erschrockenen Liebe*] which all of my life I cherished for him in my heart. [*DF*, Ch. 8]

Zeitblom's "perhaps I loved him for its sake. Yes, that is how it was" is formally equivalent to Nick Carraway's conclusion, "I see now that this has been a story of the West after all," and to John Dowell's first narrative insight, "I see that I have unintentionally misled you. . . . Yet that was the impression that I really had until just now." All three insights reveal to the narrator in the fictional present the meaning of some aspect of the fictional past. The revelations in each case concern the nature of past traits of character and past relationships of which the narrator was then unaware. Zeitblom's insight differs from the others mainly in that the human insight is not integrated with a concomitant aesthetic one, an insight into the nature of the tale itself. The reason for this difference is that in *Doctor Faustus* the goal of Zeitblom's tale from here on is to reach this aesthetic insight. Speaking functionally, Zeitblom's hero's quest is an aesthetic one so that Zeitblom can resolve in aesthetic terms at the end of his narration the personal and cultural catastrophe that his initial insight reveals.

The personal catastrophe is defined by Zeitblom's discovery that in spite of his conscious humanistic beliefs, he also admires Leverkühn's "claim to ironic remoteness" and his "*privilege* of keeping a distance"; in short, Zeitblom admires arrogance for its own sake. This is a characteristic in himself that he has not

heretofore been aware of. He was—and, even more disturb-
ingly, to some degree he still is—powerfully attracted to a
human trait quite the contrary of and antithetical to the beauty
and dignity of human reason. Like Dowell, Nick, and Jack
Burden, Zeitblom suffers from the love of an idealized self
perceived in the character of another person. This state of
obsessive projection would be burden enough. But the truth
about Zeitblom's state of mind is still worse. With a short spec-
ulative leap, he reaches the shocking conclusion that his love
for Leverkühn was abject. He was more than impressed with
Leverkühn's arrogance. He passionately humbled himself before it. He adored it. And he still does.

Between this first narrative insight and the second one at
the end of the novel, Zeitblom's tale explores a series of at
least four incidents in the fictional past when he experienced
confrontations between the two contradictory sets of values
implied in his "fearful love" of Leverkühn. In the course of
this exploration, one or the other of these sets of values emerges
without warning, as if from hiding. Through this exploration,
Zeitblom discovers in himself a complex, powerful unconscious self which appears to have, so to speak, a mind and will
of its own. This discovery explains why in spite of his conscious
beliefs, Zeitblom fearfully loved Leverkühn's arrogance. The
explanation, briefly, is that unconsciously he shared that
arrogance.

The first incident in which Zeitblom's conscious mind confronted this contradictory self occurred when he decided to
follow Leverkühn to the university at Halle. Zeitblom had to
decide at that time between a rational desire to live an independent life, and an obsessive, irrational desire to maintain a
close, proprietary, dependent relationship with Leverkühn:
"to see how he went on, . . . to watch over him, to have an eye
on him from nearby, . . . [to be] at the side of a childhood
companion to whom I clung [an dem ich hing], yes, whose life
problem [Lebensfrage], his being and becoming, at bottom interested me more than my own," (DF, Ch. 11).

In this first incident of inner conflict, Zeitblom's irrational
desire was uncomplicated by any necessary contradiction with
reality. There was no reason why he should not go to Halle.

It was a good university. His purposes were served as well by studying there as anywhere else. Thus Zeitblom was able to resolve the conflict easily by satisfying the irrational desire and by rationalizing it. He followed Leverkühn to Halle. In the second incident, however, the inner conflict could not be resolved so easily, and it produced effects on Zeitblom that he could not account for. In Halle, Zeitblom heard the lecturer Schleppfuss tell a grotesque story about the "daemonic possession" that afflicted a young man and his girl friend. The young man was impotent with women other than the one he loved, he accused his girl friend of bewitching him, and as a result, she was burned at the stake. The story equated loving desire with witchcraft, and as told in the twentieth century it bore a message rooted in puritanical sexual revulsion.

Zeitblom records that he responded to this story, and still responds when he thinks of it, with excessive anger. Exactly what caused the anger is not immediately clear. Soon, however, evidence appears which suggests that the source of Zeitblom's anger was, and is, his own unconscious sexual confusion. This evidence turns up shortly after Zeitblom heard the Schleppfuss story, when he was finally separated from Leverkühn by military service. At that time he received a letter from Leverkühn describing an abortive encounter with a prostitute. The letter makes clear that Leverkühn shared the puritanical sexual revulsion implicit in the Schleppfuss story. Reading the letter, furthermore, Zeitblom in imagination likewise "felt the touch of her flesh on my own cheek, and knew with abhorrence and sheer terror that it had burned upon his ever since" (*DF*, Ch. 15). By identifying imaginatively with both Leverkühn's desire and his distress, Zeitblom reveals that at some level, despite his protestations to the contrary, he too shared the sexual ambivalence implicit in the Schleppfuss story.

The terms in which he describes his response to Leverkühn's letter reveal, furthermore, something of the nature and cause of Zeitblom's sexual ambivalence, and illuminate also his desire to "cling" to his childhood friend. He read the letter, he tells us, "with feeling such as might move a mother at communication of that kind from her son" (*DF*, Ch. 16). That at some level Zeitblom's adoration of his heroic friend involves "motherly" concern seems to suggest a degree of sexual confusion, perhaps even an element of unresolved latent homosexuality. And it suggests still further implications of my observation that elegiac romance often involves a displacement of the primary Oedipal relationship. Zeitblom, it seems—like Nick, Jack, and John Dowell—is a victim of a sort of arrested emotional development, what Mann calls "a certain mighty immaturity [*gewaltige Unreif*]" (*DF*, Ch. 14). At some level of his inner life he remains at an emotional stage normal in boyhood but disturbing in an adult. This continued investment of his friendship with Leverkühn with a confused, immature sexual obsession also helps to explain Zeitblom's desire, expressed elsewhere in his tale, to compete with both women and men for Leverkühn's affection: Zeitblom's jealousy of Leverkühn's relationship with Rudi Schildknapp (itself probably homosexual), and Zeitblom's resentment of the attention paid Leverkühn by women who sought a central position in his life as patron or lover.

A third confrontation between Zeitblom's conscious and unconscious selves occurred during a series of conversations with a group of parlor proto-Nazi intellectuals who celebrated "the absolute, the binding, the compulsory" in German culture. Zeitblom's conflict over whether or not to criticize and refute their "old-new world of revolutionary reaction" caused him to lose twelve pounds. Holding "the conviction that these gentlemen were talking nonsense," Zeitblom's conscious, rational self confronted a powerful unconscious willingness to submit to imperious social pressure by members of the discussion group, who had mocked his one attempt to criticize their views (*DF*, Ch. 34 Cont.).

This incident differs from the first two in the degree to which Zeitblom was able to understand the conflict between his conscious and unconscious values. He reached this partial understanding by comprehending a message that his unconscious self delivered through his body. What caused Zeitblom's loss of weight is exactly what caused the young man's impotence in Schleppfuss's tale: not "daemonic" influence but the psychosomatic influence of unconscious feeling, "a certain natural wonderworking of the spiritual [*eine gewisse natürliche Wun-*

derkraft des Seelischen], its power to affect and modify the organic and corporeal in a decisive way" (*DF*, Ch. 13). The note of self-mocking, comic objectivity in Zeitblom's narrative here (his dismay over the loss of twelve pounds), furthermore, suggests that in the fictional present, by telling the tale, he is approaching a state of mind in which he will be able to formulate at last the meaning that these incidents of inner confrontation cumulatively convey.

The fourth incident of inner conflict in the tale suggests Zeitblom's gradual development in another way. The most important difference between this fourth incident and the first three is that Zeitblom's unconscious self formerly expressed values—dependence, sexual confusion, and brutal authoritarianism—that were less humane than the values they opposed,—independence, loving desire, and equitable kindness. Here these poles are reversed. Zeitblom's unconscious values are in this instance more humane than those he holds consciously. Zeitblom tapped this new-found unconscious resource of humane values for the first time during a debate with Rudi Schwerdtfeger about the insanity of Ludwig II. In this debate, Rudi took the "not so much popular as bourgeois and official" position that Ludwig had been properly diagnosed as "mad." Zeitblom took the unconventional position that Ludwig had been forcefully "deprived of the right to dispose of his own person" for political reasons. He maintained that Ludwig had been just one more victim of the old-new German obsession with "the absolute, the binding, the compulsory," and he held that, in effect, Rudi was a victim of the same obsession in arguing the conventional view of insanity. Zeitblom's position attacked that obsession: "Insanity, I explained, was an ambiguous conception, used quite arbitrarily by the average man, on the basis of criteria very much open to question" (*DF*, Ch. 40).

Even more forceful than the substance of Zeitblom's argument in attacking "the absolute, the binding, the compulsory" was his unconscious self, becoming suddenly articulate and assuming rationally comprehensible form in speech. The result seemed wholly unprecedented: "I must say that I surprised even myself by the eloquence which the subject aroused in me, although before that day I had scarcely given it a thought. I found that unconsciously [*unterderhand*] I had formed quite decided opinions" (*DF*, Ch. 40). Thus Zeitblom implicitly accepted at this point in his experience what would become the epistemological premise of his tale. It is the premise, as we have seen, of John Dowell's tale as well, and it also presupposes the premises of "organic realism" that Jack Burden arrives at through quasi-philosophical speculation. Zeitblom acknowledges "intentions," unconscious thoughts and feelings, that have the integrity and propriety of rational thought, and the coherence and complex substance of conscious knowledge.

This recollection of "unconsciously . . . formed" opinions expressible with "eloquence" prepares Zeitblom for his second dramatized insight, his own "breakthrough" (in Chapter 46). There, in accordance with the nature of the aesthetic quest of the hero of his tale, Zeitblom solves in aesthetic terms the problem raised by his first dramatized insight, his discovery of his "fearful love" of Leverkühn's arrogance.

It is typical of Zeitblom's mentality, his unconscious sympathy with "the absolute, the binding, the compulsory," that throughout his tale he tends to divide art and life into conventional pairs of absolute, irreconcilable extremes having no gradations of value between. The central figure in this formulaic, polarized view of the world is Wendell Krechmar. Early in his life, Zeitblom accepted Krechmar's view of music as representative of art in general. On one hand, Krechmar said, music's "deepest wish" is "not to be heard at all, nor even seen, nor yet felt; but only . . . to be perceived and contemplated as pure mind, pure spirit." On the other hand, Kretchmar said that music is "bound . . . to the world of sense," striving for "the most seductive sensuous realization: she is a Kundry, who wills not what she does and flings soft arms of lust round the neck of the fool" (*DF*, Ch. 8).

Following this paradigm, Zeitblom tended to perceive in polar extremes also the contexts of values in which art is created and enjoyed. One of these contexts is a polar morality that posits a "beautifying, veiling, ennobling" life of the soul or spirit in exclusive opposition to a life of "desire" subject to gross, naked, shameless, defiling animal instinct. Politically, he tended to see the world as divided into irreconcilable classes of servants and masters, automatons and gods. His conception of the human mind tended to allow only two conceivable states: the absolute extremes of "the unconscious [*Unbewusstsein*] or an endless consciousness [*Bewusstsein*]" (*DF*, Ch. 30). And not least in importance, Zeitblom's polar epistemology conceived of human knowledge as built exclusively either upon the folkish, reactionary "community-forming belief" or else upon "decent objective truth" (*DF*, Ch. 34 cont.).

In his second and final dramatized insight, Zeitblom envisages a "breakthrough" that not so much reconciles the artificial mutual exclusivity of these extremes as it displaces them altogether. "Breakthrough" is an appropriate term for this radical displacement because in a number of contexts in the novel the word represents a sort of cataclysmic, revolutionary change that antiquates and obviates everything that has gone before.

Zeitblom's "breakthrough" comes about in the following manner. Earlier in his tale, he quotes Leverkühn's youthful sketch of a sort of "breakthrough" that should occur in art, calling for "an art without anguish, psychologically healthy, not solemn, unsadly confiding, an art *per du* with humanity [*eine Kunst mit der Menschheit auf du und du*]" (*DF*, Ch. 31). Zeitblom suggested at this time, to Leverkühn's evident discomfort, that this aesthetic "breakthrough" could serve also as a model for an analogous revolutionary event in other contexts.

Although Leverkühn could perceive the need for such an art, its accomplishment seems to have been beyond him. His final work, "The Lamentation of Doctor Faustus," intended to fulfill Leverkühn's desperate boast to "take back" the Hymn to Joy of Beethoven's Ninth Symphony, was emphatically not "*per du* with humanity." It was a limited personal triumph of the sort that "the devil" (presumably representing the agenda of Leverkühn's unconscious self) had promised him during their "dialogue." It was merely a "breakthrough" to "giddy heights of self-admiration" (*DF*, Ch. 25).

Leverkühn's masterwork did not accomplish a more significant "breakthrough" in part because it was nostalgic in intent, not elegiac. It was a lament expressing unrelieved regret. In contrast, Zeitblom's more tentative, more modest, more humane work, the tale we read, succeeds where Leverkühn's work failed. Zeitblom's tale succeeds because it is truly elegiac. The purpose of Zeitblom's tale is not helplessly to lament the lost past but to overcome the afflictions of the past by rooting them out of hiding and using them to understand the present. Zeitblom's goal, like Dowell's, is to get the sight of the past out of his head; like Jack's it is to relieve himself of the burden of the past. Zeitblom strives to escape "that corner of German antiquity where we were brought up," to which Leverkühn retreated and regressed. Zeitblom's goal is to overcome the "old-world underground neurosis" which, he realizes, still "survives in us all," himself as well as his hero (*DF*, Ch. 6).

Zeitblom defines precisely this process of escaping the past. His tale, its review of the past and its examination of developments in Zeitblom's own character, are themselves

> the recovery, I would not say the reconstitution—and yet for the sake of exactness I will say it—of expressivism, of the highest and profoundest claim of feeling to a stage of intellectuality and formal strictness, which must be arrived at in order that we may experience a reversal of this calculated coldness and its conversion into a voice expressive of the soul and a warmth and sincerity of creature confidence. Is that not the "breakthrough"? [*DF*, Ch. 46]

To the problem raised by his own "fearful love" of arrogance, Zeitblom formulates his solution here as a tentative but carefully worded rhetorical question. Shouldn't we try to make feeling a respected formal and intellectual resource for art? Unpacking this question reveals the depth and complexity of Zeitblom's insight. By "feeling" here, Zeitblom means personal feeling, feeling toward other human beings. He defines this feeling negatively in describing its opposite, the one-way intimacy between himself and his hero. Leverkühn's most disturbing, and to Zeitblom his most attractive, trait is his "absentness" [*Einsamkeit*]. Zeitblom compares this "absentness," as I have said "to an abyss, into which one's feeling towards him [*Gefühle, die man ihm entgegenbrachte*] dropped soundless and without a trace" (*DF*, Ch. 1).

Zeitblom's final dramatized insight is that feeling toward others should become a formal and intellectual resource for art. The proposal may seem both self-evident and beside the point until we recall the epistemological function of art in this novel. What Zeitblom has in mind is Leverkühn's early, hopeful view that art should aspire to become more than a "construction, self-sufficing, harmonically complete in itself" (*DF*, Ch. 21). Art should aspire, Leverkühn said, to "knowledge." The term Mann uses in this passage is not *Wissen*—the static conception of what-we-know. It is *Erkenntnis*—the dynamic process of knowing, perceiving, realizing, understanding. What Zeitblom proposes, therefore, is that art should rediscover "the claim of feeling to a stage of intellectuality and formal strictness" in order to serve as an active means of understanding the objective world.

Zeitblom's final dramatized insight, then, rejects knowledge derived and organized through rigid, sterile, stereotypical formulas of thought and value. Instead, Zeitblom's insight rediscovers unconscious sources of thought, integrating them into everyday thought and action. These unconscious sources are the wellspring of felt response to what in *Lord Jim* Marlow calls "merely the human being" (*LJ* 69). That is, they are in large measure and in many respects a function of intimate human relations. Zeitblom illustrates these unconscious sources of knowledge at several levels in his tale. He illustrates them in the tale's deeply personal subject and motive, and in Zeitblom's life-long effort to maintain faithfully the most intimate possible relationship with another person.

In pursuing this theme of the salutary force of intimacy, *Doctor Faustus* follows one more among many precedents set by Conrad. In both *Heart of Darkness* and *Lord Jim*, Marlow reaches out to create or maintain intimacy with other characters in the tale. Even with Jim, whose life Marlow finds so obscure and for whom he felt a "dull resentment," he experiences at the moment Jim leaves for Patusan "a moment of real and profound intimacy, unexpected and short-lived, like a glimpse of some everlasting, of some saving truth" (*LJ* 173). And Marlow's lie to Kurtz's Intended at the end of *Heart of Darkness*, an impulsive act the roots of which are traceable to unconscious memory, was also a compassionate act. Marlow protected Kurtz's Intended with "a sheltering conception of light and order" at a moment when her emotional equilibrium and feelings were profoundly threatened by the chaotic darkness of "inner truth." Not incidentally, Jack Burden's lie to his mother at the end of his tale in *All the King's Men* has a similar source and serves a similar purpose.

The saving truth underlying the effort by Marlow and other elegiac romance narrators to create and maintain intimacy with other human beings is, as Marlow puts it, that we all of us "exist only in so far as we hang together" (*LJ* 160). In both *The Great Gatsby* and *The Good Soldier*, for example, one principal concern of the narrators is to examine and if possible reassert the coherence of the community of which they are members. Nick's insight concerns the community of Midwesterners transplanted to the East. Dowell's insights concern the corrupt superficiality of the wealthy, leisured international community to which he belongs. As this underlying truth is expressed in the narrative experience rendered in the narrator's tale, it is expressed at another level also in the narrator's attempt through the artifices of aesthetic form to draw the audience into complicity and sympathy with himself as he tells the tale. Elegiac romance narrators try by telling their tales to reach out beyond their own experience to form, among other sane, humane, contemplative, but otherwise ordinary people like themselves, people who are sensitive, careful, and persistent readers, a community of mutual understanding.

This aspect of the form too has precedence in Conrad. Daniel R. Schwarz points out that "Conrad's early artistic code, the 1877 Preface to *The Nigger of the 'Narcissus,'* is remarkable for its emphasis on creating a community of readers. . . . Surely one reason that Conrad uses a voice . . . who has a distinct personality and a characteristic speech pattern is to give his reader a figure with whom he can identify and establish a sense of solidarity."[14] Marlow's tendency to bully and cajole his au-

14. Daniel R. Schwarz, *Conrad*, pp. 23-24. This emphasis on a "community of readers" is part of Conrad's belief in what Avrom Fleishman describes as "the crucial need for social roots, . . . the primacy of community, which gives life its possibility and value," a belief that underlay Conrad's sympathy for

dience, and in elegiac romance generally the narrator's "rhetorical judo," is part of this effort to establish this "sense of solidarity" with the reader.

The narrator's attempt in elegiac romance to create a community of readers is of course a fictional act, as some recent critical theory has insisted, not a "real" one. Gerald Prince has pointed out:

> Any narrative presupposes not only a narrator but also a 'narratee,' a receiver of the narrator's message, and, just as the narrator in any tale is not its real author but a fictional construct having certain characteristics in common with him, the narratee in any tale should not be confused with a real reader or listener though he may very closely resemble him.[15]

But if, as Michael Oakeshott suggests, communities are created through the "conversation of mankind," and if as Stanley Fish, Richard Rorty, Lewis Thomas, and others have recently argued, language is the medium of community-making, then the elegiac romance narrator's fictional effort to establish a community with his audience may be more "real" than it may seem at first.[16] Indeed, this speculation seems to imply further that narrative fiction serves a social function and has a referentiality through this social dimension that critics have seldom explored.

The ability of elegiac romance narrators to engage their audiences in fictional and yet somehow "real" conversation, that is, to implicate them in the web of illusion and disillusion of hero-worship that is the central issue in elegiac romance, may have still another dimension. It may be one of the conditions Wayne Booth has sought that determine success among works of modern "novelist-hero" fiction. In a certain "large

---

political views influenced by philosophical organicism (*Conrad's Politics*, pp. 53-77).

15. "Notes toward a Categorization of Fictional 'Narratees,' " *Genre*, 4 (1971), 100. See also Simone Vauthier, "The Case of the Vanishing Narratee: An Inquiry into *All the King's Men*," *The Southern Literary Journal*, 6 (Spring, 1974), 42-69.

16. Oakeshott, "The Voice of Poetry in the Conversation of Mankind," in *Rationalism in Politics* (New York: Basic Books, 1962), especially part 1, pp. 197-204; Fish, *Is There a Text in This Class*, pp. 14-15, 303-71; Rorty, *Philosophy and the Mirror of Nature*; Thomas, *The Lives of a Cell* (New York: Bantam, 1975).

group of modern novels," Booth says, "the search for truth is answered with the discovery that truth is found not in concepts but in the reality of artistic activity. No one seems to have discovered what it is that distinguishes the few successes in this mode from the innumerable failures."[17] Booth mentions Proust's *Remembrance of Things Past* as representative of this group of novels, a suggestion I will entertain in the following chapter. In the meantime, it seems worth pointing out that one thing that distinguishes most successes in this type of fiction, such as the four novels discussed in this chapter, is the rigorous, integrated, contrapuntal structure of elegiac romance. Elegiac romance can integrate artistic activity and a search for truth by integrating structurally the narrator's insights into himself and into his hero as dramatized in the novel's narrative present, with past events occurring in the narrator's tale. That is, in elegiac romance, narrated matter that renders a "search for truth" is revelatory not directly, in an expository fashion, but indirectly, by virtue of the dramatic structure, the dramatized narrative process, the act of "authoring" itself, into which it is cast.

17. *The Rhetoric of Fiction* (Chicago, Ill.: University of Chicago Press, 1961), p. 292.

CHAPTER 6

Varieties of Elegiac Romance

It seems reasonable to suppose that the basic dramatic situation in elegiac romance, the narrator's need to reconcile himself to loss and change, is an almost universal one in the modern world, and that the narrative structure of elegiac romance may grow in some spontaneous way out of its dramatic situation. This universality may account for the fact that many novelists and short story writers, with or without Conrad's influence, have hit upon the form, discovered its usefulness, and explored many of its thematic implications. The result, as the outline of elegiac romance in Chapter One and the handlist in the Appendix to this volume suggest, is a fairly large canon of structurally similar works.

For the sake of understanding better the potential of the form, this canon may be subdivided in several ways. The simplest division is by length or scale. Short stories in the form of elegiac romance tend to be structurally clear and thematically uncomplex. They tend to stress one or two of the several thematic strands implicit in the form, the rest appearing, if at all, as undeveloped submerged motifs. In Faulkner's short story "Uncle Willy," for example, the narrator, a fourteen-year-old boy, seems to have but one obsessive concern—to reassure himself that he has been a satisfactory ally of a person he calls "the finest man I ever knew," a man who he once believed could "do anything."[1]

1. William Faulkner, "Uncle Willy," in *Collected Stories* (New York: Random

Uncle Willy's erratic and irresponsible escapades (he has been a dope addict and an alcoholic by turns, and kills himself trying to fly a small airplane) seemed adventurous to the boy when he was younger. They were "too fine to be true," and represented indomitability and freedom, especially freedom from what the boy then perceived to be "all the old terrified and timid clinging to dull and rule-ridden" adult life. The central issue in the story appears to be the boy's need to believe that in the old man's attempt to escape the prison of adulthood, he "couldn't have done it without me" (pp. 242, 239, 247).

Beneath the boy's desire to feel that he had been of service to his hero, however, lies a deeper concern, the anxiety that underlies the narrator's tale in every elegiac romance. The real reason Faulkner's narrator allies himself with Uncle Willy is to fend off his own fear of change and loss, his fear of growing up. In telling the tale, he finally reconciles himself not so much to his hero's death as to the inevitability of his own. Uncle Willy, the boy tells us, "had had fun all his life in spite of what they had tried to do with him or to him." For this reason the boy hoped:

> Maybe if I could stay with him a while I could learn how to [have fun], so I could still have fun too when I had to get old . . . It was like I knew even then that, no matter what might happen to him, he couldn't ever die and I thought that if I could just learn to live like he lived, no matter what might happen to me I wouldn't die either. [pp. 239, 242]

In the course of telling the tale, Faulkner's narrator overcomes his fear of growing up and dying by discovering that "dying wasn't anything," because after all "it just touched the outside of you." This resolution inevitably comes across as formulaic.

House, 1950), pp. 225-47, quote p. 245. Faulkner has not written a novel-length elegiac romance, although traces of the form appear in several of his works. In *Conrad the Novelist*, Albert Guerard suggests that Faulkner's *Absalom, Absalom!* may be a member of the "new form" of fiction that Guerard identifies there, which is substantially the form I am calling elegiac romance. In my view, however, *Absalom, Absalom!* is too complex and eclectic structurally to be discussed profitably as an elegiac romance. For an explanation of these structural complexities and their relation to Conrad, see Stephen M. Ross, "Conrad's Influence on Faulkner's *Absalom, Absalom!*," *Studies in American Fiction*, 2 (1974), 199-209.

Still, Faulkner's basic theme here is what most deeply concerns the speaker in every pastoral elegy and the narrator in every elegiac romance. Read for what it is, a brief comic tale, the story reaches a conclusion that renders movingly the boy's adolescent confusion and grief.

At the opposite extreme in length and scale from short stories in the form of elegiac romance lie long works of fiction in this form, such as *Doctor Faustus*, which are ambitious technically, thematically, and aesthetically. These longer works of elegiac romance tend to develop more of the thematic strands implicit in the form and develop them in more complex, sophisticated, and significant ways. The length and complexity of these novels may also, however, make them formally somewhat difficult to grasp. That is, the more expansive the work, the harder it may be to see that the underlying structural elements are those of elegiac romance.

The best example of structure obscured by length, narrative richness, and welter of detail is Proust's *Remembrance of Things Past*.[2] In this enormous novel, the narrative structure of elegiac romance is difficult to see, for two reasons. First, the structure is vastly attenuated by the interposition of events in the narrator's life and in the lives of his acquaintances, by minutely analyzed social relations, and by long passages on human feeling, social mores, and art. Second, the conditions specific to elegiac romance that motivate the narrator's tale in *Remembrance of Things Past* are thoroughly de-emphasized. It may distress some readers to be told that Proust's narrator has a "hero" at all, other than perhaps himself. Yet the formal equivalent of an elegiac romance narrator's hero exists in the novel in the character of Charles Swann. To understand Swann's formal importance we must distinguish between the momentary experience that sets off the narrator's flood of involuntary memory, when he catches the aroma of a madeleine dipped in tea, and the dramatic conditions that motivate the narrator to tell the tale, admiration of Swann in childhood and youth, and the death of Swann, which the nar-

2. Guerard lists *Remembrance of Things Past* along with *Heart of Darkness, Lord Jim*, and *The Great Gatsby* as examples of a "new form" of fiction traceable to Conrad (*Conrad the Novelist*, pp. 126-27). I have not discovered evidence that would link Proust and Conrad in the way Guerard suggests.

rator had felt as "a crushing blow" (m'avait à l'epoque bouleversé).[3] Without these conditions, the crucial moment of involuntary memory evoked by the madeleine might never have occurred.

Proust's narrator makes this basic premise of the novel explicit only toward the end of his tale, in the final volume. In the first volume, as he begins the tale, he is evidently not fully aware of Swann's influence on his life as a whole. He is aware at this point only of Swann's influence on a particular phase of his life as a child. Swann enters the tale as a visitor to the narrator's family. His importance seems at first to be merely that he aggravated the narrator's childhood bedtime travails. Whenever Swann visited the family, the narrator's mother did not come to his room to kiss him good night. This fact establishes firmly in the narrator's experience the sort of triangular Oedipal tension characteristic of many elegiac romances. Swann is of course totally unaware of this effect, since, typical of elegiac romance, in Proust's novel the relationship between the narrator and narrator's hero is limited and one-sided. Although the narrator says that he knew Swann well (avec exactitude) later in life,[4] when as a young man the narrator met Swann shortly before Swann's death in the library of the Duke de Guermantes, Swann did not recognize him.[5]

The effect of this early one-sided relationship never entirely disappears from the novel. Indeed, the narrator's discovery of the full impact of the relationship at the end of the tale constitutes the major dramatized narrative insight in the work. It is an insight formally equivalent to Nick's insight at the end of *The Great Gatsby*, when Nick says "I see now" that the tale had after all been about people from Midwestern America contending with the alien culture of the East Coast. Proust's narrator says:

3. Marcel Proust, *The Captive*, trans, C. K. Scott Moncrieff (New York: Modern Library, 1928), p. 267; *A la recherche du temps perdu*, vol. 3 (Paris: Gallimard, 1954), p. 199.

4. Marcel Proust, *Swann's Way*, trans. C. K. Scott Moncrieff (New York: Modern Library, 1928), p. 26. *A la recherche du temps perdu*, vol. 1 (Paris: Gallimard, 1954), p. 34.

5. Marcel Proust, *The Guermantes Way*, trans. C. K. Scott Moncrieff (New York: Modern Library, 1925), part II, pp. 371-72. Swann is of course extremely ill at the time of this encounter.

It occurred to me, as I thought about it, that the raw material of my experience, which would also be the raw material of my book, came to me from Swann, not merely because so much of it concerned Swann himself and Gilberte, but because it was Swann who from the days of Combray had inspired in me the wish to go to Balbec, where otherwise my parents would never have had the idea of sending me, and but for this I should never have known Albertine. . . . Swann had been of primary importance, for had I not gone to Balbec I should never have known the Guermantes either, for my grandmother would not have renewed her friendship with Mme de Villeparisis nor should I have made the acquaintance of Saint-Loup and M. de Charlus, and it was through this that I had got to know the Duchesse de Guermantes and through her her cousin, so that even my presence at this very moment in the house of the Prince de Guermantes, where out of the blue the idea for my work had just come to me (and this meant that I owed to Swann not only the material but also the decision), came to me from Swann.[6]

Thus in *Remembrance of Things Past*, as in most elegiac romances, the narrator subordinates the story of his hero to the narrator's own sense of loss, to the rapid flight of his own life, and to the passing of the society and culture that his hero represents. By noticing the structural elements of elegiac romance underlying and supporting the massive expression of these concerns, we gain at least three insights. First is recognition of this novel's place in the development of quest romance tradition. *Remembrance of Things Past* is part of the fourth phase of that tradition, in which the questing hero reappears merely as a provocative element in the fiction and as a screen on which the squire-narrator projects his own inner needs. Second, reading the novel as an elegiac romance confirms that *Remembrance of Things Past* is not an exercise in nostalgic reverie but part of the early twentieth-century effort to find in the past the means for coping with a rapidly changing present.

Our third and perhaps most rewarding insight is a fuller, more accurate sense of the novel's integration of structure and theme.

6. Marcel Proust, *The Past Recaptured*, trans. Andreas Mayor (New York: Random House, 1970), p. 167; *A la recherche du temps perdu*, vol. 3 (Paris: Gallimard, 1954), p. 915.

The remarkable unity of *Remembrance of Things Past* derives in large measure from the consistency of Proust's concerns and his copious, steady flow of memory. But the novel's unity derives also from the fact that its chronological narrative sequence, its explicit thematic exposition, and its stylistic oddities and anomalies together form a carefully architected, monumental edifice supported by a well-concealed foundation. If success in what Wayne Booth calls "novelist-hero fiction" depends on the integration of artistic activity and the search for truth, then *Remembrance of Things Past*, like other elegiac romances, achieves this integration through structural counterpoint, maintaining throughout the fiction a parallel between events in the past and the narrator's insights into himself, dramatized in the narrative present. The sheer length of this novel makes its structure unobtrusive but in no way diminishes its influence.

The End of Childhood: "Seymour: An Introduction," *A Separate Peace, The Real Life of Sebastian Knight*

More revealing than length in classifying elegiac romances, however, are criteria based on the age of the narrator and hero. Here there are two possibilities: first, the narrator's age when he met his hero; second, the narrator's age compared with that of his hero, whether he was older or younger than his hero and by how much. A system of genre subclassification based on the age of characters may seem simplistic at first. But as a genre, elegiac romance focuses structurally and thematically on loss and regeneration over time. The passage of time is an abstraction. Its concrete, personal correlative, the handle we grasp it by, is aging. We may read time by clock and calendar, but we feel time by getting older. Since the effect of the passage of time is a key issue in elegiac romance, the age of the narrator and the narrator's hero offer categories for subclassification indigenous to the genre. To subclassify elegiac romances by the age of the narrator and hero helps account for some important thematic variations among elegiac romances because aging itself helps determine the nature of the central relationship in the fiction.

Adult Hero Worship. This sub-category of elegiac romance includes *Heart of Darkness, Lord Jim, The Good Soldier, The Great Gatsby,* and *All the King's Men.* What these five novels have in common from this point of view is that in each the narrator was an adult when he first met his hero. That is, by the time the narrator contracted the hero-worshiping dependency that afflicts him as he begins telling his tale, his self-concept and his public role—other people's conception of him—were already well formed. He thought he knew who he was. He was confident that he knew what his capacities and peculiarities were and that he understood his inner life.

The narrator's self-confidence is disturbed, however, by the person who becomes the hero of the narrator's tale in these novels. He "claim[ed] the fellowship" of a deeply hidden, un-acknowledged trait or set of illusions. He touched a "secret sensibility" (*LJ* 110), as Marlow puts it, or in Warren's words, he reveals "secret needs"[7] that the narrator had "repressed or maybe ignored more than half a lifetime" (*LJ* 33). Meeting that person destroyed the narrator's complacency. In short, adult hero-worship brought out an as yet still immature element of the narrator's inner nature. In telling the tale, the narrator strives to make this underdeveloped aspect of himself congruent with his more mature outward appearance.

In the elegiac romances in this subcategory the scene in which the narrator first caught sight of his hero is usually rendered in the narrator's tale as a moment of high drama. The adult narrator remembers vividly the initial "vision" that affected his life so suddenly and so profoundly: Marlow's first wholly imaginary "distinct glimpse" of Kurtz, Dowell's first impression of Ashburnham in the hotel dining room at Nauheim, and Nick's first sight of Gatsby staring at the green light across the bay. In each case what clinched the narrator's initial attraction to his hero was his sense that his hero immediately took him into confidence or service. Willie Stark commanded Jack with a wink the first time they shook hands, Ashburnham took Dowell in immediately with his savoir faire, Jim "bullied" Marlow into becoming his "ally" by appealing to his curiosity. Saint-Exupéry's brief elegiac rom-

7. See Chapter One, note 36.

ance, *The Little Prince*, a deceptively innocent children's story for adults, gently parodies this conventional scene of first meeting, when the narrator describes the first service demanded of him by the little prince: "You can imagine my surprise at dawn when an odd little voice woke me up saying "Please . . . draw me a sheep! [Alors vous imaginez ma surprise, au lever du jour, quand une drôle de petite voix m'a réveillé. Elle disait: S'il vous plaît . . . dessine-moi un mouton!]"[8]

Childhood or Adolescent Hero-Worship. In the contrasting subcategory of elegiac romance, this important initial scene usually is not described. Here, the narrator's hero-worship began during childhood or early adolescence. Because of its early origin, the narrator's deep emotional attachment seems to him to have emerged fully developed from the dark chaos of his own past—to be without origin, without beginning. The narrator seems to remember no time in his life when he was not dominated by his hero's personality. Works in this category include *The Last Tycoon*, *Doctor Faustus*, *The Real Life of Sebastian Knight*, *Remembrance of Things Past*, and "Seymour: An Introduction."

In place of a dramatic scene of first meeting, elegiac romances in this category must suggest in some other way the overwhelming power of the narrator's attraction to his hero. Often they do so with a description of the hero's person in which the narrator implies his hero's great physical allure. In Fitzgerald's *The Last Tycoon*, Cecilia feels especially drawn to Stahr's hands, "delicate and slender" (*LT* 20). Buddy Glass similarly remembers the beauty of Seymour's hands and registers his "personal admiration" of Seymour's nose, hair, and other physical attributes (*SI* 177). The narrator of *A Separate Peace*, Gene Forrester, admires Finny's "bold nose and cheek bones" and the way his "back muscles [worked] like a panther's" (*SP* 19). Even more detailed is V's memory of his brother, Sebastian Knight: his

dark hair, closely cropped, [that] renders a small birthmark visible above his rose-red diaphanous ear, . . . the black regulation uniform with that leather belt I secretly coveted.. . .Then later on,

8. Antoine de Saint-Exupéry, *The Little Prince*, trans. Katherine Woods (New York: Harcourt, Brace & World, 1971), p. 6; *Le Petit Prince* (New York: Harcourt, Brace & World, 1943), p. 9.

when he was sixteen and I ten ... he was tall and sallow com-
plexioned with a dark shadow above his upper lip. His hair was
now glossily parted ... [SK 11]

Partly because of this strong element of physical attraction in
hero-worship begun in childhood and adolescence, elegiac romances in this subcategory also suggest the narrator's own development in physical terms. More particularly, the narrator is likely
to measure his own growth against, as it seems to him, his hero's
diminished physical power and stature. He feels as Gene Forrester does that "the giants of your childhood, whom you encounter
years later ... are not merely smaller in relation to your growth,
but ... absolutely smaller, shrunken by age" (SP 6).

Commonly, then, in elegiac romances where the narrator's
hero-worship begun in childhood or adolescence, the narrator
is fairly explicit about overcoming his hero's influence by sup-
planting him. Nabokov's V. says in the end "I am Sebastian
Knight" (SK 205). Zeitblom expresses discreet satisfaction over
the fact that he has survived his hero and has taken up the
"burden" of his hero's life and times in telling the tale (DF, Ch.
26). Buddy Glass asserts this new primacy bluntly:

Always I'll be aware, and so, I believe, will the reader, if rather
less partisanly, that a somewhat paunchy and very nearly middle-
aged man [Buddy Glass] is running this show. . . . I must tell you
that I know as well as I know anything that if our positions were
switched around and Seymour were in my seat, he would be so
affected—so stricken, in fact—by his gross seniority as narrator
and official shot-caller that he'd abandon this project. [SI 169-70]

The narrator's growing self-confidence is the signal that he is
breaking out of a state of childish dependency into something
closer to emotional maturity. Fitzgerald's Cecilia suggests the
true nature of this new freedom when she tells us that her fantasy
"picture" of Monroe Stahr first began to fade when she realized
for the first time that she had lost the capacity to "cut out pictures" of idealized, heroic figures like those she had once "pasted
inside of my old locker at school." That moment "I'll always
think of," she says, "as the end of childhood" (LT 87).

That "end of childhood" may be specific, as in these stories, or it may be highly abstracted and displaced, as in *Doctor Faustus*. Because Zeitblom and Leverkühn grew up together as children, Zeitblom's acquaintance with his hero was throughout Leverkühn's life a constant reminder of his own provincial German view of the world, a view locked in the presuppositions of the hometown milieu he and his hero grew up in. These narrow presuppositions at one time served Zeitblom adequately. Now he knows that he held on to them too long. Applied to modern life and adult needs, they are restrictive, corrupt, socially dangerous, and self-destructive. Yet they remain in his mind persistently, associated with the figure of his hero. Similarly, Swann's life as dilettante and snob represents an aspect of Proust's narrator's own aspirations, to which he is, at the very least, ambivalent.

The unusual complexity of many novels in this subcategory has its origin in part in the lost initial moment of the narrator's infatuation with his hero. The narrator overlays his tale in *Doctor Faustus* with encyclopaedic commentaries on music, demonology, and magic. In "Seymour: An Introduction," the narrator repeatedly alludes to tenets of oriental mysticism and other occult phenomena. Nabokov weaves into the fabric of his narrator's tale anagrams, word-play, puzzles, and tricks. Proust's narrator richly embroiders his tale with social commentary and reflections on time, memory, and art. These devices and tropes are not superficial, unintegrated embellishments. They suggest how obscure the experience still seems to the narrator himself, and represent his effort to grasp it and make sense of it by casting it in a variety of metaphorical forms. In this type of elegiac romance more than any other, we follow the narrator as he undertakes an almost impossible task: to write himself out of his own childhood by telling the tale, and at the same time to try to discover the true nature of aspects of that childhood that persist into adulthood as demanding emotional predispositions.

The strain this task places on the narrator in elegiac romances of childhood hero-worship is evident in Buddy Glass's frenetic tone in "Seymour: An Introduction." Throughout his life, growing up with Seymour as a member of a show-business family living on New York's Upper West Side, Buddy admired his older brother and hopelessly competed with him. Buddy believes that this was a happy childhood. As he begins his tale, he is trying to convince himself that his extreme agitation at the moment is the result of still being "ecstatically happy" (*SI* 98). But Buddy was and is far from happy. He reveals in every sentence his insecurity as a person and as a narrator. He grossly overstates his case. He harangues the reader. He finds fault with himself over his evident inability to tell the tale adequately, or at least coherently. He needlessly apologizes for his limitations. He repeats himself over and over, announcing and reannouncing parts of the tale yet to be told, revising and denying his assertions in the very act of making them.

Buddy implicitly passes off this obsessive self-criticism as a product of his highly refined "scruples" as a writer. He claims that the obscure epigrams drawn from Kafka and Kierkegaard which open his tale "suggest very plainly how I think I stand in regard to the over-all mass of detail I hope to assemble here" (*SI* 101). He identifies himself as "the true artist-seer, the heavenly fool who can and does produce beauty," and who is "dazzled to death by his own scruples, the blinding shapes and colors of his own sacred human conscience" (*SI* 105). He identifies himself, that is, with his childhood image of Seymour, who was a writer and a poet, but who also from Buddy's point of view was a "liege lord," a "sage," a Zen Master, an artistic "Sick Man":

> our blue-striped unicorn, our double-lensed burning glass, our consulting genius, our portable conscience, our supercargo, our one full poet, and, inevitably, I think . . . our rather notorious "mystic" and "unbalanced type" . . . [He] was the only person I've ever habitually consorted with, banged around with, who more frequently than not tallied with the classical conception, as I saw it, of a *mukta*, a ringding enlightened man, a God-knower. [*SI* 106]

In identifying himself with this idealized image of his brother, Buddy reveals somewhat more baldly than others of these narrators his rivalry with his hero. Buddy insists that he always intensely admired Seymour's ability to win games using an unorthodox style of play and yet remain above the satisfaction of winning: to be "all smiles when he heard a responsive click of glass striking glass" in shooting marbles, and yet appear to be so uncertain as to "*whose* winning click it was" that "someone almost inevitably had to pick up the marble he'd won and *hand* it to him" (*SI* 209). This professed admiration reveals Buddy's greatest self-deception with regard to his brother, and reveals also therefore, the subject of his most significant dramatized insight as he tells the tale. His tale is in fact a record of being defeated and overshadowed throughout his childhood by an older brother who, maddeningly, always made a conspicuous point of avoiding taking credit for his superiority and success, thereby never allowing his younger brother a means of saving face in his inevitable defeat, and forcing him always into a posture of subservience and hero-worship.

This insight comes to Buddy only gradually as he works his way through the tale. Eventually he stops protesting his ecstatic happiness, and discovers instead the compulsion which underlies his agitation. Narration itself forces him to recognize the important, "terrible and undiscountable fact" that "has just reached me, between paragraphs, that I *yearn* to talk, to be queried, to be interrogated, about this particular dead man" (*SI* 143). His confession, to himself and to his readers, that his tale is a "compulsive, and I'm afraid, occasionally somewhat pustulous disquisition," leads then to the final and central dramatized insight in the work (*SI* 136).

Buddy's final insight is that his greatest motive for telling the tale is not a desire to celebrate the brother's greatness, but a "perpetual lust to share top billing with him" (*SI* 212). He achieves just this end by outliving Seymour and becoming the "official shot-caller" in telling the tale. Buddy has already hinted at this motive early in the tale when he calls himself "a narrator . . . with extremely pressing personal needs" (*SI* 107), needs much like the "secret needs" Warren attributes to Jack Burden. Buddy's pretense of ecstatic happiness covers an exhausted life of grief, anger, and guilt. At the age of forty he is a nervous wreck— sleepless, obsessively self-abnegating, sickly, hysterical, and desperate.

These symptoms are clues to what Buddy warns us from the beginning of his tale not to miss. "The thing to listen for, every time, with a public confessor," he says, "is what he's *not* confessing to" (*SI* 167). What Buddy is not confessing to is his feeling that he was not "much more than lukewarmly tolerated" at home as a child, because he lived then, and in imagination still lives, until he completes his tale, in Seymour's shadow. As he begins to overcome this despair in telling the tale he gradually accomplishes what he set out covertly to do from the first. He succeeds in "nosing [Seymour] out in popularity on page" as he could never do in life (*SI* 168). Having proven himself equal to some of his dead hero's talents by taking up his hero's Herculean burden in telling the tale, Buddy can at last feel that he is "done here," and turn to his daily work of teaching with a renewed sense that "there is no single thing I do that is more important" (*SI* 212-13).

In Nabokov's *The Real Life of Sebastian Knight*, the narrator and the hero of his tale are brothers, just as Salinger's principal figures are. But as examples of elegiac romance in the subcategory of childhood hero-worship, these novels differ in an interesting way. "Seymour: An Introduction" emphasizes brotherly rivalry, with brotherly identification a secondary, aggravating issue. In *Sebastian Knight* identification is the central issue and rivalry secondary, although, as we have seen earlier, we are likely to find some confusion of identity in every elegiac romance. Marlow recognizes some of Jim's characteristics in himself. Zeitblom sees his own love of arrogance in Leverkühn's. Dowell acknowledges that he loved Ashburnham "because he was just myself." But the pressure on Nabokov's narrator to reconcile himself to loss is greater than that of almost any other elegiac romance narrator. At the end of his tale, Nabokov's narrator, V., says unequivocally:

> I am Sebastian Knight. I feel as if I were impersonating him on a lighted stage, with the people he knew coming and going. . . . They move round Sebastian—round me who am acting Sebastian. . . . They all go back to their everyday life . . . but the hero remains, for, try as I may, I cannot get out of my part: Sebastian's mask clings to my face, the likeness will not be washed off. I am Sebastian, or Sebastian is I, or perhaps we both are someone whom neither of us knows. [*SK* 205]

As this passage suggests, V.'s success in clarifying his identity is severely limited. It is nevertheless a success, and one similar to John Dowell's in *The Good Soldier*. The success of the narrators in these novels lies in their gaining distance on the nature of their confusion of identity, even though at the end of their tale, they both still adamantly maintain that confusion.

The evidence that in *The Real Life of Sebastian Knight* V. understands his confusion of identity lies in the effort he makes to ensure that the reader will see through his confusion and distinguish clearly between himself and the hero of his tale. The feature V. emphasizes that clearly distinguishes V. and Sebastian is thematically the most important. Loss is a conspicuous influence on the lives of both, but the way they experience loss and respond to it is significantly different. Sebastian was nostalgic. Like Gatsby, Sebastian was obsessed with having lost "the freshest and the best forever." Sebastian was a novelist, and in his "most autobiographical" novel, *Lost Property*, he contended that "one of the purest emotions is that of the banished man pining after the land of his birth, . . . straining his memory to the utmost in a continuous effort to keep alive and bright the vision of his past" (*SK* 26-27). This passage is reminiscent of Marlow's description of the "real sentient man" who remembers "vaguely having been deserted in the fullness of possession by someone or something more precious than life" (*LJ* 199). But although the awareness of loss may seem similar in narrator and narrator's hero in Nabokov's novel and other elegiac romances such as *The Great Gatsby*, the feeling underlying the awareness of loss of narrator and narrator's hero is quite different. Sebastian and Gatsby recalled the past in order to maintain their vision of it. In contrast, V. and Nick actively revisit the past not to keep it alive but to cast it off.

In Nabokov's novel especially, this distinction between narrator and narrator's hero is reflected in details of their lives. Sebastian Knight was a lonely, self-conscious, "very high-strung and nervous" person who sought obsessively for unattainable satisfaction. His personality and the goal of his quest were defined by the central experience of his childhood—the disappearance of his mother from his life when he was four years old. He saw his mother again only once, for a brief, teasing moment. This reappearance seemed to him gratuitous and without perceivable cause. It was the first and most important of what he called aleatory (chance) occurrences in his life the aetiological (causal) secret of which Sebastian attempted as a novelist to discover. His mother's visit and the sugared violets she gave him haunted him for the rest of his days.

Sebastian's unabating love for his lost mother made him hate his father for remarrying after Sebastian's mother left him. When Sebastian found out that his father subsequently died in a duel defending his mother's honor, his hate abruptly changed to love. And at the end of his life, Sebastian gave up a relationship with a woman he had lived happily with for years in order to pursue a woman who, like his mother, had "left husband and child" when "one day it occurred to her that she might be in love with another." Thus Sebastian derived from his mother the key element in his imaginative life, his "capricious and rambling" quest (*SK* 9, 8).

In contrast, V. was timid and retiring as a child, and, until Sebastian's death, uncertain, self-depreciating, and seemingly passionless. His life lacked motivation and goal. He endured Sebastian's indifference to him without complaint: even though he loved his brother "dearly," his one-way "life-long affection" for Sebastian, typical of the relationship of elegiac romance narrators with their heroes, had been "somehow or other . . . always . . . crushed and thwarted" (*SK* 33). Another key difference between V. and Sebastian is the nature of their childhood bereavement. Whereas Sebastian lost his mother when he was still a child, V. was, he tells us, "still a child when I lost my father" (*SK* 8). In place of his lost mother, Sebastian created idealized surrogates in the women he loved and in characters in his novels. In place of his lost father, V. created an idealized surrogate also—Sebastian. Nabokov's novel, indeed, is unusual in making so explicit this aspect of the primary Oedipal relationship underlying the structure of elegiac romance. V. says, "Every time I open one of [Sebastian's] books, I seem to see my father dashing into the room" (*SK* 7). The first chapter of V.'s tale, purporting to narrate the early years of Sebastian's life, is more accurately described as V.'s story of their father's death.

In accordance with these differences in their past, Sebastian and V. have different characteristics as authors. Sebastian's novels, written under the pseudonym of his mother's name, reiterated the two most important events of his childhood: the loss of his mother and her momentary return. Her "capricious and rambling" quest, "now swerving wide off the mark, now forgetting it midway," appeared as the "wavy" plot lines of Sebastian's fiction (*SK* 8). In Sebastian's autobiographical novel, *Lost Property*, furthermore, his quest to recapture the lost past failed because he could not solve, by the means at his disposal, the riddle of the past. He could only elevate the present to an ideal. For him, "time . . . was never 1914 or 1920 or 1936—it was always year 1" (*SK* 65). Sebastian's mind remained locked in a timeless period in which "time and space [are] . . . measures of the same eternity" (*SK* 66). Sebastian, like the young Jack Burden, repetitively sought the falsely profound, "the aetiological secret of aleatory occurrences" (*SK* 96). And like Swann, Sebastian's emotional and aesthetic life repeated throughout his life the patterns that had been already clearly established in his youth.

Sebastian the novelist borrowed his mother's capriciousness, but V., the "biographer" of Sebastian, pursued his brother's identity with their mother's fretting conscientiousness. As "a traveller . . . in the past" (*SK* 127), for V. time was never "year 1," as it always was for Sebastian. V. sought to determine exactly what did happen in 1914, 1920, 1936. Believing that the past constitutes the "interchangeable burden of the soul" of which we are "unconscious" (*SK* 204-05), V.'s purpose in writing Sebastian's biography is to recapture and "animate the past." To do so, he exercises his "imagination—the muscle of the soul" (*SK* 83).

It is this muscle that Sebastian allowed to atrophy in himself, with the effect that he wrote "Conradish" books concerned more with the "con" than with the "radish," books that left his readers "puzzled and cross" (*SK* 42). But after Sebastian's death, when V. set out to discover and then write the story of Sebastian's life, V. began to use his imagination with "a blaze of emotional strength" (*SK* 33). In short, exercise of imagination allows V. to transform a confusion of identity into a profound conception of shared human life. V.'s concluding statement, "I am Sebastian, or Sebastian is I," represents success in his quest because it dramatizes V.'s insight into the past, the unconscious, "interchangeable burden of the soul" that all people share. Identifying with Sebastian at the end of his tale is V.'s way of making his art "*per du* with humanity" and of coming to terms with the inevitability of his own death, that moment when finally "the masquerade draws to a close."

There remains to be discussed in this subcategory a small group of elegiac romances of childhood or adolescent hero-worship in which the whole experience, from first encounter through the hero's death, and perhaps including the telling of the tale, is confined to the adolescence of both hero and narrator. Here too, the crucial moment when the narrator met and identified with the person who becomes the hero of his tale remains hidden in unawareness, obscured by the rapid and confusing onset of puberty. But elegiac romances of hero-worship among adolescents are distinctive in tone, because the narrator does not have to try to reconstruct his whole childhood in order to free himself from his delusion, and because the initial experience did not occur at an age of utter unself-consciousness. As a result, elegiac romances of hero-worship among adolescents tend to enjoy greater clarity of style and form that those of hero-worship begun in childhood. The narrator, such as Gene Forrester in John Knowles's *A Separate Peace* or the boy who narrates Faulkner's "Uncle Willy," reveals readily and explicitly the fantasies underlying his experience.

Knowles's novel, the story of the friendship between two boys at an American prep school during World War II, is the best known work in this subcategory. Its narrator's subservience to his hero is clear and unequivocal. Gene felt he was "trapped" by his hero, Finny, "in his strongest trap, that is I became his collaborator" (*SP* 11). He describes Finny as "a river god, . . . his whole body hanging between river and sky as though he had transcended gravity" (*SP* 67). He makes the discovery, as Marlow does in *Heart of Darkness* and *Lord Jim*, that he is himself "like a savage underneath" (*SP* 137), that the real significance of his experience lies at a "level of feeling deeper than thought, which contains truth" (*SP* 40), and that this significance is expressed in his life through "a complex design I had been weaving since birth with all its dark threads, its unexplainable symbols" (*SP* 92). He begins his tale feeling "isolated from everything," an isolation caused by betraying his friend. And he strives, by telling his tale, to "achieve" in the end "growth and harmony" (*SP* 4).

The formal and thematic clarity of the novel extends even to an unabashed statement of what Warren calls the narrator's "secret needs." The physical basis of Finny's appeal is indicated in

Gene's admiration of Finny's "penetrating voice," his "unthink-
ing unity of movement," his "back muscles working like a panther's," and his "uninterrupted, emphatic unity of strength" which
"flowed from his legs to torso around shoulders to arms and full
strong neck" (*SP* 8, 10). This overt physical attraction was in-
tensified and offset by Gene's overt rivalry with his hero. Gene
strove unsuccessfully to match Finny's athletic ability and to out-
shine him in his studies. Conflict of rivalry and attraction culmi-
nated in a scene that expresses an identification as potent as V.'s
identification with Sebastian. Gene dressed himself in Finny's
clothes, looked at himself in a mirror, and was shocked to see
reflected there—it seemed to him—"Phineas to the life" (*SP* 54).

Conflict of rivalry and attraction resulted also in the suppressed
hostility that finally drove Gene to cause Finny's injury and ultimately his death. Thus Knowles represents unequivocally the
climactic event of the Oedipal rivalry implicit in every elegiac
romance by the fact of the hero's death and the narrator's survival. Iceberg-like, the narrator's hostility to his hero remains
mostly under the surface, emerging only in, for example, Marlow's resentment of Jim and the responsibility Dowell takes for
knowingly delivering to Ashburnham the telegram that drove
him to suicide.

Yet even in his hostility the force of identification prevails. At
the end of his tale, Gene expresses, once again with the greatest
possible clarity, the sense of release from his past life that every
elegiac romance narrator experiences. He tells us he cannot "escape the feeling" that Finny's funeral was really "my own funeral" (*SP* 186). In losing Finny, he feels, what he actually lost
was part of himself.

"The Illusions of My Beginnings": Huxley, Bromfield, Saint-
Exupéry

The thematic emphasis of an elegiac romance is affected not
only by the narrator's age at the time his hero-worship began,
but also by the relative ages of the narrator and his hero throughout the experience. In other words, it can make a difference
which of the two, narrator or narrator's hero, is older.

Hero Older than the Narrator. In most of the elegiac romances discussed in this book, the narrator's hero is roughly the same age or older than the narrator. Nothing in the basic nature of hero-worship in this type of elegiac romance is problematical. It is the relationship we would most expect. With regard to the narrator in each case, the narrator's hero—Kurtz, Gatsby, Willie Stark, Sebastian Knight, Stahr, Seymour, Swann, Uncle Willy, and Finny—this heroic figure is, as John Dowell puts it in *The Good Soldier*, a sort of "large elder brother who took me out on several excursions and did many dashing things whilst I just watched him robbing the orchards from a distance" (*GS* 253-54).

Hero Younger than the Narrator. From the point of view of classification by age, however, this quotation points up an interesting irony in *The Good Soldier*. Although Dowell describes the hero of his tale as "like an elder brother," Ashburnham is in fact slightly (three years) younger than Dowell. The significance of this fact to the novel is that Ashburnham's relative youth places him nearer in age to Dowell's wife and therefore suggests a reason, or a rationalization perhaps, for Ashburnham's greater sexual vitality. Nevertheless, Dowell and Ashburnham are so close in age that for adults whose "friendship" is "a young-middle-aged affair" the difference can be discounted. In *Doctor Faustus*, where the difference in age is also slight, that Leverkühn is the younger of the two helps Zeitblom to maintain his peculiar motherly feeling toward his hero.

In a number of elegiac romances, however, the narrator's hero is significantly younger than the narrator. These are works such as *Lord Jim*, Melville's "Bartleby the Scrivener," and a small group of short stories in which the narrator is an adult and the narrator's hero a child. This group includes Willa Cather's "Jack-a-Boy," Aldous Huxley's "Young Archimedes," Louis Bromfield's "Kenny," and Antoine de Saint-Exupéry's *The Little Prince*.[9]

9. In this section I have used the following texts: Louis Bromfield, *Kenny* (New York: Harper Brothers, 1944), pp. 9-96; Willa Cather, "Jack-a-Boy," in *Collected Short Fiction, 1892-1912* (Omaha, Neb.: University of Nebraska Press, 1965), pp. 311-22; Aldous Huxley, "Young Archimedes," in *Little Mexican* (London: Chatto and Windus, 1959), pp. 271-340; Herman Melville, "Bartleby," in *The Complete Stories of Herman Melville*, ed. Jay Leyda (New York: Random House,

Lord Jim establishes the thematic tenor of this category. Jim's youthfulness is a repeated motif in the novel. Jim had "blue boyish eyes," a "young face," and a "fresh young voice" with a "boyish intonation." He and Jewell greeted each other as "boy" and "girl." Jim seems at times to be almost a Dorian Gray, frozen in youth: "It's extraordinary," Marlow exclaims, "how very few signs of wear he showed" (*LJ* 193). Even Jim's enemies noticed his youthfulness. Cornelius, the cringing trader whom Jim displaced in Patusan, wondered angrily what Stein meant "sending a boy like that to talk big to an old servant" (*LJ* 223). Cornelius is certainly an unpleasant, treacherous character, but he must be credited with the accurate perception that Jim in many respects was indeed "like a little child," because he knew "no more than a child" (*LJ* 236). For example, Jim's values were still rooted in adolescent adventure fiction. Part of Marlow's ambivalence to Jim is based on the fact that although he finds Jim appealing, Jim's boyish "attitude of mind in a grown man . . . had in it something phenomenal, a little mad, dangerous, unsafe" (*LJ* 168).

Marlow is aware that he, not his hero, is the "large elder brother" in his tale, In fact, he once refers to Jim in an affectionate moment as "my very young brother" (*LJ* 160). Yet, to paraphrase Ford's Dowell, it was Jim who took Marlow out on excursions—to witness the Patna disaster (in imagination), and later to visit Patusan. Jim did the dashing things, while Marlow watched him rob the orchards from a distance. The reason Marlow watched Jim passively and served Jim's practical needs was to serve Marlow's "secret needs," those that originated in his own childhood and youth. Jim revealed a flaw in character that Marlow feared discovering in himself, one that lay "unknown, but perhaps suspected . . . more than half a life time."

Although it is not a twentieth-century work, and thus is somewhat beyond the scope of this book, Melville's "Bartleby the Scrivener" also illustrates this type of elegiac romance in a suggestive way. Melville's narrator discovers a weakness in his own character reflected in the hero of his tale. The narrator, an elderly lawyer who had "a profound conviction that the easiest

---

1949), pp. 3-47. An unpublished essay by Thomas Friedmann has been especially helpful in my discussion of "Bartleby."

way of life is the best," prided himself on avoiding conflict and the "turbulence" of his profession. He rationalized this life of avoidance by cultivating a reputation for being "prudent" and "*safe*." But self-knowledge entered "the cool tranquility" of his "snug retreat" in the form of a man who was even more given to a life of avoidance than the narrator himself, who in fact took such a life to its logical extreme. By responding to all requests for action, "I would prefer not to," Bartleby remained "permanently exempt from examining the work" he did and avoided being "dispatched on the most trivial errand of any sort." He refused all "common usage" (pp. 4, 20). The narrator had achieved the same effect in his own life by more sophisticated means. What Melville's narrator sees in Bartleby's life to his consternation and terror is what Marlow in *Lord Jim* calls a hint of the possible fate that might befall himself, he whose youth in its fundamental nature resembled Bartleby's youth. The tendency to retreat leads not to ease and safety as the narrator had assumed, but ultimately to death.

In its more extreme form, the narrator in this subcategory of elegiac romance is an adult, and his hero is a child. In this form, the narrator seems to have responded not to a latent weakness in the child's character but to a perceived, perhaps a fantasized, strength. Again, although in *Lord Jim* the narrator's hero is not a child but a somewhat childish young adult, this novel illuminates elegiac romances of this type. To Marlow, Jim was "a youngster of the sort you like to imagine your self to have been," and he represented "the illusions of my beginnings." Part of Jim's youthful illusions was belief in "unlimited power over natural instincts" (*LJ* 93, 95). Similarly, when the narrator's hero is a child, the child represents to the narrator a talent or force of character that defies natural limitations, but that, in the event, turns out so great as to be incompatible with life. What the child seems to have rekindled in the narrator are recollections of the numinous quality of life as we sometimes experience it, or seem to recall experiencing it, in childhood. Typically, the narrator takes credit for discovering a virtue in this special child that disappeared from the earth with the child's death. The child-hero entered the narrator's life "trailing clouds of glory." The now dead child is a ghost of the narrator's own idealized childhood.

The narrator in this type of elegiac romance often displays a remnant of talent or sensibility of the sort he recognized in the child. Willa Cather's narrator in "Jack-a-Boy" is marginally an artist, making her living as a neighborhood music teacher. Huxley's narrator in "Young Archimedes" establishes his claim to sensibility with an introductory description of the Italian countryside in which his experience with the child, Guido, occurred. Bromfield's narrator in "Kenny" is a farmer who prides himself on his human insight, based, he believes, on what he calls the "*animal* thing" in his own character, something "stronger than my own conscious judgment or my intelligence," that "had always played a big part in any decision I had ever made and almost anything I have ever done" (pp. 31-32).

These narrators also have in common a strong explicit animistic sense that their surroundings are "possessed" by spirits and primitive gods, of which, they suspect, their child-hero may have been one. In the child as Cather's narrator puts it, "the old divinities reveal themselves" (p. 320). Each of these child-heroes seemed, in the words of Bromfield's narrator, to be "some creature out of another world and another age" almost "as if he were not quite human" (pp. 45-57). The god revealed by the narrator's hero in Huxley's story is not a god of place, but rather a quality, "genius," conceived of as "distinct and separate from the rest of the mind, independent, almost, of experience" (p. 325).

In one of these stories the child's extraordinary nature is expressed as an idealized future. In Huxley's story, the narrator speculates that Guido "was going to be a genius at forty" (p. 315). Bromfield's narrator does not try to imagine his young hero's future, but insists instead on Kenny's profound and almost supernatural understanding of wood lore, and on the godlike intensity of Kenny's love affair with a neighboring farm girl. This affair was "something wild and filled with beauty," the narrator says, "a romance . . . which belonged to the remote past in which none of us had had any fear of that in us which lies so near to the very core of the earth and the pattern of the universe" (p. 68).

This response reveals the underlying meaning of the child-hero in this type of elegiac romance. Bromfield's narrator is a bachelor who accidentally sees these lovers together for a brief moment. This leads him to ask why he himself had never married. Perhaps, he supposes, it was

> because, without even knowing it, I had been searching all my life
> for what I had seen during that brief second and had never found.
> The memory . . . would remain with me as long as I lived, a kind
> of symbol of those things which had been lost out of the lives of
> all of us in a world in which machinery had made slaves of us and
> time and speed had become our rulers. [P. 69]

Bromfield lets his narrator off the hook somewhat here by making him generalize his fears and inadequacies. Cather is more rigorous. Her narrator feels that Jack-a-Boy "looked down into your soul's secrets and made you remember things you had not thought of for years" (p. 311). And Huxley makes his narrator reveal his (the narrator's) insecurity by reflecting that when the child-hero "grows up, [he] will be to me, intellectually, what a man is to a dog" (p. 321).

Insecurity in these narrators runs very deep. Each reveals his rivalry with his child-hero, a rivalry in which the narrator takes second place. Bromfield's narrator feels that Kenny's "*animal thing*" is more intense than his own, and that Kenny was somehow "far wiser and older than myself" (p. 58). This sense of inferiority to his child-hero sometimes drives the narrator to odd rationalizations. When Huxley's narrator compares Guido to himself as a man to a dog, he quickly reassures himself with the hopeful possibility that "there are other men and women who are, perhaps, almost as dogs to me" (p. 321). And after Cather's narrator tells us that Jack-a-Boy's eyes "made you remember things you had not thought of for years," she implies her ambivalence to the child by expressing her ambivalence to these memories: "there were things in my own life I had no desire to remember" (p. 311).

Perhaps it is their rivalry with the as-yet-undiminished hopes of these remarkable children that leads two of these narrators to feel responsible in part for the children's deaths. The sense of responsibility on the narrator's part is less clear here, though, than it is for example in *A Separate Peace* and *The Good Soldier*.

Cather's narrator tells us that she fled the summer heat alone, even though she knew that Jack-a-Boy might die if he did not find relief from the oppressive weather. And when she returned, she forgot the gift she had promised to bring him (p. 218). Huxley's narrator realizes that he "ought to have thought of the possibility" that Guido might attempt suicide, "and somehow guarded against it" (p. 132). In this feeling of guilt, each of these narrators reveals the fear that he has snuffed out his own archaic, ideal image of himself that the encounter with the child had rekindled. When the child is father to the man, the tensions of the primary Oedipal relationship are no less affecting and somewhat more complex. Once again we are led to feel that what these narrators grieve for ultimately is having lost, to some degree intentionally and necessarily, the illusions of their own beginnings.

Much of what we have observed in these short stories in which the narrator's hero is younger than the narrator applies as well to Saint-Exupéry's *The Little Prince*. In Cather, Huxley, and Bromfield, however, a pretense to reality prevails, despite supernatural overtones in the narrators' descriptions of their miraculous child-heroes. Saint Exupéry drops this pretense, with the result that the story seems entirely fantastic. *The Little Prince* is of course usually considered a children's story. Reading it as an elegiac romance, however, helps explain why the book impresses many readers as a sophisticated fable for adults.

Saint-Exupéry's aviator-narrator tells his tale, by his own account, for very much the same reason that Buddy Glass tells his in "Seymour," not to bury his hero but to exhume him. After asking us to read his book carefully and telling us that he finds narration painful, the narrator says that he describes his hero "to make sure that I shall not forget him" (p. 18). What Saint-Exupéry exhumes, though, is his own sense of the "essential" and the "invisible," which seems to have diminished in adulthood. As he followed the little prince, he says, he learned from an assortment of fantastic characters and beasts how to live his life properly. For example, he learned from the fox that "one sees well only through the heart" and that "you become responsible, forever, for what you have tamed" (p. 71). What the narrator learns in general from these messages is that, alas, he is "a little like the grown ups. I have had to grow old" (p. 19). Thus, this narrator too painfully roots out of himself childhood illusions of invulnerability and unfettered licence, and renders them imaginatively in telling the tale.[10]

10. *The Little Prince*, pp. 18, 81, 19.

"Interiorized" Form: Borges, Kafka, Landolfi, Nabokov

Many of Borges's stories concern private miracles, private obsessions, private prisons, and private forms of heroism. Borges's characters evidence what he calls a "stammering greatness" in their attempts to face threats to the coherence of their lives and to their sanity. The narrator's hero in both "Funes, The Memorious" and "The Other Death" is a character whose private problem involves the workings of memory. Funes remembers too much; Damian, in "The Other Death," remembers imperfectly. This subject, the workings of memory, and the form of these stories gives them a good deal in common with the early work of Conrad. An allusion to *Lord Jim* in "The Other Death" (p. 106) reminds us that the narrators of both *Lord Jim* and one of the short stories that immediately precedes it in Conrad's career, "Karain, A Memory," are also men who cannot forget men who could not forget.

Borges's elegiac romances differ conspicuously from Conrad's, however. Borges's narrators perceive in their hero's life quite a different class of implication. Whereas Marlow and the Karain narrator see serious flaws in the imaginative process of their heroes, what Borges's narrator sees in "Funes, The Memorious," for example, is limits to the hero's intellectual vitality. Funes's "garbage disposal" memory makes him "almost incapable of general, platonic ideas," "incapable of thought," and unable to "live by leaving behind" (pp. 40-43). Borges's narrator can also accept the fact that his hero's state of mind is almost entirely self-inflicted.

Grove Press, 1967), pp. 35-43; "The Other Death," in *The Aleph and Other Stories, 1933-1969*, trans. Norman Thomas di Giovanni (New York: Dutton, 1968), pp. 103-11; Willa Cather, *My Mortal Enemy* (New York: Vintage, 1961); Mark Harris, *Bang the Drum Slowly* (New York: Dell, 1973); the commercial film version of this book, "Bang the Drum Slowly," screenplay by Mark Harris, produced by Maurice and Lois Rosenfield, directed by John Hancock (Paramount Pictures, 1973), and also an earlier television dramatization, "Bang the Drum Slowly," adapted by Arnold Schulman, directed by Daniel Petrie, broadcast September 26, 1956, first rebroadcast (by National Public Television) May 6, 1982; Franz Kafka, "Josephine the Singer, or the Mouse Folk," in *The Penal Colony*, trans. Willa and Edwin Muir (New York: Schocken, 1943), pp. 256-77; Tommaso Landolfi, "Gogol's Wife," trans Wayland Young, in *Gogol's Wife and Other Stories* (Norfolk, Conn.: New Directions, 1961), pp. 1-16; Vladimir Nabokov, *Pale Fire* (New York: Berkeley, 1962); and Peter Shaffer, *Equus*, in *Equus and Shrivings* (New York: Atheneum, 1975), pp. 1-106.

Although Funes's flawless memory compensates in part for his crippling injury, it was not caused by that injury and in fact has no observable origin. Conrad's narrators, in contrast, cannot accept the possibility that their heroes' state of mind might have no "real" cause. When a friend asks the Karain narrator whether he thought what Karain told them "really happened," the narrator refuses to consider the possibility that Karain's mental state may have been even more disturbed than it seemed: that he may have been plagued not by guilt for a real crime but by a fantasy guilt for a fantasy crime. And Marlow confidently attributes the flaws that Kurtz and Jim display to "haggard utilitarian lies" maintained by the "European mind."

In "The Other Death," Borges's narrator faces even more directly the issue that Conrad's narrators avoid: whether or not a certain remembered event "really happened." Did Damian die heroically in battle, or was he a coward who died in his bed, an old man dreaming of heroism? At first the narrator explores several supernatural "solutions" to this problem. The most plausible of these from his point of view is that there may be "two universal histories," one in which "we are living now," and the other, suppressed, producing "the odd contradictions that I have related." In the end, however, the narrator entertains the more likely possibility that he himself has not "always written the truth" (p. 110).

This statement may be read as an extreme form of the elegiac romance convention that the narrator feels insecure as a narrator. Still, Conrad's narrators never admit that they may not be telling the truth. Indeed, even as Marlow seeks "inner truth" he reaffirms his belief in concrete reality. In *Lord Jim*, Marlow doubts but never gives up his professional loyalty to the "fixed standard of conduct." In *Heart of Darkness* he doubts that "the world of straight-forward facts" comprises the whole of reality, but he still seeks refuge in that world. And while the narrator in "Karain, A Memory" listened to Karain's story of fatal delusion and penetration of the present by the past, he was given "protection and relief" by the "invisible presence [of] the firm, pulsating beat of the two ship's chronometers ticking off steadily the seconds of Greenwich Time."[3]

3. *Tales of Unrest*, p. 64

In contrast, Borges's narrator in "The Other Death" accepts implicitly at the end of his tale that the story he has told may be a fabrication of his own mind. He suggests, by alluding to the belief that when "in all innocence Virgil believed he was setting down the birth of a man and foretold the birth of Christ," that in a similar way his own imagination has exerted power over his memory of past events sufficient to make "fantastic" events "real." What Borges's story demonstrates is the element of imagination, of wishful, myth-informed memory, in our reconstructions of the past, private and intimate as well as public and universal. Together, Borges's two short variations of elegiac romance suggest one thematic direction that radical variation of elegiac romance may take. This direction is to examine the nature of what in "Funes, The Memorious" Borges calls the "sacred" or "venerable" (*sagrado*) act of remembering (p. 35).[4]

Kafka's story, "Josephine the Singer, or the Mouse Folk," also examines memory and shows why memory deserves the epithet, *sagrado*, that Borges applies to it. The problem in Kafka's story is neither too much memory nor faulty memory, but an almost total lack of it.

Kafka's anonymous narrator tells the tale, ostensibly, of a person, Josephine, admired as a singer by a community of "mouse folk." Oddly, Josephine has "disappeared." She has presumably already died by the time the tale begins. The narrator tells the tale almost entirely in the present tense. Only at the end of the tale do we find out that the last time anyone saw Josephine, helped off a stage in a state of near collapse, was "a day or two ago" (Kafka, p. 276). The significance of the present-tense narration, then, is that the mouse folk seem to be able to live only in the present. In contrast to Funes the Memorious, their lives are untouched by the past. The narrator tells us that they "ignore historical research entirely," and that they reproduce so rapidly that "one generation . . . treads on the heels of another." As a result, each individual's experience of life is almost entirely im-

4. Di Giovanni somewhat misleadingly translates *sagrado* as "ghostly." The passage in question is the first sentence of "Funes el Memorioso": "Lo recuerdo (yo no tengo derecho a pronunciar ese verbo sagrado, sólo un hombre en la tierra tuvo derecho y ese hombre ha muerto) . . . " (*Ficciones* [Buenos Aires: Emecé Editores, 1956], p. 117).

mediate. The mouse folk "have no time to be children" and have "no age of youth, scarcely the briefest childhood," so that they are "all at once grown up and then . . . stay grown up too long" (pp. 264-67).

Kafka's story is about a people who experience no development in their individual lives, no sense that each moment has been prepared for by previous moments and leads in turn to moments that will certainly follow. It is an elegiac romance set in a world in which elegiac romance is all but impossible. The past for the mouse folk is what happened "two or three days ago," because that is as far as their memory reaches. For them, as for the young Jack Burden and for Sebastian Knight, the future is inconceivable except as more of the same. As a result, the mouse folk are a people whose lives are characterized by "unexpended, ineradicable childishness" combined with a mental state of being "prematurely old" (pp. 267-68).

The style of the narrator's tale in this story formalizes this uncomfortable state of mind as a cautious, well-hedged, somewhat pretentious disquisition on the meaning of the relationship between the mouse folk and their heroine, Josephine. He discusses the matter as though Josephine is alive, because being almost entirely memoryless, he can neither understand nor grieve. Although along with the other mouse folk he can "admire" Josephine, he cannot understand her because understanding requires reflection. Even the opposition to Josephine is "fleeting and transient," since her opponents can only give an unreflecting "impression" couched in phrases they are "in the habit of saying" (p. 261).

Kafka's narrator cannot grieve because, lacking a sense of what is past, he lacks a sense of loss. This fact makes Kafka's story a highly ironic variation of elegiac romance. It is an elegiac tale told by a narrator who has experienced loss but who is incapable of comprehending it. At the end of his tale he does not seek "fresh Woods, and Pastures new." He merely shrugs: "Perhaps we shall not miss her so very much after all" (p. 277). The significance of Borges's epithet is now clear. Memory is "sacred" because it gives dignity and meaning to both life and death, qualities which are beyond the scope of the mouse folk. The elegiac romance narrator's effort to remember the past in order to destroy its deleterious effects is a cultural ritual of the highest importance.

Still, even this *sagrado* cultural ritual is subject to burlesque, and burlesque is what Nabokov accomplishes in *Pale Fire* and what Landolfi accomplishes in "Gogol's Wife." Nabokov's central character, Kinbote, is a stereotypical pedantic scholar, the self-styled "friend" of the poet, John Francis Shade, who is ostensibly the subject of Kinbote's work. In this role of scholar, Kinbote is like V. in *The Real Life of Sebastian Knight*, Zeitblom in *Doctor Faustus*, and Foma in "Gogol's Wife." The difference is mainly one of technical device. Whereas V., Zeitblom, and Foma reveal themselves by narrating tales purporting to be scholarly biographies of the artist's life, Kinbote reveals himself by purporting to edit a "definitive" edition of an autobiographical poem, Wordsworthian in tone, that Shade completed (we are told) just before he died.

Nabokov's technique, in short, is to extract a single convention of the genre and inflate it. It is not at all unusual in elegiac romance for the narrator to retell, reorder, edit, criticize, or interpret his hero's artistic work, in the end making his dead hero's product serve the ends of the narrator's own autobiographical statement. V. quotes passages from Sebastian Knight's novels to explain his procedure in writing Knight's "biography." Buddy Glass explicates Seymour's poems to explain himself. Jack Burden elaborates upon Willie Stark's speeches to demonstrate why they affected him. Zeitblom uses his analyses of Leverkühn's musical compositions to explain the state of mind he and his hero share with their German compatriots. What is unique about *Pale Fire* is that Nabokov has made this fragment of the convention the basis of the fiction as a whole. Doing so allows him to place his narrator at two removes from reality instead of just one: Kinbote is clearly insane.

Landolfi's story "Gogol's Wife" is in form more easily recognizable as elegiac romance than *Pale Fire*, but its narrator, Foma Paskalovitch, is no less insane. The narrator's tale in "Gogol's Wife" is presented as a chapter of an otherwise unwritten scholarly biography of Gogol. The narrator's reticence at the beginning of the tale is a form of the elegiac romance narrator's self-conscious fear of not telling his tale adequately, and of failing to produce the proper effect. His ambivalence toward his hero's "wife" and his eagerness to demonstrate his profound intimacy with his hero burlesque the emotional triangle that informs the narrator's tale in many elegiac romances. Even the love-hate relationship between the narrator's hero and his "wife" burlesques an elegiac romance convention. She is a product of Gogol's own creative afflatus ("she" is a balloon) just as Jim's fantasy world, the voices which plague Karain, and Leverkühn's conversations with the devil are those heroic figures' own private creations.

Thematically, however, "Gogol's Wife" is a somewhat more radical variation of the genre than Nabokov's novel is. As insane as Kinbote certainly is, we have a good deal more evidence in *Pale Fire* than we have in "Gogol's Wife" that the narrator had some sort of relationship with the hero of his tale. In *Pale Fire*, Shade's poem and the unmistakable irony of the scenes between narrator and hero that Kinbote recounts suggest that their relationship was real, if tenuous and superficial. In "Gogol's Wife" all we have is Foma's word that he ever knew Gogol and that the scenes he narrates are more than fabrications of his own mind. Both these works, however, contrast with, say, Borges's "The Other Death," where the narrator questions his own veracity, since Kinbote and Foma are taken in totally by their own fantasies.

Symbolic Modulation: Film and Drama

In addition to these formal variations, elegiac romance may also be varied by translating it out of its native medium, prose fiction, into another medium. One instance of this is the successful commercial film and the earlier television play entitled *Bang the Drum Slowly*.

Mark Harris's novel *Bang the Drum Slowly*, from which both film and play were adapted, is itself an effective, clearly constructed elegiac romance. Harris's narrator, Henry Wiggen, intends to tell the story of his friend Bruce Pearson, who died of Hodgkin's disease. But as a choral character named Red Traphagen tells Wiggen after reading part of his manuscript, the book is not so much about Pearson "as about you" (p. 243). The novel varies the form of elegiac romance in an interesting way by making the narrator's hero apparently less extraordinary than the narrator. The narrator is a professional baseball pitcher at the peak of his career. His hero is a mediocre catcher, who is "not a bad fellow, no worse than most and probably better than some" (p. 284). What makes Pearson heroic in Wiggen's eyes is his ability to face death courageously, struggling to live as intensely as he can, and even grow, right up to the moment the disease fells him. His heroic quest is to live fully and decently within his limitations until he dies. The narrator's insight in the course of telling the tale is uncomplicated but proportionate—acknowledging death has a strong effect on the way people behave toward one another, and on the way they lead their lives.

As prose fiction, *Bang the Drum Slowly* is therefore a successful elegiac romance. It is also to my knowledge the only elegiac romance in prose fiction that has reached the screen with its form intact. There have been a number of bad or mediocre movies made of elegiac romances: *Moby-Dick, The Great Gatsby, Lord Jim, All the King's Men*. What usually happens is that the film capitalizes on the glamorous, traditional, and highly visual heroic action of the narrator's hero, wrenching it from its narrative context, and either minimalizes or suppresses entirely the figure of the narrator. Both the commercial film version and the television play of *Bang the Drum Slowly* are successful because they maintain the basic narrative structure of the novel, giving the dramatization a clear point of view and confining the significant action to its appropriate sphere, the inner world of the narrator.[5] One value of this film is that it suggests that if other works of elegiac romance were to be treated similarly, they might enrich the film medium by providing a new means of integrating subjective action—feeling, insight, and inner change—with the

5. Another recent, partially successful dramatization of an elegiac romance is the British television production of Ford's *The Good Soldier* (produced by Peter Eckersley [Granada Television], adapted by Julian Mitchell, directed by Kevin Billington, aired on Public Television on January 8 and 9, 1983). This adaptation retains the narrator and suggests his confusion, but fails to suggest his change through telling the story. Francis Ford Coppola's "Apocalypse Now" dramatizes (or perhaps more accurately, exploits) *Heart of Darkness* with similar partial success.

more normal material of film, visual action. A film about Ishmael, for instance, might have a chance of matching the effect of Melville's monumental work, as no film about Ahab ever could.

The television play of *Bang the Drum Slowly*, furthermore, suggests rarely exploited possibilities for drama, as does Peter Shaffer's play *Equus*. This is the one instance to my knowledge in which elegiac romance structure has been used directly in drama, or for that matter in any medium other than prose fiction. In this play, a psychiatrist narrates his encounter with a deeply disturbed adolescent boy who has been convicted of blinding several horses with a metal spike. The characters act out scenes from the boy's past as the boy described them to the psychiatrist. The audience witnesses the action firsthand at the same time that it hears about it secondhand through the psychiatrist's tale. In this way the audience experiences dramatically the inherently contrapuntal nature of the genre.

To discuss the play as an elegiac romance, however, we must view it not as the story of the boy, Alan, but as the story of Dysart, the psychiatrist who narrates. Also, since Alan does not literally die at the end of the play (literally, we are to suppose, he is cured), we must accept the boy's fate as Dysart views it, as a ritual death. We are encouraged to take this view by Alan's cry at the end of his therapeutic experience, "KILL ME," and by Dysart's conclusion that his job is to do "ultimate . . . irreversible, terminal things" to his patients. In making the boy "normal," he says, he will have made him into "a ghost" (Shaffer, pp. 104-06). Finally, we must accept that as in many elegiac romances the narrator's hero has only one real distinction, his fatal limitation or obsession. Alan is a very solitary boy but is otherwise a rather ordinary adolescent. At the same time, he is "a modern citizen for whom society doesn't exist," a person who has retreated into an extremely violent, private world (p. 79).

Once we accept these premises the form of the play becomes clear. Alan passes through his harrowing emotional experience gaining no real insight. Dysart is the only self-aware character in the play. He is the one who realizes what Alan's experience implies about his own and others' lives. Echoing Marlow's recognition that he sought to exonerate Jim because he felt his own integrity and values threatened, Dysart says that Alan is "the most alarming" case of his career because "it asks questions I've avoided all my professional life" (pp. 74-75).

As in *Lord Jim* and other elegiac romances in which the narrator's hero is significantly younger than the narrator, the narrator's hero in Shaffer's play embodies virtues the narrator wishes had been his in his own youth. Dysart is a competent professional who recognizes the limitations of his craft and of his own "educated, average head." His hero represents the illusions of Dysart's beginnings, ideals that as an adult Dysart feels he has betrayed. He acknowledges that he is "all reined up in old language and old assumptions," and that although he may be "straining to jump clean-hoofed on to a whole new track of being I only suspect is there . . . I can't jump because the bit forbids it" (p. 18). He admires the revelatory primitive passion of ancient Greek ritual, but himself can only visit the monuments of ancient Greece in "cautious jaunts in hired Fiats, suitcase crammed with Kao-Pectate" (p. 81).

The dramatized insight that comes to Dysart as he narrates the play is therefore a horrible one. He is not led by his new insight to graze in "Pastures new." Much like Marlow toward the end of *Lord Jim*, Dowell at the end of *The Good Soldier*, and Zeitblom at the end of *Doctor Faustus*, Dysart has learned to accept the bit in his teeth, a bit that now "never comes out" (Shaffer, p. 106). More self-aware at the end of the play, he understands that he continues to plod the old pasture, to which, he now knows, he will forever be confined.

"An Intelligent and Observant Woman"

These formal variations of elegiac romance, like the more conventional examples of the genre, are mostly about the mind of men. Elegiac romance appears to be, until recently at any rate, a conspicuously "male" form of fiction, used to work out peculiarly male problems of hero-worship, rivalry, fear of impotence, and fear of adult relations and responsibilities.

This observation seems true of most existing elegiac romances. But as a reflection on the basic nature of the genre and its potential to represent more broadly human, nonsex-differentiated issues, to say that elegiac romance is a form of fiction limited to stories about distinctively male sorts of problems and anxieties would severely misrepresent the genre. In fact, there are several elegiac romances by women, and there are also elegiac romances in which the narrator or the narrator's hero, or both, are female. Patricia Merivale has discussed perceptively one such elegiac romance, Joan Didion's A Book of Common Prayer.[6]

Another is Willa Cather's My Mortal Enemy.[7] In this elegiac romance, the narrator, Nellie Birdseye, is a naive girl of fifteen given adult "advantages" by her Aunt Lydia. One of these advantages is the chance to meet the imposing Myra Henshawe. Typical of elegiac romances of adult hero-worship (even though Nellie is still an adolescent when she first meets Myra), that meeting is vividly remembered, and it had a traumatic effect on Nellie. She immediately perceived in Myra "a compelling, passionate, overmastering something for which I had no name." Myra's very physical presence had an enormous impact on Nellie. Myra had a "beautiful voice" but an "angry laugh," and had "deep-set, flashing grey eyes." "I felt quite overpowered by her," Nellie says, "and stupid, hopelessly clumsy and stupid" (p. 6).

Both Nellie's awe and her sense of being weakened and unnerved in the presence of the person who is to become the hero of her tale are typical of the way the elegiac romance narrator's experience begins, an experience that resolves in telling the tale. Thus, the end of Nellie's experience is typical of elegiac romance as well. Nellie tells us Myra Henshawe's story in heroic terms after Myra's death, and in the end Myra's tragic decline leaves Nellie in a state of profound disillusionment with love and life.

"My Mortal Enemy" exemplifies, therefore, the potential of elegiac romance to express a set of experiences dealing with death, loss, regeneration, and emotional maturation—broadly human experiences, of course, confined in no sense to one sex

6. "Through Greene-Land in Drag: Joan Didion's A Book of Common Prayer," Pacific Coast Philology, 15 (October, 1980), 45-52.

7. Patricia Lee Yongue notes Carlyle's influence on several of Cather's major works in which heroic figures are prominent ("Willa Cather on Heroes and Hero-Worship," Neuphilogische Mitteilungen, 79 [1978], 59-66). She does not, however, mention My Mortal Enemy, one of the few of Cather's works that is a study in hero-worship per se.

alone. A work of fiction that still more clearly exemplifies this broader nature of elegiac romance is Fitzgerald's *The Last Tycoon*. Here, Fitzgerald's narrator is female and his narrator's hero male. The novel comes across first as a love story. In the fantasy-charged relationship between narrator and narrator's hero there is clearly a strong element of physical attraction. But examined more closely, the nature of that relationship turns out to be less a case of unrequited love than of hero-worship.[8]

In *The Last Tycoon*, the career of a Hollywood film producer, Monroe Stahr, is told by Cecilia Brady, the daughter of one of Sahr's business associates. Near death herself as she tells the tale, Cecilia adorns it with imagery of loss as Nick Carraway does in *The Great Gatsby*. Almost immediately she describes herself as "a ghost assigned to a haunted house" (*LT* 5). She dwells gratuitously on her sister's death. The characters in her story discuss the Depression, towns they have left behind, and lost lovers. They listen to songs entitled "Lost" and "Gone." In the lugubrious finale Fitzgerald planned for the novel, possessions of Stahr and his companions killed in a plane crash were to have been looted by children.

Like Nick, Cecilia yearns at first for the recovery of lost innocence. As she tells her tale, again like Nick, her nostalgic note turns elegiac. But Cecilia differs from Nick and appears to be unique among elegiac romance narrators in one particular respect. A victim of tuberculosis, her reflections on loss are explicitly generated by the imminence of her own death. This universal need to come to terms with the inevitability of one's own death

8. The evidence that Cecilia's attitude toward Stahr is hero-worship exists first in her inability to affirm the possibility that they might marry. Her daydream about marrying Stahr, Cecilia says, always lacked a satisfactory ending. Always "somebody came in" to interrupt the scene as she imagines it. But second and more important, Cecilia herself recognizes that Stahr is a hero, not a potential lover. She tells us that when she actually did try to propose to Stahr, she suddenly realized that she was not addressing a man but an image, "a picture of him I cut over and over" (*LT* 87). The element of heterosexual appeal in *The Last Tycoon* is therefore no more surprising or revealing of the underlying issues in the novel than the latent homosexual appeal implicit in the relationship between narrator and narrator's hero in, say, *A Separate Peace, The Great Gatsby, Doctor Faustus*, or *My Mortal Enemy*. The sexual content of the narrator's dependency upon the hero is there, and it matters, but it is far from the central concern of the fiction.

is always implicit in elegiac romance. In Cecilia's case, making that need explicit compounds and deepens the process by which the narrator reconciles her inner life to another person's death, that of the hero of her tale. Even Mann's narrator in *Doctor Faustus*, who writes among the rubble of the collapsing Third Reich, does not face death so certainly as Cecilia does.[9]

In spite of the imminence of Cecilia's death, Fitzgerald insisted that he did not intend the novel to be "the story of deterioration." Cecilia's character was to evolve *"away from"* her earlier adolescent views of life and love. Fitzgerald tells us that Cecilia "was

---

9. This fact, the imminence of Cecilia's own death, seems recently to have taken on new significance in critical discussion. If the subclassification of elegiac romance I have attempted in Chapter Six is valid, it tends to confirm several of Patricia Merivale's insights into Joan Didion's *A Book of Common Prayer*. But it also suggests the possibility of another conclusion than the one Merivale draws regarding "the distinctively 'feminine' variant of the contemporary identity quest" ("Through Greene-Land in Drag," p. 45).

Certain characteristics of Didion's novel seem more typical of its genre than Merivale allows. Didion's narrator, Grace Strasser-Medina, was older than her hero, Charlotte Douglas. This age difference leads Grace to see Charlotte as a "daughter," much as Marlow sees Jim as "my very young brother." It also leads her to regard Charlotte as Marlow regards Jim, as "a little mad, dangerous, unsafe." At the same time, Grace was an adult when she formed her attachment to Charlotte. This fact seen from the point of view of elegiac romance helps account for the possibility that Grace may bear some responsibility for the nefarious political events that take place in Boca Grande. This possibility comes to light, Merivale points out, as Grace tells the tale. What is true of other adult hero-worshipers such as Marlow, Dowell, Nick, and Jack Burden, is true also of Charlotte. The experience of telling the tale and what telling the tale reveals inevitably deal a serious blow to her self-esteem. The tale brings to light elements in her inner self that had heretofore lain safely hidden from conscious awareness.

Where Didion's Grace and Fitzgerald's Cecilia do seem to differ markedly from male narrators of elegiac romance is in their state of being while they tell the tale: the fact that they are themselves dying. This fact infinitely intensifies one fundamental theme of the genre—accommodation to change and loss. Based on Thomas Rosenmeyer's observation that there are two possible currents in pastoral elegy—one in which nature revives and the other in which nature dies in sympathy with the person whose death is lamented (*The Green Cabinet*, p. 113; see Chapter One, note 28)—it seems possible to speculate that Fitzgerald and Didion are in these works writing in the second of these two currents. It seems premature at this time, however, with so few elegiac romances in which the narrators portray themselves as about to die, to carry this speculation further. It seems premature also, with so few elegiac romances by and about women, to ask whether female narrators are more likely than male narrators to be found in this current of the tradition, and if so, whether that fact might reveal significant differences between "the contemporary identity quest" as pursued by female and male narrators in elegiac romance.

twenty when the events that she tells occurred, but she is twenty-five when she tells about the events, and of course many of them appear to her in a different light." She was to become "intelligent, cynical, but understanding, and kindly towards the people, great or small, who are of Hollywood" (*LT* 166). Fitzgerald intended, furthermore, that in synthesizing Cecilia's experience, her tale would both bring her to a mature reconciliation with "the end of childhood" and dramatize the process of imagination, memory, and growth of identity by which that coming of age occurs (*LT* 87).

With these intentions fulfilled, Fitzgerald hoped, this novel might "perhaps" lead to "a new way of looking at certain phenomena" and "arouse new emotions" (*LT* 172). The sort of phenomena he appears to have had most in mind are reconciliation to death and the achievement of a kind of consummate maturity. Finished, *The Last Tycoon* might have led also to a new way of looking at still another important phenomenon implicit in the portion of the novel Fitzgerald left us: the inner development of a central female character, the narrator, Cecilia Brady. It is the novel's potential for rendering this particular development that makes Cecilia an important figure in modern American literature, and certainly a unique figure in Fitzgerald's work.

Fitzgerald was clearly aware of this potential. He recognized that the novel was his second work in a form pioneered by Joseph Conrad. It was to be "more 'like' *The Great Gatsby*," he notes, "than any other of my books." He seems to have seen Cecilia as a sort of female Marlow who is "at the moment of telling the story, an intelligent observant woman" (*LT* 168). If he had completed the novel successfully, therefore, Fitzgerald would have had to develop Cecilia's inner world much more fully than he had any of his earlier female characters.

His notes show, in fact, that to create a female character with such a distinct, independent identity was a challenge that attracted him. In describing Kathleen, the woman whom Stahr makes love to, Fitzgerald expresses impatience with the stereotypical traits of his female characters who "were all so warm and full of promise. What can I do," he asks himself, "to make it honest and different?" (*LT* 182). What he had to do, and evidently intended to do, seems clear when we look at *The Last*

Tycoon as an elegiac romance. If he was to follow Conrad's precedent, Fitzgerald had to insure that his *narrator* attained inner freedom and independent identity in the novel's fictional present through the dramatized process of telling the tale.

We can infer this direction of Fitzgerald's development of the novel from Cecilia's character and from her role in the novel's structure. Cecilia begins her tale believing that she took "Hollywood for granted" as an adolescent, and suffered under "the young illusion that most adventures are good" (*LT* 5, 15). By the end of the first chapter she already recognizes that, although she was drawn to Stahr, because she had known him since childhood her attraction has had a peculiar, worshipful quality. What she felt was neither simple admiration nor a "crush." It involved obsessive imaginative identification—hero-worship—that blocked her own self-discovery. "The pictures that Stahr himself conceived," she observes, "had shaped me into what I was" (*LT* 23). Obsessive identification resulted in something like the state of arrested emotional development Carol Ohmann attributes to Ford's narrator in *The Good Soldier*.

Cecilia's most important insight in the part of the novel we have is her recognition that for her Stahr was not a man but a projection of her own dependency and insecurity: "I'll always think of that moment when I felt Miss Doolan behind me with her pad, as the end of childhood, the end of the time when you cut out pictures. What I was looking at wasn't Stahr but a picture of him I cut out over and over" (*LT* 87). If Fitzgerald had completed *The Last Tycoon*, he would have had to examine what this narrator's immature "picture" of her hero implies, not about the hero but about the narrator herself. Just as the heroic mental images of Kurtz, Jim, Gatsby, and Myra Henshawe serve as ironic mirrors reflecting the inner lives of Marlow, Nick, and Nellie Birdseye, Cecilia's idealized image of Stahr reflects a level of her own inner life of which she is not fully conscious.

It reflects, in short, what Conrad called "inner truth," in contrast with the "surface truth" of "straightforward" everyday experience. It is through dramatizing an insight of this sort that, as Fitzgerald hoped, *The Last Tycoon* might have led to "a new way of looking at" an important aspect of human development. Had Fitzgerald completed the novel, Cecilia Brady might have become one of the most interesting of elegiac romance narrators, "an intelligent and observant woman," as well as one of the most deeply and subtly developed female figures in American fiction.

Why Write Elegiac Romance?:
The Biographical Dimension

With this account of some of the variations possible in elegiac romance, my argument ends. A number of issues remain that I have barely touched upon. Some are mainly aesthetic in nature, such as the tendency of elegiac romance to synthesize two kinds of prose fiction, the "objective" and the "subjective"; such as the part the genre has played in the twentieth-century tendency for the author to withdraw, as Joyce put it, to some position above and behind the fiction, paring his nails; such as the value of elegiac romance for maintaining a place in realistic fiction for "the romantic" as Henry James defined it: the "things that, with all the facilities in the world, all the wealth and all the courage and all the wit and all the adventure we never *can* directly know."[1] Other relevant issues are found at the frontier between aesthetics and social science, such as the cultural value that this elegiac form may have for us today at a time when, as Auerbach has put it, "the tempo of [social, cultural, and political change continues to demand] a perpetual and extremely difficult effort toward inner adaptation and produces intense concomitant crises";[2] such as the role that elegiac romance might play in an attempt to understand and affect adult attitudes toward child-

1. Preface to *The American*, in *The Future of the Novel*, ed. Leon Edel (New York: Vintage, 1956), p. 45.
2. *Mimesis*, p. 404.

218

hood and children, toward the elderly and aging, and toward death; and such as the significance and nature of the process by which we tend to transmute artists into heroic figures.[3]

I will not consider these and other related issues further in this volume. But there does remain one more issue I would like to raise and discuss briefly here, because it bears directly upon the central topic of this book: the basic structural and thematic outline of a genre concept as, in Claudio Guillén's phrase, an "invitation to the actual writing of a work." Elegiac romance appears to have a biographical dimension of a sort that to my knowledge few other literary forms have. Several works in the genre mark the climax of their authors' careers. Still more to the point, writing an elegiac romance has in several cases signaled some sort of aesthetic or emotional crisis in the author's life.

This effect seems to begin with Conrad. In the "Author's Note" to *Nostromo*, Conrad tells us that when he completed the sequence of fiction that includes *Heart of Darkness* and *Lord Jim*, he experienced "a subtle change in the nature of the inspiration" that compelled him to write. When he "finished the last story of the Typhoon volume," he says, "it seemed somehow that there was nothing more in the world to write about."[4] Sometime later, Ford Madox Ford seems to have undergone a similar experience. Ford began *The Good Soldier* on his fortieth birthday, and he intended it to be his "formal farewell to literature." It was to contain all he knew about writing. After completing it, he says, he regarded himself "as the Great Auk . . . having reached my alloted, I had laid my one egg and might as well die" (*GS* xix). Carol Ohmann points out that *The Good Soldier* does indeed seem revolutionary in comparison with Ford's earlier work, where there is no precedent for its coherence and quality.[5]

The experience of some other writers of elegiac romance seem similar. Writing *The Great Gatsby* deeply affected F. Scott Fitzgerald's life and career. *Gatsby* was his most concentrated literary

3. See for example Robert F. Lucid's pioneering work in this area, "Norman Mailer: The Artist as Fantasy Figure," *The Massachusetts Review*, 15 (Autumn, 1974), 581-95).

4. *Nostromo* (Garden City, N.Y.: Doubleday Page, 1929), p. vii.

5. Carol Ohmann, *Ford Madox Ford*, pp. 76-77. See also Frederick R. Karl, "Conrad, Ford, and the Novel," *Midway*, 10 (1969), 34.

effort and, as Arthur Mizener tells us, after Fitzgerald completed it "there was a long spell when he appeared to be petering out."[6] And when Vladimir Nabokov abandoned his mother tongue, the first novel he wrote in English was an elegiac romance: *The Real Life of Sebastian Knight*.[7] Thomas Mann's experience in writing an elegiac romance is perhaps the most telling of all. The Faust theme, Mann has said, seemed to have "long roots [that] reached far down into my life." A novel on this theme was one that "from the start" he had kept "for the end." He feared he would die if he wrote it, and indeed he did literally almost die while he was writing *Doctor Faustus*. Mann claimed that "the book itself had made him ill." In Erich Kahler's estimation, *Doctor Faustus* is a "terminal book." It is, he says, Mann's last "summing up."[8]

Ford Madox Ford, furthermore, established what is in a sense an entirely new, related genre, the "real" or nonfictional elegiac romance. At Conrad's death, Ford, who had worked closely with Conrad for many years, wrote a book-length epitaph, *Joseph Conrad: Personal Remembrance*. This book marked still another turning point in Ford's professional life, since immediately after writing it he began his major work, the tetralogy *Parades End*. In *Joseph Conrad: A Personal Remembrance*, Ford perceives his long relationship with Conrad in terms of the relationship between the elegiac romance narrator and his hero. Ford sets out with good intentions to talk about his dead friend. He winds up, true to the elegiac mode, talking about himself. In the course of this reminiscence, furthermore, Ford forges an explicit link between the form he so directly inherited from Conrad, the intimacy he recalls enjoying as Conrad's collaborator, and the history of the quest romance tradition as I have sketched it in Chapter One. Recollecting their many conversations while taking the air together in Conrad's horse cart across the Kentish downs, Ford says:

6. *The Far Side of Paradise* (Boston: Houghton, Mifflin, 1965), p. xxv.
7. Conrad Brenner, "Introduction" (*SK* vii).
8. Thomas Mann, *The Story of a Novel*, pp. 19-20; Erika Mann, *The Last Year of Thomas Mann*, trans. Richard Graves (New York: Farrar, Straus, 1958), p. 25; Kahler, *The Orbit of Thomas Mann* (Princeton, N.J.: Princeton University Press, 1969), p. 43.

I will never see Joseph Conrad again, the last Don Quixote de la Mancha of the *mot juste* in England. Let's say that the mare was his Rosinante, the indescribable fields of grain his windmills, his black wicker cart the triumphal chariot of his apotheosis on the island . . . and myself, surely his Sancho.[9]

I hesitate to press the significance of this scattered evidence. There are certainly contingencies enough in every case. There are certainly causes beyond the coincidence of form. And certainly authors have met crises without writing elegiac romances. Yet it does seem reasonable to infer from the evidence compiled here that for some modern authors sometimes, writing fiction in the form of elegiac romance has coincided with the end of a phase of creative life, after which the writer was either propelled into a new and still more fruitful phase of work, or else came to the end of creative life altogether, at least for a time. If this phenomenon has occurred with some regularity, perhaps it has done so because in elegiac romance the form and its subject are, as Jim's life seemed to Marlow, momentous enough to affect deeply the author's own conception of himself.

That is, writing an elegiac romance seems to have done for some authors something of what narrating the tale does for the narrators of elegiac romance. The death of the narrator's hero, representing both personal loss and change of a larger, more

9. My translation of the original, which reads as follows: "Et jamais je ne reverrai Joseph Conrad qui était le dernier Don Quixote de la Manza du mot juste en Angleterre. Mettez vi [sic] vous voulez que la jument fut sa Rossinante, les champs de blés indescriptibles ses moulins à vent, sa voiture en osier noir le char triomphal de son apothéose sur l'Ile . . . et moi-même sûrement son Sancho." Ford Madox Ford, *Joseph Conrad: A Personal Remembrance* (Boston: Little, Brown, 1924), p. 275. This passage is part of a note that Ford wrote originally for the *Journal Littéraire*, Paris, August 16, 1924, immediately following Conrad's death, and republished untranslated in the *Remembrance*. Another nonfictional elegiac romance is Lillian Hellman's "Julia," in *Pentimento: A Book of Portraits* (New York: Signet, 1974), pp. 83-121. There are also, of course, some "real" biographies in which biographers play themselves off against their subjects or in which the biographers' own concerns encroach upon the narrative. In these biographies the biographer sometimes emerges as interesting in some respects as the subject. Examples of this type are Boswell's *Johnson*, Lockhart's *Scott*, and Jones's *Freud*. Ford's perception of his relationship with Conrad in Cervantean terms suggests that what I have outlined as the typical experience of elegiac romance narrators may shed some light on the motivation of biographers such as these.

far-reaching nature, presumably demonstrates to those authors as to their narrators, the limits of our power to direct our lives. We have very few ways of dealing with the powerlessness we feel in the face of death or other far-reaching changes that we have not caused ourselves and would not choose to cause. One of these ways, evidently, is to recreate and come to terms with a remembered heroic figure, as elegiac romance narrators do, or to create a fictional artifact in which that memory is evoked and dealt with, as the authors of elegiac romances do. By thus governing the heroic figure's life through the process of narration, authors, like their narrators, perhaps reclaim a degree of power over their own lives, that not inconsiderable degree of power that lies in gaining one more jot of self-knowledge. Thus it is that some authors of successful elegiac romances seem to have found that by telling this complex tale they too free themselves, as their narrators do, to seek once again their own mature powers in "fresh Woods, and Pastures new."

A Handlist of Elegiac Romances

This is a list of works that evidence the main characteristics of elegiac romance. No claim is made as to their historical relationship with other such works, except as discussed in the argument of this book. Nor does the list pretend to be complete. It should be considered a work in progress offered for use as a reference and study guide. It may also suggest in brief form the possible scope of the genre.

Novels

Saul Bellow, *Humboldt's Gift*
Myles Connolly, *Mr. Blue*
Joseph Conrad, *Lord Jim*
Joan Didion, *A Book of Common Prayer*
F. Scott Fitzgerald, *The Great Gatsby*
F. Scott Fitzgerald, *The Last Tycoon*
Ford Madox Ford, *The Good Soldier*
Gunter Grass, *Cat and Mouse*
Mark Harris, *Bang the Drum Slowly*
Nikos Kazantzakas, *Zorba the Greek*
John Knowles, *A Separate Peace*
Thomas Mann, *Doctor Faustus*
Herman Melville, *Moby-Dick*

Vladimir Nabokov, *Pale Fire*
Vladimir Nabokov, *The Real Life of Sebastian Knight*
Marcel Proust, *Remembrance of Things Past*
Robert Penn Warren, *All the King's Men*
Christa Wolfe, *The Quest for Christa T*

Novellas

Louis Bromfield, "Kenny"
Truman Capote, *Breakfast at Tiffany's*
Willa Cather, *My Mortal Enemy*
Joseph Conrad, *Heart of Darkness*
Julio Cortázar, *The Pursuer*
Herman Melville, "Bartleby the Scrivener"
Antoine de Saint Exupéry, *The Little Prince*
J. D. Salinger, "Seymour: An Introduction"

Short Stories

Louis Auchincloss, "The Cathedral Builder" (*Second Chance*)
Louis Auchincloss, "Foster Evans on Louis Bovee" (*Tales of Manhattan*)
Jorge Luis Borges, "Funes, The Memorious" (*A Personal Anthology*)
Jorge Luis Borges, "The Other Death" (*The Aleph*)
Louis Bromfield, "The Cat That Lived at the Ritz" (*Awake and Rehearse*)
George Gordon, Lord Byron, "A Fragment" (*Works: Letters and Journals,*
    III)
Willa Cather, "Jack-a-Boy" (*Collected Short Fiction*)
Julio Cortázar, 'There, But Where, How?" (*A Change of Light*, trans.
    Gregory Rabassa)
Harlan Ellison, "All the Lies That Are My Life" (*Shatterday*)
James T. Farrell, "Monologue of an Old Pitcher" (*Childhood Is Not Forever*)
William Faulkner, "Uncle Willy" (*Collected Stories*)
Elma Godchaux, "The Horn That Called Bambine" (*A Southern Harvest,*
    ed. Robert Penn Warren)
Ernest Hemingway, "My Old Man" (*Collected Short Stories*)
Aldous Huxley, "Young Archimedes" (*Little Mexican*)

Franz Kafka, "Josephine the Singer, or the Mouse Folk" (*The Penal Colony*, trans. Willa and Edwin Muir)

William Melvin Kelley, "Cry for Me" (*Dancers on the Shore*)

Tommaso Landolfi, "Gogol's Wife" (*Gogol's Wife*, trans. W. Young)

Bernard Malamud, "The German Refugee" (*Idiots First*)

Indro Montanelli, "His Excellency" (*Modern Italian Short Stories*, ed. M. L. Slonim, trans. Uguccione Ranieri)

Stefan Zweig, "Buchmendel" (*Kaleidoscope*, trans. Eden and Cedar Paul)

Index

Library of Congress Cataloging in Publication Data

Bruffee, Kenneth A.
  Elegiac romance.

  Includes bibliographical references and index.
  1. Fiction—20th century—History and criticism. I. Title.
PN3503.B765 1983   809.3′9353   83-45140
ISBN 0-8014-1579-9 (alk. paper)